Practical Flutter

Improve your Mobile Development with Google's Latest Open-Source SDK

Frank Zammetti

Apress®

Practical Flutter: Improve your Mobile Development with Google's Latest Open-Source SDK

Frank Zammetti
Pottstown, PA, USA

ISBN-13 (pbk): 978-1-4842-4971-0   ISBN-13 (electronic): 978-1-4842-4972-7
https://doi.org/10.1007/978-1-4842-4972-7

Managing Director, Apress Media LLC: Welmoed Spahr
Acquisitions Editor: Louise Corrigan
Development Editor: James Markham
Coordinating Editor: Nancy Chen

Cover designed by eStudioCalamar

Cover image designed by Freepik (www.freepik.com)

Distributed to the book trade worldwide by Springer Science+Business Media New York, 233 Spring Street, 6th Floor, New York, NY 10013. Phone 1-800-SPRINGER, fax (201) 348-4505, e-mail orders-ny@springer-sbm.com, or visit www.springeronline.com. Apress Media, LLC is a California LLC and the sole member (owner) is Springer Science + Business Media Finance Inc (SSBM Finance Inc). SSBM Finance Inc is a **Delaware** corporation.

For information on translations, please e-mail rights@apress.com, or visit http://www.apress.com/rights-permissions.

Apress titles may be purchased in bulk for academic, corporate, or promotional use. eBook versions and licenses are also available for most titles. For more information, reference our Print and eBook Bulk Sales web page at http://www.apress.com/bulk-sales.

Any source code or other supplementary material referenced by the author in this book is available to readers on GitHub via the book's product page, located at www.apress.com/9781484249710. For more detailed information, please visit http://www.apress.com/source-code.

Printed on acid-free paper

I'd like to dedicate this book to butterflies, which flutter in the wind.

No, wait, that's too easy.

I'd like to dedicate this book to gamblers who, the British people might say, make "a flutter on the horses."

Yes, that's actually a real usage of the word flutter, but that too is too easy.

No, I'd like to dedicate this book to all the unknowns the human race has yet to discover and, in some cases, create. I am a pessimist by nature, but I fight that nature each and every day because I also recognize that the universe is a wondrous place and, despite what the evening news tells us, the human race is capable of great beauty and wondrous creation.

And, with my stated goal of being immortal, because death just isn't me – it's been done before, so I'm just gonna go ahead and skip it – I look forward to seeing it all!

Table of Contents

vi

About the Author

Frank Zammetti is a technical author of some renown – and by *some* I mean very little. But hey, a guy's gotta eat, right? Frank has been a programmer in one fashion or another for nearly 40 years, about 25 of that professionally. These days, you'll actually find *architect* on his business card, but he's still a code monkey at heart and twiddles bits nearly every day. Frank is – and I believe I have the correct technical term here – a nerd of the highest order: when not making inanimate computing objects do his (likely evil) bidding, Frank can be found watching, reading, or writing sci-fi; building rail guns, Tesla coils, or some other contraption that will probably zap him to death at some point; quoting *Babylon 5*, *Lord of the Rings*, *Chronicles of Riddick*, or *Real Genius* to people for no apparent reason (which, of course, they just *love*); or playing video games to pretend he's a hero (of the space or guitar variety most usually). Frank is also a progressive rock musician (keyboard player) and an avid eater of pizza and all things carbohydrates. He's also got a wife, a dog, and some kids, just to round out the awesomeness, and will always be the one that stands up and exclaims "And my axe!" any time plans are being made (see, I told you, just quotes *Lord of the Rings* for no apparent reason! – what a nerd!).

About the Technical Reviewer

Herman van Rosmalen works as a developer/software architect for De Nederlandsche Bank N.V., the central bank of the Netherlands. He has more than 30 years of experience in developing software applications in a variety of programming languages. Herman has been involved in building mainframe, PC, client-server, web, and mobile applications. For the past 4 years, Herman has mainly been involved in developing applications in .NET C# and Angular after working for 15 years with Java technology.

Herman lives in a small town, Pijnacker, in the Netherlands with his wife Liesbeth and their children Barbara, Leonie, and Ramon. Next to developing software, in his spare time, he is also a soccer coach for girl soccer teams for almost 10 years now. And of course he supports Feyenoord!

Acknowledgments

If you've never done it, let me tell you a secret: when writing a book like this, the person actually doing the writing is only a small part of getting the thing done and making it as good as it can be. Sometimes, I think maybe even the smallest part!

Because of that, I want to acknowledge all the hard-working people who helped complete this project and bring it to your hands (whether physical or digital) including Nancy Chen, Louise Corrigan, James Markham, Herman van Rosmalen, Welmoed Spahr, and Dhaneesh Kumar. And, if your name isn't in this list and it should be, then I offer my sincerest apologies – you were not left out intentionally, and you have my gratitude even if you're not on the page.

I'd also like to thank Lars Bak and Kasper Lund for creating Dart, the quite elegant and not at all unpleasant to use programming language that underpins Flutter. Speaking as someone who created his own language and toolchain for it many years ago, I very much appreciate what you guys pulled off. Kudos!

And, writing a book on Flutter practically demands that I acknowledge the entire Flutter development team. I've been doing mobile development in one form or another for very nearly 20 years (take a look at etherient.com, specifically the Products page, and more specifically Eliminator, which was a game I released in 2001 for Microsoft's PocketPC platform – I believe that was my first mobile app, at least the first of any note), and I've used more mobile toolkits, frameworks, and libraries than I can count. Given all that experience, I can say with great confidence that Flutter, even upon its initial release, was head and shoulders above them all. It really is pretty amazing what you all have been able to accomplish in such a relatively short period of time, and without your hard work I obviously wouldn't have been writing this book! I look forward to using Flutter more and more to the point, and I look forward to what you folks are going to do with it!

Introduction

Creating mobile apps that look, feel, and function like native apps and are also cross-platform is a tricky proposition, even after all these years of developers working to achieve that goal. You can write native code for each platform and do your best to make them as similar as possible, and that's certainly a good way to get native performance and capabilities into your app. But, effectively, that means writing your app multiple times. Clients tend not to like having to pay for that sort of thing!

Instead, you can take the HTML route and have a single code base that works everywhere. But then, you will often be left out in the cold in terms of native device capabilities, not to mention performance frequently being subpar (there are some options that minimize these concerns to be sure, but they're still there no matter how good those options do).

I've been doing this exact thing for two decades now (seriously!), so I've seen it all, many times over. So, when I see a possible unicorn on the horizon, I'm skeptical for sure. But, when you get closer and see that the unicorn is indeed real, well, it's not really a unicorn anymore, is it? It's reality, and a wondrous reality at that.

And so, I present to you the unicorn that is the wondrous reality: Flutter!

Thanks to the talented engineers at Google, Flutter is a platform that provides a means for you to write a single code base (more or less) that works on Android and iOS equally well while delivering native performance and native capabilities. Built with modern tools and development techniques, Flutter opens up the world of mobile development to programmers that is, dare I say it, even *fun* to use!

In this book, you'll learn Flutter by building two real apps, not just grossly simplified, dumbed-down, and contrived examples (although there are a few of those early on, as concepts are introduced). No, the apps we'll build together will be practical apps that you could use for real if you want, not just simple tech demos, and along the way you'll see many aspects that went into their development, including in some cases the problems I faced in putting it together and the solutions I came up with. In doing so, you'll get solid, hands-on experience with using Flutter in a real-world way – a way that will prepare you for building your own apps later.

You'll also learn some things tangential to building the app including building a server with Node.js and WebSockets. You can consider those nice little bonuses to the real star of the show in Flutter.

On top of that, you'll get a bonus third app that's drastically different from the first two: a game! Yes, we'll build a game together using Flutter, if for no other reason than to highlight some additional capabilities of Flutter that the first two apps won't necessarily touch on and will give you a chance to see Flutter from a different angle, expanding your horizons for what's possible. A game may not be quite as "practical" in a sense, but games sure are fun to make, and a little fun never hurt anyone!

By the end, you'll have a good handle on what Flutter offers, and you'll be in an excellent position to go off and create the Next Big Thing(tm) app with it.

If you were a computer enthusiast in the 1980s, then you're probably familiar with typing in 20 small-print magazine pages of machine code to play a game or run an app for balancing your checkbook (yes, we really did that – and, entirely tangentially, there were even radio stations that would broadcast the code, similar to how a modern takes data and creates sounds from it to transmit over a phone line, which you could record and then run through a program that would spit out the code for you!). You certainly could do that with this book, type it all in by hand, but that would be a painful amount of typing!

So, before you get started, I suggest you head over to the Apress web site, search for this book, and grab the source code bundle from there. That should give you everything you need to follow along without having to type your fingers raw!

That said, don't forget that the best way to learn anything is by doing, so definitely get in there and hack at the example code and apps and see what happens when you make changes. As you finish reading the chapters associated with each app, maybe get in there and try and add a feature or two (and, I'll even make some suggestions along the way for doing just that to give you some direction). I think before long you'll realize that because of the power Flutter provides, small changes can make significant differences in what winds up on the screen.

So, get ready for what I hope you'll find to be an enjoyable and informative ride through the land of Flutter (and other stuff) that will be a rewarding experience!

I hope you enjoy this book and learn a great deal from it. That's definitely my intention! So, grab a snack, pull up a comfy chair, have your laptop at the ready, and get on it. Adventure awaits! (And, yes, I realize full well how corny that sounds.)

CHAPTER 1

Flutter: A Gentle Introduction

Welcome to the starting line!

If you ask ten different mobile developers how they develop their mobile apps for Android and iOS devices, you'll probably get ten different answers. But that may not be the case for long thanks to a relative newcomer on the scene: Flutter.

In this chapter, we'll look at mobile development and how Flutter fits into that picture and, maybe in some ways, completely changes it. We'll get up and running with Flutter, get a basic understanding of what it's all about, and generally set the stage for building some real apps in the remainder of this book.

So, let's jump right in and talk a bit about what mobile development, in general, is all about.

Meditations on the Abyss

Software development ain't easy!

That really should be the sing-song of anyone who twiddles bits, me very much included. I don't want to bore you with my personal history, but the simple fact is that I've been programming, in one form or another, since I was around 7 years old, which means I've been doing this thing for nearly 40 years (about 25 of that professionally). I've seen a lot and done a lot, and the one thing I've learned is what I said at the top: software development ain't easy. To be sure, some individual tasks and some discrete projects can be easy, but overall, this is fundamentally a pretty tough thing we code monkeys do!

And that's before we even begin to talk about mobile development, which is harder still!

1

© Frank Zammetti 2019

F. Zammetti, *Practical Flutter*, https://doi.org/10.1007/978-1-4842-4972-7_1

I started mobile development roughly two decades ago, back in the days of Microsoft's Windows CE/PocketPC and Palm's PalmPilot and it's PalmOS (primarily – there were some others around, but those were, more or less, the only real games in town, so to speak). At that point, it wasn't so bad because there was a limited set of devices and capabilities you had to be concerned with, and there was no shortage of options in terms of development tooling. To be sure, the tooling wasn't nearly as pleasant to use as what we have today, but there was basically just one way to develop a PocketPC app, one way to develop a PalmOS app, not a whole bunch of choices in how to go about it. That sounds like a bad thing, and indeed in some ways it is, but the removal of choice also has the effect of removing developer confusion, which is one of the biggest struggles we have in software engineering today.

Also, although it would be considered a definite negative today, there was no notion of cross-platform development at that point Well, other than essentially developing your app twice, which is precisely what we had to do if we wanted to run on both platforms. But, given the differences between them, that wasn't all that typical. You were more likely back then to find an app that was exclusive to one platform or another because the developer couldn't be bothered, or wasn't capable, of porting it to other platforms (or it just wasn't worth the time and effort, which may, in fact, have been the most common reason).

Since then, the mobile space has undergone a lot of evolution, seen a lot of change, expansion, and contraction. For a while, we had a lot of platforms to support: Android, iOS, webOS, Tizen, Windows Mobile, and maybe a few others that even I can't remember. All that time, porting apps between platforms was still the norm because there wasn't a good cross-platform approach, at least none without significant compromises. Yes, it got more comfortable over time because at least the native tooling improved so even though you had to write the same app multiple times, each time was a bit more pleasant than in the past. Apple released their iOS SDK in 2008, and Google released their Android SDK a year later in 2009 and developing apps for both platforms meant (and still means) using both SDKs, since iOS development is based on the Objective-C language (or Swift more and more today), while Android development is based primarily on the Java language.

Eventually, the number of platforms started to get widdled down as winners and losers in the space were determined. Nowadays, it's basically a two-horse race with Android and iOS ruling the roost (there's still others to consider, but they're really kind of niche at this point, and many developers, even most I'd say, tend to ignore them unless they have particular goals that *must* include them). And with that, the notion of true cross-platform development starts to become more attractive and more viable.

The rise of the Internet provides one option because you can write an app using the technologies that underpin the Internet and wind up with an app that looks and works roughly the same on both platforms (and even others). But that comes with compromises that, even though over time are being minimized, still do exist. Things like performance and true native capabilities are still a bit difficult to do with web technologies.

Aside from web technologies though, in the last few years, we've seen the birth of several cross-platform development techniques and tools that allow you to write an app once and have it work roughly the same on all devices while still providing a native-like experience. Popular options are Corona SDK (primarily for games, though not exclusively), Xamarin, PhoneGap (which is really still just web technologies cleverly wrapped up in a native WebView component), Titanium, and Sencha Touch (again, based on web technologies, but with a nice layer of abstraction above it), just to name a few. There's no shortage of options nowadays, all with their pros and cons.

And into this arena steps a new competitor, anxious to slay all other options and provide the One True Way™ to write cross-platform mobile app:

Flutter.

I know, it's a somewhat silly name... but you know, for all the benefits it brings, I think we can more than live with an arguably silly name!

What's in a (Silly) Name?

Flutter is the creation of Google – you know, the company that pretty much controls the Internet, for better or worse (in the case of Flutter, I think for the better). Flutter began its life under the name "Sky" in 2015 at the Dart developer summit (don't forget that word, Dart, because we'll be coming back to that before long). At first, it ran only on Google's own Android operating system, but was before long ported to Apple's iOS, which covers the two leading mobile operating systems today.

Various preview versions of Flutter were released subsequent to its initial announcement, culminating in the December 4th, 2018, release of Flutter 1.0, the first "stable" release. That signaled that Flutter was ready for prime time and it was time for developers to jump onboard – and jump onboard they have! The popularity of Flutter could realistically be described as meteoric, and for some pretty good reasons.

One of which is this: the original stated goal of Flutter, or at least one of the main ones, was being able to render app UIs at a consistent 120fps no matter what. Google very much understands that a consistently smooth UI is one that users will be delighted by and want to use, so it was at the forefront of their thinking with Flutter. This is a lofty goal to be sure and few cross-platform mobile frameworks ever achieve it (even ones that aren't cross-platform often have a tough time of it).

One of the key decisions Google made when designing Flutter is something that differentiates it from most other mobile development options, and that's the fact that Flutter renders its own UI components. Unlike most other frameworks, Flutter does not use native platform components. In other words, when you tell Flutter to display a button, for example, Flutter itself renders that button, it's not just asking the underlying OS to render the button, which is what most other frameworks do. This represents a big difference between Flutter and nearly anything else out there and is primarily what allows Flutter apps to be consistent across platforms. This also has the benefit that new UI components, or widgets (remember that word too because like Dart it's gonna come back in a big way shortly) can be added to Flutter quickly and easily without worrying about whether the underlying platform supports them.

This also allows Flutter to provide design-specific widgets. What this means is that Flutter offers two sets of widgets: Material design widgets and Cupertino design widgets. The former implement Google's own Material design language, which is the default design language for Android. The latter implements Apple's iOS design language.

Under the covers, Flutter can be conceptualized as being comprised of four main parts, beginning with the Dart platform. I'm going to skip this until the next section because it's big on its own to warrant a separate section, so let's move on to the second component, the main Flutter engine. This is a (mostly) C++-based codebase, so performance is near-native levels at the core, and this codebase uses the Skia graphics engine to do its rendering. Skia is a compact, open-source graphics library, also written in C++, that has evolved to have excellent performance across all supported platforms.

Flutter also provides, as its third major component, an interface over the native SDKs of both platforms which is called the foundation library. This library has the goal of obviating the differences between the APIs of the native platforms in favor of a Flutter-supplied API that is consistent. In other words, you don't need to worry about how to launch the camera app on iOS vs. how you launch it on Android, you don't need to think about what API to use on one platform vs. another. You merely need to know the Flutter API call to make to launch the camera app, and it'll work on both platforms.

The final component is the widgets, but like Dart, they too deserve their own section, so let's come back to that in a bit.

That, in a tiny nutshell, is what Flutter is all about. To be clear, there's not too much of that information that you need to internalize to develop Flutter apps. However, I think it's always useful to know a little history and a bit of the internals of the tools we use. Hopefully, you agree!

Now, let's parse some of the words I threw out, plus a few more, and look at them in detail, beginning with Dart.

Dart: Language of the Gods?

When Google started working on Flutter, they had an early decision to make: what programming language would it use? It could be a web-based language like JavaScript, or perhaps the natural choice would have been Java given that Android uses that. Or, since support for iOS was something that they of course desired, maybe Objective-C or Swift would be a good choice (after all, Swift is ostensibly open-source, so a good argument, I'd wager, was made by some on the Flutter team for it early on). Maybe something like Golang or Ruby would be better. What about going "old-school" with C/C++? Or take a cue from Microsoft and go with C# (since it too is open-source)?

I'm sure there were a lot of choices available, but in the end, Google decided (for reasons!) to go with a language that they themselves had created a few years earlier: Dart.

The entire next chapter is devoted to Dart, so I'm going to refrain from going into too many details here, but at the least, I think a quick sample is in order, so have a look at this:

```
import "dart:math" as math;

class Point {

  final num x, y;

  Point(this.x, this.y);

  Point.origin() : x = 0, y = 0;
```

```
  num distanceTo(Point other) {
    var dx = x - other.x;
    var dy = y - other.y;
    return math.sqrt(dx * dx + dy * dy);
  }

  Point operator +(Point other) => Point(x + other.x, y + other.y);

}

void main() {
  var p1 = Point(10, 10);
  var p2 = Point.origin();
  var distance = p1.distanceTo(p2);
  print(distance);
}
```

It isn't terribly important to understand every last thing you see here. Actually, at this point, it's not important for you to understand *any* of it! That said, if you have experience with any Java or C-like language then I'm willing to bet you can actually follow this without too much trouble, and that's one of the big benefits of Dart: it's similar enough to what most modern developers know for them to be able to pick it up pretty quickly and easily.

Note   It's interesting that we call then C-like languages, but C itself, along with other C-like languages, are descendants of ALGOL, a much older language. It never seems to get the historic respect it deserves though, so I threw this note in to try and change that and get ALGOL some love!

Without getting into all the nitty-gritty details (that's what the next chapter is for), I think a little background on Dart is in order. As I mentioned, Google created Dart back in 2011, and it was initially unveiled at the GOTO conference in Aarhus, Denmark. The initial 1.0 release took place in November 2013, roughly two years before Flutter was released. You have Lars Bak (also the developer of the V8 JavaScript engine underpinning chrome and Node.js) and Kasper Lund to thank for Dart by the way!

Dart is a neat language that is rapidly gaining a lot of traction, thanks in no small part to Flutter, though being a general-purpose language, it can and is used to build all sorts of stuff, from web apps to server code to IoT (Internet of Things) apps, and so on. At around the time I was writing this chapter, a survey about which languages are most important to developers in 2019 (in terms of their own interest in it) came out, published by JAXenter (see `https://jaxenter.com/poll-results-dart-word-2019-154779.html`) with the pertinent result being that two languages stood out by quite a bit from the rest: Dart and Python, with Dart winning out overall. It also says that Dart experienced the most growth in 2018 and while Flutter is almost certainly the single biggest driver, it's probably not enough on its own to account for those results, so it's fair to say Dart is coming on strong from all corners!

So, yeah, Dart is getting a lot of attention for sure.

What's Dart all about? Well, in a nutshell, there are a few key points about it, and the preceding code sample demonstrates much of it:

- Dart is fully object-oriented.

- It's a garbage-collected language, so no memory allocation/ deallocation worries.

- It has a C-based syntax style that is easy for most developers to pick up (that said, it does have a few peculiarities that might throw you at first, but it's no worse than any other language with a similar syntax).

- Supports common language features like interfaces, mixins, abstract classes, reified generics, and static typing.

- A sound typing system (but with flexibility around typing at the same type that makes it not a burden but a genuine help for developers).

- Isolates for concurrency so that you can have independent workers that do not share memory but instead use message passing for communication, yielding good performance while reducing the risk typically associated with other forms of concurrent programming paradigms.

- Dart can use ahead-of-time compilation to native code in order to reach the highest levels of performance this side of Assembly. It compiles to ARM and x86 code, but it can also transpile to JavaScript so your Dart code can run, after a fashion, on the web even. Putting aside that transpilation (is that even a word?!), with Flutter targetting a mobile platform, you'll wind up with AOT-compiled Dart code.

- Dart supports a rather large package repository that provides additional functionality on top of the core language for virtually anything most developers would need and makes it easy to bring those packages to bear in your projects.

- Tooling support from a lot of popular developer tools including Visual Studio Code and IntelliJ IDEA.

- Snapshots as a core part of the Dart VM, which are a method to store and serialize objects and data at runtime (Dart programs can be compiled to snapshots, which contain all the program code and dependencies pre-parsed and ready to execute at startup, and snapshots are also used heavily in the use of isolates).

Dart is now an ECMA standard under technical committee TC52, and you can view the latest specification at `www.dartlang.org/guides/language/spec` (and, more generally, `www.dartlang.org` is the home page of the Dart language).

As I said, the entire next chapter is devoted to getting you up to speed with Dart enough to tackle the Flutter code to come, but for now, I think this should serve as a decent enough introduction.

Widgets to the Left of Me, Widgets to the Right!

Let's get back to talking about the real star of the show here, Flutter, and the one concept that, more than any other, really underpins what flutter is all about: widgets.

In Flutter, everything is a widget. When I say *everything* is a widget, I mean... well, I mean that *almost* everything is a widget (it's far harder to find something that *isn't* a widget in Flutter than to find all the things that are!).

And what's a widget, you ask? Well, they are chunks of your UI (though it's true that not all widgets manifest on the screen, though that's rare). A widget is also, obviously, a chunk of code, like so:

```
Text("Hello!")
```

…and this is also a widget…

```
RaisedButton(
  onPress : function() {
    // Do something.
  },
  child : Text("Click me!")
)
```

…this, too, is a widget…

```
ListView.builder(
  itemCount : cars.length,
  itemBuilder : (inContext, inNum) {
    return new CarDescriptionCard(card[inNum]);
  }
)
```

…and finally, this is also a widget:

```
Center(
  child : Container(
    child : Row(
      Text("Child 1"),
      Text("Child 2"),
      RaisedButton(
        onPress : function() {
          // Do something.
        },
        child : Text("Click me")
      )
    )
  )
)
```

9

This last one is interesting because it's actually a hierarchy of widgets: a `Center` widget, with a `Container` widget underneath it, and that `Container` widget with a `Row` widget underneath it, and two `Text` children under the Row plus a `RaisedButton` too. It's not important what those widgets are (though the names pretty much give them away) but what *is* important is that the entire hierarchy of widgets you see there is *itself* considered a widget in the realm of Flutter.

Yes, widgets are everywhere in Flutter! Widgets to the left of me, widgets to the right! Flutter is basically the Oprah of UI frameworks: you get a widget! And you get a widget! And YOU get a widget – you ALL get widgeeeeeeeets!

As I said at the start, virtually everything is a widget in Flutter. There are the obvious things, the things that people think of when you say the word widget in the context of a user interface: buttons, lists, images, text form fields, all that sort of stuff. Those are widgets for sure. But, in Flutter, things that you don't typically think of widgets are still widgets, stuff like the padding around an image, the state of a text form field, the text displayed on the screen, even the theme an app is using, all of those are widgets in Flutter too.

Given that everything is a widget, a natural consequence is that in Flutter, your code, to a substantial degree, turns out to be nothing but a giant hierarchy of widgets (and this hierarchy has a particular name in Flutter: the "widget tree"). You see, most widgets are containers, meaning they can have children. Some widgets can have but a single child while others can have many. And then, those children can each have one or more children, and so on and so on – its widgets all the way down!

All widgets are Dart classes, and widgets typically have only a single concrete requirement: they must supply a `build()` method. This method must return... wait for it... *other widgets*! There are a very few exceptions to this, some low-level widgets like the Text widget, which returns a primitive type (a String in this case), but most return one or more widgets. Aside from this requirement, at a code level, a widget is just a plain old Dart class (which isn't any different, minor syntax aside as the next chapter will show, from a class you've seen in any other object-oriented language).

A Flutter widget extends one of a handful of standard classes, as is typical in the object-oriented paradigm, classes which Flutter itself provides. The class extended determines what kind of widget we're dealing with a fundamental level. There are two that you'll use probably 99% of the time: `StatelessWidget` and `StatefulWidget`.

A widget that extends StatelessWidget never changes and is called a stateless widget because it has no state. Things like Icon widgets, which display small images, and Text widgets, which of course display strings of text, are said to be stateless widgets. An example of such a class might be this:

```
class MyTextWidget extends StatelessWidget {

  Widget build(inContext) {
    return new Text("Hello!");
  }

}
```

Yep, there's not much to it!

By contrast, the StatefulWidget base class has the notion of state in it, that is, it changes in some way when the user interacts with it. A CheckBox, a Slider, a TexField, these are all well-known examples of stateful widgets (and when you see them written with this sort of capitalization going forward it means that I'm referring to actual Flutter widget class names, not generic fields like a text form field, by contrast). When you code such a widget, you actually have to create *two* classes: the stateful widget class itself, and a state class to go along with it. Here's an example of a stateful widget and its associated state class:

```
class LikesWidget extends StatefulWidget {
  @override
  LikesWidgetState createState() => LikesWidgetState();

}


class LikesWidgetState extends State<LikesWidget> {
  int likeCount = 0;

  void like() {
    setState(() {
      likeCount += 1;
    });
  }
```

```
  @override
  Widget build(BuildContext inContext) {
    return Row(
      children : [
        RaisedButton(
          onPressed : like,
          child : Text('$likeCount')
        )
      ]
    );
  }

}
```

As before, don't get too hung up on the details of this because there's no expectation that you should understand this code yet as we'll get into it all in later chapters, beginning with the next chapter with which you'll build up some Dart knowledge. But, also as before, I'd bet you get the basic idea of what's going on here anyway because it's fairly obvious I think. At least for the most part that is – how the widget code and its state object interact and relate probably is a bit less than obvious, but not to worry, that won't be the case for long!

Going back to stateless widgets for a moment, it should be noted that the term "stateless" is a little bit of a misnomer here because being Dart classes, which can have properties and data encapsulated in them, stateless widgets do, in a sense, have state. The core difference between a stateful and a stateless widget though is that a stateless widget doesn't automatically get re-rendered by the Flutter core framework when its "state" changes, whereas a stateful widget does. When the state of a stateful widget changes, regardless of what causes the change, certain lifecycle events fire. Those trigger lifecycle event hook functions getting called, which results, ultimately, in Flutter re-rendering the portion of the screen where the widget resides (assuming a change was necessary – Flutter makes that determination for you because it knows what the state of the widget was before as well as after the event).

Think of it this way: both types of widgets can in a sense have state, but only a stateful widget has state that Flutter it aware of and even manages to some extent. Therefore, only a stateful widget can be automatically re-rendered when appropriate, all controlled by the Flutter framework itself, rather than you having to do anything manually in your code.

You may be inclined to think that you always want to deal with stateful widgets since it should mean less work on your part, but as you'll see as we build the applications in later chapters, that's not always the case. As a result, you'll use a stateless widget a lot of the time even though it might seem counterintuitive to do so. But, that's a discussion for another day.

There are two main things you probably should have noticed at this point that are important about all of this. First, Flutter UI's are built by composing widgets. That results in the widget tree that I mentioned earlier. While the code for the widgets themselves is object-oriented, a compositional paradigm is how the UI is built. This is important because most Flutter widgets are quite simple in and of themselves and it's only through composition that you can build up a robust UI with them. Some frameworks have what you could rightly call "god components," elements that are practically full applications all by themselves. That's very much not the case with Flutter, and even a relatively trivial UI will likely combine several widgets in Flutter.

Second, Flutter UIs are built from code. I know that seems obvious, but think about it for a second: there's no separate markup language for a Flutter UI like there is in web development. The benefit of this is there's only a single language to learn, a single paradigm to comprehend. It may not be apparent at first blush, but this is a big advantage of Flutter over many competing options.

For now, this is just about all you need to know about widgets. We'll get into more detail starting in Chapter 3 as we survey the Flutter widget catalog, which is the list of widgets that ship with Flutter, and of course as we look at using each of the widgets from Chapter 4 on when we're building the three applications with them. By the end, you'll have a good knowledge of the most common widgets you'll use as you develop with Flutter, as well as a few others, and good foundational knowledge about using and building widgets generally.

Brass Tacks: The Pros and Cons of Flutter

As with any framework, as good developers, we need to evaluate the benefits and pitfalls of any option we might consider, and Flutter is no different. I for one think Flutter has a lot going for it, but it's not a panacea, and it's not without its blemishes, and anyone that says it's perfect is a snake oil salesman (and that goes for anything, not just Flutter). Flutter has its issues, and it won't fit every single project, though I would humbly suggest that there are few where it wouldn't be an excellent choice, if not *the best* choice.

As such, let's talk about the pros and cons of Flutter and, where it makes sense, compare to some of the other options available:

- Pro: Hot reload – This is something I'll come back to after we've walked through getting set up for Flutter development and had a look at a first sample app, but this is a big advantage for Flutter, as you'll see. React Native can have this capability as well if you use the third-party Expo component, but what Flutter provides is arguably better and, indeed in my experience, is much more consistent. Few other frameworks have anything similar.

- Con: Mobile only – As of this writing, you can only use Flutter to develop iOS and Android mobile apps. If you come to love Flutter, you'll be disappointed that you can't use it for all your development needs. However, note that I started by saying "as of this writing"? That's because there are initiatives to allow web development and even native Windows, Mac, and Linux development to be done with Flutter. Before long, this con may be a pro because all the computing world may be built with Flutter (which, for some people, will be a more significant con: Google having more control than they do now – you'll have to make that determination for yourself).

- Pro: Properly cross-platform – Your Flutter apps will, with minimal effort, work correctly on iOS and Android (and, eventually, Android's successor Fuscia). Flutter, out of the box, supplies two sets of widgets, one specific to iOS and one to Android, so not only will your apps work the same, but they can also look appropriate for each platform (although that's entirely up to you, it's not a requirement). Few other frameworks can manage this with the ease Flutter does (you typically must write a lot of branching code to make it happen, and while that's still true with Flutter, the degree to which it's true tends to be a bit less).

- Con: Comingling of code – Some developers, especially those that come from a web development background where separation of UI from logic code is common (vis-a-vis, HTML/CSS defines the UI, JS, and then whatever runs on the back end defines the logic), tend to have a visceral reaction to seeing all of it more or less mixed together in Flutter code. This isn't specific to Flutter of course: React Native, for example, suffers the same complaints sometimes.

- Pro: Dart – Dart is simple and powerful, object-oriented, and strongly typed, allowing developers to be very productive very quickly and to do so with safety. Once you get over the (not unusually large) initial learning curve, most developers tend to like Dart as compared to languages like JavaScript, Objective-C, or Java.

- Con: Google – I'm listing this as a con, but it's very much a subjective thing, and you definitely may or may not agree (to be honest, I argue with myself about it all the time). Some people are uncomfortable with the amount of control Google has over the Internet, even if that control isn't something they actively cultivate. When you're the dominant player, you tend to have the majority of control. However, some people will look at the notion of using something created by Google to build mobile apps and think that's a bridge too far. Others, of course, will look at it and say it's great that such a big player is backing this technology. So, this "con" is very much up for debate. But it's a debate you must answer for yourself.

- Pro: Widgets – A rich set of widgets come with Flutter, and it may, in fact, be all you ever need to build any app. However, you can also create your own (in point of fact, you'll *always* create your own, but to what level they go can vary) and you can even pull in many third-party widgets to extend Flutter's capabilities. Those widgets are just as easy to use as any that ship with Flutter. Compared to React Native, for example, which has a relatively sparse set of widgets without adding third-party widgets, Flutter provides much more power out of the box.

- Con: The widget tree – This can become a con because you wind up sometimes with a very deeply nested hierarchy and, if for no other reason, it can be challenging to look at the code and understand the structure. We've kind of become used to this sort of thing over the past two decades with the rise of the World Wide Web because HTML itself is the same sort of thing. But, because virtually everything is a widget in Flutter, the hierarchy can sometimes be deeper even than HTML, and the code style of Dart sometimes makes looking at such a thing tricky. There, of course, are techniques you can use to alleviate this somewhat, and I'll talk about those later as we look at real application code in later chapters, but it's still a con because you have to be consciously aware of it and deal with it yourself. Neither Flutter nor Dart will do you any favors in this regard.

- Pro: Tooling – As you'll see in the next section, getting a basic development environment setup for Flutter is easy. However, you can move beyond that basic environment and use many of the same tooling you're used to doing other development with. This, again, means low developer friction.

- Con: Reactive programming and state management – Flutter is generally considered to be a reactive programming paradigm, which means that you define your UI in Flutter in terms of the current state of a given widget. The build() method that you saw earlier takes as an argument the current state, and what it returns is a visual representation of that widget incorporating that current state. When the state changes, the widget "reacts" to the change by being re-build via a call to build() again, passing it the new state. This all happens as a function of Flutter and the event lifecycle it presents; it's not something you (usually) have to think much about aside from supplying the build() method. Contrast this to frameworks where you construct a widget, then call some series of mutator methods on it to set it up in the proper state. This paradigm is compelling, in Flutter and elsewhere, but it can be a con in Flutter too because it sometimes makes doing trivial things more difficult than it arguably should be (you'll see some of this difficulty in later chapters, and ways to deal with it). Related to this is the topic of state management, which, at least at the time of this writing, is a deficiency in Flutter in the sense that there is no canonical right and wrong way to do it. There are numerous approaches, each with pluses and minuses, and you'll need to decide which fits your needs best (and yes, I'll be providing what I see as being a good approach). Google is working on such a canonical approach right now, but it's not ready yet, so until it is, I'll consider this lack of solid direction as something of a con (though to some ways of thinking such flexibility can be regarded as a pro, and I wouldn't get into any barroom brawls over it either way!).

- Pro: Platform-specific widgets – Since Flutter UIs are constructed in code, it becomes straightforward to have a single codebase that supports both iOS and Android, even where there are differences you need to account for. As an example, you can always interrogate the `Platform.isAndroid` and `Platform.isIOS` values at runtime to determine what your code is running on, and then branch based on the value to construct a platform-specific widget. Maybe you want a RaisedButton on Android but a plain Button on iOS. There's no need to create two different codebases; just a simple branch will do the trick in many cases.

- Con: App size – Flutter apps tend to be a bit larger than their purely native counterparts because they have to include the core Flutter engine, the Flutter framework, support libraries, and other resources. A dirt simple "Hello, world!" Flutter app can be upward of 7mb in size. It's a trade-off for sure, so if you have a use case where app size is really a driving factor, then Flutter may not be your best choice.

Okay, I think by this point it's safe to say you've got a basic Flutter vocabulary, so to speak, built up, and you have an idea of what Flutter is all about. Let's get do to work now and get to some real code!

Ok, Enough Talk, Let's Get Going with Flutter!

Oops, before we can get to real code though, we probably should get Flutter installed, plus whatever tooling we're going to need, huh? As I'm sure you can imagine, it's not especially easy to build Flutter code into an executable app without that step being done first!

Fortunately, as I mentioned earlier, getting our development environment set up for Flutter is pretty easy.

Flutter SDK

The first step you absolutely must accomplish is downloading, installing, and configuring the Flutter SDK. Everything hinges on this! The second step, which technically is optional but which we're going to consider required for the purposes of this book, is downloading, installing and configuring Android Studio (and as part of this will be setting up an Android SDK and emulator).

First, head over to `https://flutter.io`, which is your "one-stop shopping" location for Flutter installation and documentation. There, hit the Get Started button at the top. You'll find yourself on the Install page where you can select which operating system you're using (Windows, MacOS, or Linux).

Note   I'm not at all ashamed to admit that I am primarily a Windows user. It's what I know best and – gasp – even prefer! As such, this book will be somewhat Windows-centric, and if you're using another OS, you will, to some extent, be on your own. With that said, I will be diligent about trying to point out any areas where there are significant differences. There really shouldn't be any, and what you see here *should*, by and large, apply whether you're using Windows or not. How you install software is one area where there clearly are differences, but the Flutter web site will alert you to the proper procedure if it's something you need assistance with.

Choose the appropriate link and the Flutter web site will provide you with information about downloading and installing the SDK. It's not unlike any other SDK or software, so you will likely have little difficulty. One thing I'll make note of however is that part of the instructions indicates adding the SDK to your path. While this certainly makes things a bit easier, that's one step that you can skip if you prefer to. Just note that if you do skip it, all commands will need to be executed from the SDK directory, or you'll need to specify the full path to the SDK if you aren't in that directory. Once we get to the Android Studio step though you'll discover that adding the SDK to the path really doesn't matter, it's only if you're going to be executing SDK commands from the command line rather than having Android Studio effectively do it for you, that it might matter.

And speaking of commands, one command that you *will*, in fact, execute from the command line, and one you'll do right after installing the SDK according to the instructions on the Flutter web site, is `flutter doctor`. Most commands you'll issue to the SDK, if not all of them, begin with `flutter`, which is the actual executable you're executing, and `doctor` is one command you can issue to it. It's also probably the most important because it runs through a series of checks and configuration steps to get you up and running.

At first, you'll run it and see some failures, and this is to be expected at this point because the next step takes care of that: installing Android Studio.

Android Studio

Once again, the instructions on the Flutter site walk you through this, and it's slightly different for each OS, but once you get it installed, you're going to fire it up and walk through the Android Studio Setup Wizard. This will download Android SDKs and emulator images and everything else required for it to work. You'll also need to install some plugins specifically for Dart and Flutter, and the documentation again details that.

Now, after that, if you continue following the instructions there, it will run you through the process of hooking up your Android phone or tablet to your computer and making sure `flutter doctor` can see it. This step, however, is one you can skip! Of course, if you do have an Android device, then you're entirely free to do so.

However, if you're an iOS devotee, or if you'd prefer not to use a real device when developing your Flutter code – I prefer not to have to plug my phone in all the time to be honest – then my suggestion is to go into Android Studio, fire up the AVD (Android Virtual Machine) manager, which you can find on the Configure menu on the startup screen, and create yourself an Android virtual device. I suggest making a Pixel 2 virtual device, using API level 28 (make sure you've installed that particular SDK, which you can do in the SDK Manager, also found on the Configure menu) and give it a resolution of 1080x1920 (420dpi) and target Android 9. Select one of the x86 (ABI x86_64) images. Android virtual devices for a long time had a bad reputation when it comes to performance, but this type of virtual device performs exceptionally well, achieving nearly native performance in most cases. Although it won't really matter, go ahead and configure it for a 512Mb SD card. For the most part, the defaults should be what you want, but the key ones are the API level and the CPU type.

When that's done, you'll be ready to go and will be able to run Flutter code on that virtual device from Android Studio. Or, you can do this all from the command line using the SDK, though I won't be describing interacting with the SDK from the command line beyond flutter doctor. We'll be in Android Studio for the remainder of this book.

Note that if you rerun it, `flutter doctor` will still flag a problem, namely that it can't find an Android device, assuming the virtual device you created isn't running. If it is, however, `flutter doctor` should detect it, and you'll get a clean bill of health. Finally, if the virtual device is *not* running, and assuming you didn't plug a real Android device into your computer, then as long as that's the only problem flutter doctor reports then you're still good to go.

If you're wondering about iOS at this point, don't! Just because we're using Android Studio, that in no way, shape or form means that what you do in it can't be used on iOS. The only time it matters that our deploy target is iOS is if you want to test on an actual iOS device, or build your application for distribution, at which point you'll need a Mac machine and Apple's Xcode IDE installed. Distributing apps is not a topic covered in this book though, whether for iOS or Android, so the emulator will suit our needs just fine.

The (Slightly Less) Typical "Hello, World!" App

If you continue with the instructions on the Flutter web site, it will, as a final step, have you create a little Flutter app. While the documentation there is excellent, I'd suggest skipping that step and instead let me walk you through it. I gotta sing for my supper here after all, right?

The first step will, indeed, be to let Android Studio (in conjunction with the SDK) build an app for us. The process is quite simple, and once we have that basic app up and running in our virtual device, we'll modify it a bit so we can see hot reload at work.

But, first things first, let's create a project! When you first start Android Studio, you should see a window like in Figure 1-1.

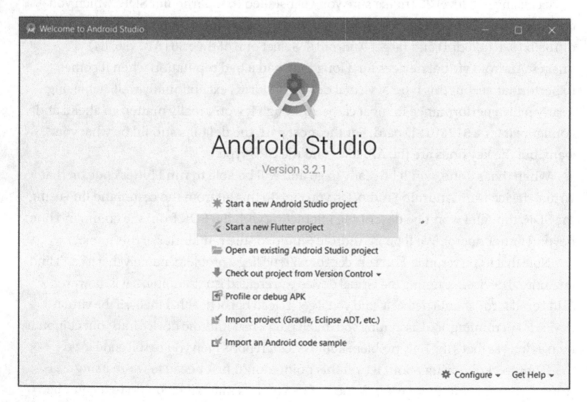

Figure 1-1. *Kicking it off in Android Studio*

See that *Start a new Flutter Project* line? That's the one you want, so go ahead and click it! You'll be met with the new application wizard's starting screen as you can see in Figure 1-2.

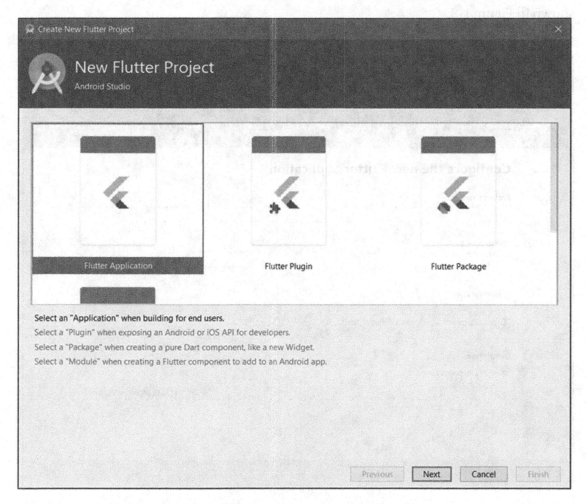

Figure 1-2. *Select the type of Flutter project you want to create*

There are four types of Flutter projects you could create:

- Flutter Application (which is what we'll use throughout this book)

- Flutter Plugin (a plugin allows you to expose native Android or iOS functionality to your Dart-based Flutter applications)

- Flutter Package (this is only necessary if you want to distribute a custom widget independent of an application)

- Flutter Module (which allows you to embed a Flutter app into a native Android app)

Select Flutter Application and click Next and you'll wind up with the window as shown in Figure 1-3.

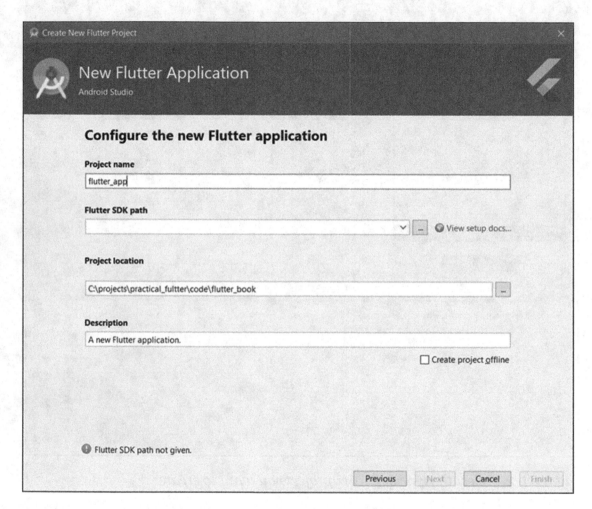

Figure 1-3. Entering some necessary information about our new app

Here, you'll enter some essential information about the application being created. The defaults may be fine, or you can give the project whatever name you'd like, and the same for the description. Also, update the Project location field as necessary (or just use the default). Do you see that error on the bottom? If you don't, that's fine; it likely means you already set up your path correctly. But, if you do see it, that's because Android Studio doesn't yet know where the Flutter SDK is, so you'll need to tell it. Simply browse to the SDK that you should already have installed by clicking the three-dot button next to the field and make sure Android Studio is happy with it (read: the error goes away), and click Next again to get to the screen from Figure 1-4.

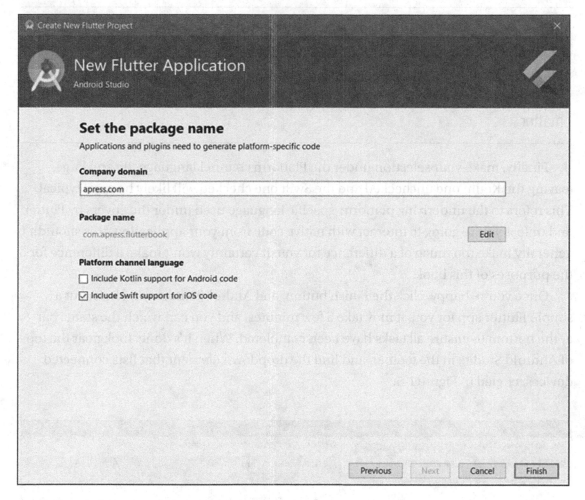

Figure 1-4. *Final details about the project*

This last screen requires a little more information, primarily the Company domain. This doesn't need to be a company of course, but the point is that it needs to be a value in the typical "dot" form, which generally means an Internet domain. If you don't have a domain though, you can put any value you like there. Is your name Jim? You could enter Jim! Well, you *could* enter Jim even if that's not your name of course, though that would be a little weird. The point being: enter a value that makes sense to you, whatever it is, and note that the Package name value updates accordingly, concatenating the Project name you entered on the last screen with the Company domain value here. This Package name value must be unique should you want to publish this app to an app store, though for our early testing here it doesn't make a difference.

Note   You may also see a Sample Application field, depending on the version of Android Studio and the Flutter plugin you have installed. It's okay either way, that's for having the wizard generate some sample code for you if you wish, but it's not something we need for this book, so whether it's there or not, it doesn't matter.

Finally, make your selection under the Platform channel language. By and large, leaving the Kotlin one unchecked and the Swift one checked will likely be most typical. This refers to the underlying platform-specific language used under the covers by Flutter, and unless you're going to interact with native code from your application, this shouldn't generally make too much of a difference for you. It certainly won't make a difference for the purposes of this book.

Once you're happy, click the Finish button, and Android Studio will churn out a simple Flutter app for you. It may take a few minutes, and you can watch the status bar at the bottom to ensure all tasks have been completed. When it's done, look near the top of Android Studio, in the toolbar, and find the dropdown element that lists connected devices, circled in Figure 1-5.

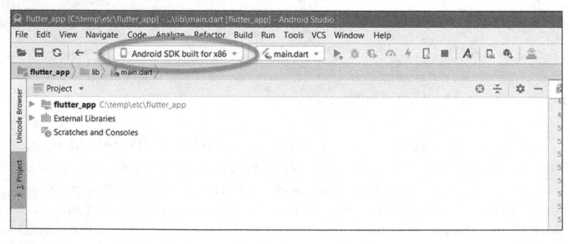

Figure 1-5.   *The virtual machine dropdown in Android Studio*

You should see the emulator you created earlier listed. Select it, and if it's not yet running, it should start up before long. Once it does, click the green arrow next to the dropdown that says `main.dart` next to it (that's the entry point of the app), which is the Run icon. Then, sit back for a bit while the app is built, deployed and started on the emulator (depending on your machine, it could take up to a minute, so be patient – it's much faster after the initial build though). You should see something like Figure 1-6 in the emulator.

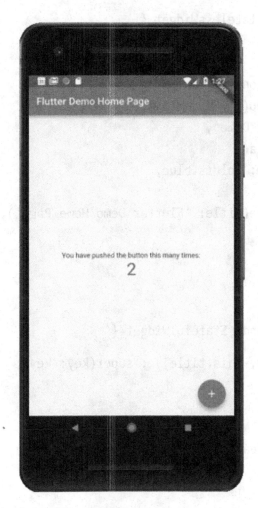

Figure 1-6. *Fisher Price's My First Flutter App!*

It's a simple app, but it shows a lot. Click the circle button at the bottom with the plus sign (called a Floating Action Button, or FAB), and notice that the count goes up with each click.

The code produced, which should open automatically in Android Studio (but if it doesn't find `main.dart` under the `lib` directory, should be as followed (though note that I've removed comments and reformatted some things too, hopefully, make it a little nicer to look at on the page):

```dart
import 'package:flutter/material.dart';

void main() => runApp(MyApp());

class MyApp extends StatelessWidget {

  @override
  Widget build(BuildContext context) {
    return MaterialApp(
      title: 'Flutter Demo',
      theme: ThemeData(
        primarySwatch: Colors.blue,
      ),
      home: MyHomePage(title: 'Flutter Demo Home Page'),
    );
  }

}


class MyHomePage extends StatefulWidget {

  MyHomePage({Key key, this.title}) : super(key: key);

  final String title;

  @override
  _MyHomePageState createState() => _MyHomePageState();

}


class _MyHomePageState extends State<MyHomePage> {

  int _counter = 0;

  void _incrementCounter() {
```

```
  setState(() {
    _counter++;
  });
}

@override
Widget build(BuildContext context) {
  return Scaffold(
    appBar: AppBar(
      title: Text(widget.title),
    ),
    body: Center(
      child: Column(
        mainAxisAlignment: MainAxisAlignment.center,
        children: <Widget>[
          Text(
            'You have pushed the button this many times:',
          ),
          Text(
            '$_counter',
            style: Theme.of(context).textTheme.display1,
          ),
        ],
      ),
    ),
    floatingActionButton: FloatingActionButton(
      onPressed: _incrementCounter,
      tooltip: 'Increment',
      child: Icon(Icons.add),
    ),
  );
}
}
```

While not all that much code, there's quite a bit going on. At this point though, you don't really have the vocabulary, so to speak, to be able to deep-dive into it because we haven't talked about Dart in detail yet. But, I don't want to leave you with absolutely no explanation at all, so there are a few key things that I'll point out now.

First, note that every Flutter app's main entry point is a `main()` method. That method will be just a call to the `runApp()` method, provided by Flutter itself, and passing it the top-level widget. There is always a single widget at the top of the hierarchy that contains all the others, and here it's an instance of the `MyApp` class. This class happens to be a stateless widget, as previously discussed, so the only thing it must provide is a `build()` method, and that's what you see here. The widget returned from it (because remember: `build()` always returns a single widget that may or may not have children under it) is an instance of `MaterialApp`, which is a widget provided by Flutter (included in the `flutter/material` package you see imported at the top). We'll talk about that widget in Chapter 3 when we look at Flutter widgets, but the critical thing about it is that it provides the basic framework for a Material (i.e., Google UI-style) app. You can see that the `title` is set (where `title` is one of the named arguments to the `MaterialApp`'s constructor), which is what you use in the status bar with when the app is run. You can also see that you can set a `theme` for a Flutter app and provide details about that theme, such as the primary color the theme uses, blue in this case.

This `MaterialApp` widget has a single child, which is an instance of the `MyHomePage` class (not to steal the thunder of Chapter 2, but one slightly weird thing about Dart is that when you instantiate a class, you do not need to write the `new` keyword, as you do in most object-oriented languages, and that's what's happening here).

The `MyHomePage` class defines a stateful widget, so in this case, we need two classes, the "core" class that extends from `StatefulWidget` and the state class associated with it that extends `State`. It may seem a little weird at first, but it's the state class, `_MyHomePageState`, that effectively is the widget. You can tell that because it has a `build()` method. Your first instinct would probably be to expect that in the `MyHomePage` class, and then `_MyHomePageState` would contain just the data that represents the state of the widget, but it's actually the opposite.

Either way, the `build()` method of that widget again returns a single widget, this time a `Scaffold` widget. Still, don't get hung up on what his widget is because we'll get to them all in Chapter 3. But, a short and sweet description is that it provides the fundamental visual layout for the app, including things like a status bar (an `AppBar` widget in fact) where the title lives. The Scaffold also provides something to "hook" the FAB to, so to speak, the FAB being an instance of the FloatingActionButton widget, which is the value of the floatingActionButton argument to the Scaffold's constructor.

The other argument passed to the Scaffold's constructor is body, which is how we add other widgets as children of this one. Here, you can start to see the "everything is a widget" mantra in action because we have a Center widget, which is a container widget that – you guessed it – centers its one and only child. In this case, that child is a Column widget, one of the many layout-related widgets Flutter provides, this one lays out its children in a columnar arrangement. This Column has two children, both Text widgets, one for the static "You have pushed the button this many times:" text, and the other to display the number of times you've pushed the button.

All of this will become more clear as we delve into Dart and then Flutter itself over the next two chapters. And, while I've left out a lot of details, I think this explanation provides enough to have a decent idea of what's going on in this code (and, plus, those comments I removed are actually helpful and give you some more information, so do read them after you've generated this app).

Hot Reload: You'll Love It!

Now, here's where things get incredibly cool! Make sure you have the app running in the emulator, and then head on over to Android Studio and find this line of code:

```
Text(
  'You have pushed the button this many times:',
),
```

Go ahead and edit that, maybe change "button" to "FAB," and press Ctrl+S, or select Save All on the File menu. Now, watch the emulator, and almost immediately you should see your change reflected on the screen (it may take a few seconds, but it should be a heck of a lot faster than the initial run).

Pretty sweet, no?

Hot reload works only in debug mode, which you can tell you are in thanks to the debug banner in the upper right of the app. In this mode, your app is actually running in a Dart Virtual Machine (VM) rather than having been compiled to native Arm code, which is what happens when you build your app for real (so yes, your app will be a hair slower in debug mode). Hot reload works by injecting your modified source code files into the already running Dart VM that hosts your app. When that happens, the VM updates the classes that changed by updating any altered fields or methods. Then, the Flutter framework initiates a rebuild of the widget tree, and your changes are reflected automatically. You don't need to rebuild, or redeploy, or restart anything; it all happens automatically as required to get your changes on the screen as quickly as possible.

Every now and again, though pretty rare in my experience, you may find that a change doesn't hot reload as expected. If that happens, the first thing to try is to click the Hot Reload icon on the toolbar, which looks like a lightning bolt, as shown in Figure 1-7 (you can also find a Hot reload option on the Run menu, with an associated hotkey, Ctrl+/).

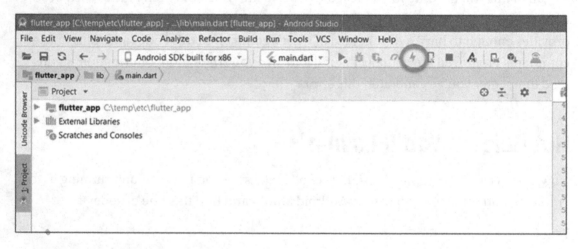

Figure 1-7. *The Hot reload icon in Android Studio*

That should get you going. Also note that in the console pane, which should automatically be at the bottom of the Android Studio window, you should see a message something along the lines of:

```
Performing hot reload...
Reloaded 1 of 448 libraries in 2,777ms.
```

Also, a little tooltip should appear near the console while the reload is in progress.

Now, an exciting thing about this mechanism, which you will have noticed if you clicked the FAB a few times and then did the text change, is that the existing state of the app is maintained. In other words, the count of the number of times you tapped the button remains after the reload. This makes it very easy to modify your UI and have it still show the current state so that you can essentially do easy A/B tests between two designs. But what if you want the state not to be maintained? In that case, you'll probably want to do a Hot restart. You'll find that option, which is something you have to trigger manually (as opposed to Hot reload, which occurs automatically when you make a change to the code and save it) by selecting the Hot restart option on the Run menu, or pressing the associated hotkey (Ctrl+Shift+/).

Interestingly, there doesn't appear to be a toolbar icon for Hot restart, but regardless, this will restart your app, but without doing a new build, and clearing state.

You naturally can trigger a build any time you want (which really is the Run command), but that will go through a compilation cycle, so it's slower. Hot restart is nearly as fast as Hot reload because it does a lot less work, but it gets you roughly the same effect (minus any pending code changes of course – you need to initiate a build for that, or let Hot reload do it, as by default is the case).

Hopefully, you're seeing how nice Hot reload can be, how efficient you can be as a developer with it doing its thing. I think you're going to come to appreciate it as you go further with Flutter!

Basic Flutter Application Structure

One final topic to touch on in this introductory chapter is the overall structure of the application that was generated for you. The primary directory structure is what you see in Figure 1-8.

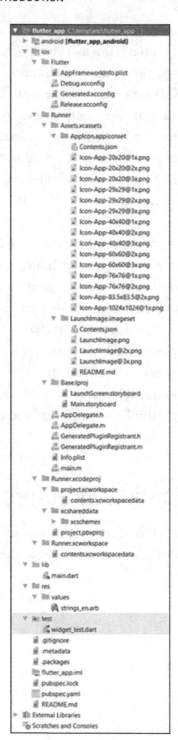

Figure 1-8. *The basic Flutter directory structure*

As you can see, there are five top-level directories. They are

- `android` – This contains Android-specific code and resources, things like application icons, Java code, and Gradle configuration and transient resources (Gradle being the build system Android uses). In fact, this is effectively a complete Android project that you could build using standard Android tools all by itself. For the most part, you should only have to modify the icons (which are in the `android/app/src/main/res` directories, where each subdirectory is a different icon resolution) and, depending on what your app does, the `AndroidManifest.xml` file in `android/app/src/main`, which is where you can set Android-specific application properties.

- `ios` – Just like the android directory, this directory contains project code specific to ios. The critical content here is the `ios/Runner/Assets.xcassets` directory, which is where the iOS-specific icons for your app are found, and the `Info.plist` file in `ios/Runner`, which roughly serves the same purpose as the `AndroidManifest.xml` file for Android apps.

- `lib` – Although it may seem odd at first, `lib` is where your application code will live! You are relatively free to organize your code any way you wish here, creating whatever directory structure suits you, though you'll need one file to serve as your entry point and most of the time that'll be the `main.dart` file that was generated for you.

- `res` – This directory contains some resources, things like strings for internationalization of your app. For this book, we won't be dealing with any of this.

- `test` – Here you will find Dart files for executing tests against your app. Flutter provides a Widget Tester utility that can make use of these tests to confirm the functionality of your widgets. As with the res directory, we won't be dealing with this testing in this book given that it's an optional part of Flutter development and could warrant a whole book on its own! Testing is essential generally of course, but until you learn to write Flutter apps, you won't have anything to test, and this book focuses on the first part of that goal.

Although hidden by default in Android Studio, there is also an `.idea` directory, which stores Android Studio configuration information and as such you can ignore it (note that Android Studio is based on the IntelliJ IDEA IDE, hence the name). There is also a hidden `build` directory that contains information used by Android Studio and the Flutter SDK to build your app. You typically can ignore this as well.

Aside from the directories, you'll also find some files in the root of the project. These are generally the only files you need to worry about outside of the `lib` directory (and others you see in the screenshot you don't need to be aware of generally), and those are

- `.gitignore` – The file Git version control uses to know what files, if any, to ignore from version control. Using Git is entirely optional when writing Flutter apps, but this file gets generated either way. Source control is a whole topic unto itself and one this book will not cover, so you can ignore this file.

- `.metadata` – Data that Android Studio to track your project. You can ignore this as you'll never edit this yourself.

- `.packages` – Flutter comes with its own package manager to manage dependencies within your project. This package manager is called Pub, and this file is what it uses to track dependencies in your project. You won't interact with this file directly, or even Pub directly, so this too can be ignored (it's not unheard of to use Pub directly from the command line, but from Android Studio it is, for the most part, abstracted away from you, along with most of the Flutter SDK's command line interface).

- `*.iml` – This file should be named after your project and is Android Studio's project configuration file. You'll never edit this directly, so ignore it.

- `pubspec.lock` and `pubspec.yaml` – Have you ever worked with NPM? Are you familiar with the `package.json` and the `package-lock.json` files it uses? Well, these are the same things but for Pub! If you aren't familiar with NPM, `pubspec.yaml` is how you will describe your project for Pub, including dependencies it has. The `pubspec.lock` file is a file Pub uses internally. You'll definitely edit `pubspec.yaml`, but not `pubspec.lock`, and we'll go over `pubspec.yaml` later on in detail.

- README.md – A readme file that you are free to use however you wish. Typically, this Markdown file is what sites like GitHub use to show information about your project when you browse to a repository where this file is in the root.

By far, the most important file here is pubspec.yaml, and it's one of the few you'll need to edit, so if you forget everything else here, just remember that! We'll get to it later, when we need to bring dependencies into our project, but for now, the generated file is quite enough for our needs.

A Few More "Under-the-Covers" Details

If you take a look at some of the files in the *ios* directory, you'll notice the word "Runner" in some. This is a hint at how Flutter apps work when building for release. As previously noted, Hot reload works because in debug mode your code is run in a VM. When assembled for release though, that's no longer the case. Then, your code gets compiled to native ARM code. It actually gets compiled into an ARM library, which explains why your code is in a lib directory: it wasn't a misnomer at all, was it?!

The Flutter engine's code, along with your application code, is Ahead-Of-Time (AOT) compiled with LLVM (Low-Level Virtual Machine, a compiler infrastructure, written in C++, which is designed for compile-time, link-time, run-time, and "idle-time" optimization of programs written in arbitrary programming languages) on iOS, and with the Android Native Development Kit (NDK) into a native ARM library. That library is included in what's called a "runner," which is just a native app that – wait for it – *runs* your application. Think of it as a thin wrapper around your app that knows how to start your app and provides some services to it. In some ways, the runner is still kind of a VM, though a very, very thin one (almost like a Docker container, if you're familiar with that).

Finally, the runner, along with the compiled library, is packaged into an .ipa for iOS or an .apk file for Android, and you have a complete, release-ready package! When the app is launched, the runner loads the Flutter library and your app code, and from that point on, all rendering and input/output and event processing is delegated to the compiled Flutter app.

Note   This is very similar to how many, if not most, cross-platform mobile game engines work. I previously wrote a book about Corona SDK, such a library that I have a lot of affection for, and it works in a very similar manner, though there the language in use is Lua instead of Dart (another one I'd bet the Flutter team considered!). It's just interesting to me that Google essentially took inspiration from game engines to create Flutter because it just proves what I've always said: if you want to be a better programmer, the one kind of project you should tackle to hone your skills is writing games. The world got a whole app framework out of the deal this time! And, if you haven't looked ahead yet, the last two chapters of this book are focused on building a game with Flutter, because I very much live that "program games" advice!

Summary

In this chapter, you started your Flutter journey! You learned about what Flutter is, what it offers, and why you might want to use it (and even some reasons you might *not* want to use it). You learned about critical concepts like Dart and widgets. You learned how to set up your development environment to be able to work on Flutter code, and you created your first very simple Flutter app and got it running in an emulator.

In the next chapter, you'll learn more about Dart, getting a good foundation in it, so that we can move on to building real apps with Flutter before long!

CHAPTER 2

Hitting the Bullseye with Dart

In the last chapter, you got a brief introduction to Dart, the language Google chose to underpin Flutter. It was a cursory introduction, just giving you a high-level overview of (some of) what Dart has to offer, but it was enough, along with some basic code samples, to provide you with a general idea what Dart is all about.

As you can imagine, given that all Flutter apps are built with Dart, it's something you must have a decent grasp of, and that's what this chapter is all about! As you read through it, you'll get to know Dart pretty well, at least well enough to get started with the code in subsequent chapters (where the knowledge from this chapter will hopefully get embedded in that brain of yours well and good). We'll get a bit more in-depth, but as we do, recall that introductory section from Chapter 1 because it, along with this chapter, forms a complete picture of Dart.

To be clear, this will not be an exhaustive look at Dart. I may fill in some gaps in later chapters as we explore application code, but some topics are either very rarely used or very specialized, and I felt it wouldn't hurt you in any way to skip them. Indeed, what's covered here is likely to be 95% of what you'll ever need to know about Dart. Naturally, the online Dart documentation that you can find at `www.dartlang.org`, which is Dart's home on the Web, has all those additional topics covered, plus in some cases expands on what's in this chapter, so if you really want to deep-dive into Dart, then stop over there when you're done with this chapter and have at it!

Now, let's start the journey by talking about some real basics, some key concepts that you must know in order to get far with Dart.

© Frank Zammetti 2019

F. Zammetti, *Practical Flutter*, https://doi.org/10.1007/978-1-4842-4972-7_2

The Things You Must Know

As with any modern programming language, Dart has a lot to offer, but it's built on a few key concepts that underpin most of it. Some of these are things that Dart has in common with other languages while some of them are things that make it stand out from the pack a bit.

But even before we start talking concepts, wanna see something cool? Take a look at Figure 2-1. This is what's known as DartPad, and it's a web app provided by the dartlang.org web site, more specifically `https://dartpad.dartlang.org`.

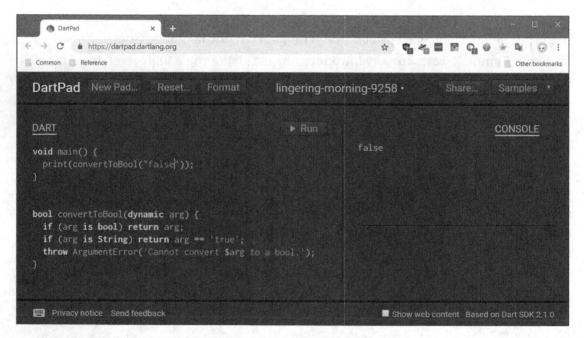

Figure 2-1. *FlutterPad, your experimental playground for Dart code on the Web!*

This neat tool allows you to play with most of Dart's capabilities in real-time without having to install any tooling at all! It's a great way to test concepts out quickly and easily. Just enter some code on the left and click Run, and you'll see the results on the right. Quick, super-useful and straightforward!

Now, on with the learning!

All languages have keywords, of course, tokens that you can't use because they have specific meaning in the language you're using, and Dart is no exception. Let's examine those keywords now. I've tried to group them into related concepts that were applicable to try and give you as much context as possible as we go through these. I've also tried to order them in a reasonable way rather than just a purely alphabetical list so that you'll learn about many of the concepts you need to know to be an effective Dart developer in a logical sequence as we go through them.

Note   This book assumes you aren't a complete beginner to programming generally and specifically that you already have some experience with a C-like language. That's especially true in this section because many of these keywords are no different than in any other language you're familiar with. For those, I'll offer only very brief descriptions, and I'll save the more in-depth explanations for those keywords and concepts that are unique to Dart, or if not unique are a little out of the ordinary at least.

No Comment: All About Comments

I want to start with our discussion by talking about comments in Dart because I feel like commenting, in general, is something that not enough developers do and do effectively. Comments are a critical part of programming whether it's something you enjoy doing or not, and as such, Dart provides three forms of comments.

First, Dart supports single-line comments using the likely familiar // character sequence. The compiler ignores anything following this on the line. As such, // can be the first thing on the line, or you can drop such a comment on the end of a line:

```
// Define the user's age.
int age = 25; // The age is 25
```

Now, don't get me wrong: I'm not suggesting this is an example of good or proper commenting! Quite the opposite in fact! I'm just using it as an example to show this form of a comment in Dart.

The second form is multi-line comments, and again here, Dart is typical by using the /* and */ marker sequences:

```
/*
  This function calculates account balance
  using the Miller-Hawthorne method
  of value calculation.
*/
```

Anything between those two sequences is ignored.

The final form of commenting provided by Dart are called documentation comments. These comments are designed to produce useful verbiage when documentation generation tooling is used on Dart code. These can be either single-line or multi-line by using the /// or /** and */ sequences:

```
/// This is a documentation comment.
/**
  This, too,
  is a
  documentation comment.
*/
```

As with the other forms, anything on a line with /// (which, again, can be the start of the line or post-fixed to the end of a line) is ignored. However, there is an exception: anything enclosed in brackets in such a comment is taken to be a reference to a class, method, field, top-level variable, function, or parameter, resolved to the lexical scope of the documented program element. So, for example:

```
class Pet {

  num legs;

  /// Feeds your pet [Treats].
  feed(Treats treat) {
    // Feed the critter!
  }

}
```

Here, when documentation is generated (which you can do with the Dart SDK's dartdoc tool) the [Treats] text will become a link to the API documentation for the Treats class (assuming dartdoc can find Treats in the lexical scope of the Pet class).

Tip   This is a bit of a tangent, but one I feel very strongly about and will use my author soapbox to espouse a bit! Please, comment your code and comment it well, most especially if anyone but you is ever going to look at it (but trust me, even if you expect it'll only ever be you, a well-written comment on code you haven't looked at in years will be a real godsend). There is an eternal ongoing debate in the programming world about commenting. Some people are completely averse to writing any sort of comments (this is the "self-documenting code" camp), others just want people to write useful comments. I'm very much in the latter camp, and I'm even a bit more extreme about it. To me, comments are just as important as code, and I've come to that conclusion based on 25 years of professional software development where maintaining other peoples' code, or just my own years later, is a huge challenge. Yes, try to write "self-documenting" code for sure, that's completely great advice. But then, once you've done so, comment anyway! Of course, don't tell me that a++; increments a in a comment, because that's pointless. You have to write meaningful comments obviously. But, if you aren't putting as much attention into writing good comments as you are writing good code then, in at least this author's opinion, you just aren't doing your job thoroughly and correctly.

Nothing Stays the Same: Variables

To begin with, everything is an object in Dart. Variables in Dart, as in virtually any language, store a value or a reference to something. In some languages, there is a difference between primitives like numbers and string and objects, which are instances of classes. Not so in Dart! Everything here is an object, even simple numbers, functions, and even null are all objects, which are always instances of classes, and all of which extend from a common Object class.

Variable Declaration and Initialization

In Dart, you can declare a variable in two ways:

```
var x;
```

...or...

```
<some specific type> x;
```

In this case, note that x has a value of null, even if it's of a numeric type. That's always the default value if you don't define the variable which, as in virtually all languages, you can combine with the declaration:

```
var x = "Mel  Brooks";
String x = "Mel  Brooks";
```

And there, you see something interesting: when you do var x, Dart will infer the type from the value assigned. It knows that x is a reference to a String in that case. But you can also declare the type explicitly, as in String x, either way works. There is a style guideline that says you should declare local variables using var and others using a type annotation (which is what the String in String x is considered), but that's a matter of preference ultimately.

Also, there is a third option:

```
dynamic x = "Mel Books";
```

Here, the dynamic type annotation tells Dart that what x references can change over time. So, if later you do

```
x = 42;
```

...Dart won't complain that x now points to a numeric value rather than a string.

There is, in fact, a fourth and final option for declaring a variable:

```
Object x = "Mel Brooks";
```

Since everything in Dart extends from the common Object class, this works too. But, as mentioned in the bullet points that started this chapter off, there is an important difference. If a variable is of type Object, and you try to call a method on the reference that doesn't exist, then you'll get a compile-time error. With dynamic, that won't be the case, and you'll only see the problem at runtime.

Constants and Final Values

Finally, related to all of this is the const and final keywords, both of which define a variable as being a constant, a final immutable value:

```
const x = "Mel Books";
```

It works with type annotations too:

```
const String x = "Mel Brooks";
```

And you can use final instead if you prefer:

```
final x = "Mel Brooks";
```

But, it's not just a preference. The difference is that const variables are constant at compile-time, which means their value can't depend on anything at runtime. So, if you tried:

```
const x = DateTime.now();
```

...that won't work. But, this will:

```
final x = DateTime.now();
```

Essentially, final means you can only set it once, but you can do so at runtime, while const means you can only set it once, but its value must be knowable at compile-time.

One final point on const: you can apply it to values as well as variable. For example (and don't worry that we haven't talked about what List is yet, we'll get to that soon – but I'm pretty sure you can figure it out anyway!):

```
List lst = const [ 1, 2, 3];
print(lst);
lst = [ 4, 5, 6 ];
print(lst);
lst[0] = 999;
print(lst);
```

That works as expected: the initial list of values (1, 2, 3) is printed, then a new list is referenced and printed (4, 5, 6), and finally the first element is updated, and the list again printed (999, 5, 6). However, what happens if you move the lst[0] = 999; line before the reassignment of lst on the third line? Well, now you'll get an exception because you're trying to alter a list that was marked as const. This is something a bit atypical in Dart (I'm sure *some* other language has his, but it's not *common* certainly).

Note   Variables and other identifiers can start with a letter or an underscore and then be followed by any combination of letters and numbers (and, of course, as many underscores as your heart desires!) Any that start with underscore have a special meaning: it is private to the library (or class) it's in. Dart doesn't have visibility keywords like public and private as is found in other languages like Java, but starting with an underscore does much the same thing as private does in Java and other languages.

Everybody Has a Type: Data Types

Dart is a strongly typed language, but curiously, you don't need to annotate types. They're optional, and that's because Dart performs type inference when annotations aren't present.

String Values

Dart offers a String type, which is a sequence of UTF-16 code units. Strings can be initialized using either single or double quotes. Strings can include expressions using the ${expression} syntax. If the expression refers to an identifier, then you can drop the curly braces. So:

```
String s1 = "Rickety Rocket";
String s2 = "${s1} blast off!";
String s3 = '$s1 blast off!';
print (s2);
print (s3);
```

You can see double and single quotes here, and you can see both forms of expressions (sometimes referred to as tokens).

String concatenation can use the + operator, as you can in a lot of languages, or it can use adjacent string literals, like this:

```
return "Skywalker," "Luke";
```

Those string literals can, of course, include expression tokens as well.

Numeric Values

Your typical integer numeric values have a type of int. The range of values is -2^{63} to $2^{63}-1$ on the Dart VM (the range will take on the range of JavaScript numbers when Dart code is compiled to JavaScript, something not discussed in this book, and it will never be larger than 64 bits, depending on platform)

A double precision floating point number, as specified by the IEEE 754 standard, has a type of double.

Both int and double are subclasses of num, so you can define a variable as num w = 5; or num x = 5.5; as well as int y = 5; or double z = 5.5; and Dart knows that x is a double based on its value just like it knows z is because you specified it.

A numeric can be turned into a string using the toString() method of the int and double classes:

```
int i = 5;
double d = 5.5;
String si = i.toString();
String sd = d.toString();
print(i);
print(d);
print(si);
print(sd);
```

And, a string can be turned into a number with the parse() method or the int and double classes:

```
String si = "5";
String sd = "5.5";
int i = int.parse(si);
double d = double.parse(sd);
```

```
print(si);
print(sd);
print(i);
print(d);
```

Note   It's a little weird to my eyes but notice that `String` is the only type
that starts with a capital letter. I'm not honestly sure why that is, but it's worth
pointing out. Well, it's also kinda/sorta not entirely true: `Map` and `List` also start
with capitals, as you'll see a few sections from now. Still, I'm not sure those
should be put in the same category as `String`, given that `String` is, to mind
anyway, a more "intrinsic" data type, like `int` and double. But we can debate
that another time – just realize that some data types start with a capital letter
and some don't!

Boolean Value

Boolean values are of type `bool`, and only two objects have boolean values: the keywords
`true` and `false` (which are compile-time constants).

   Note that Dart's type safety means that you can't write code like this:

```
if (some_non_boolean_variable)
```

   Instead, you must write something like:

```
if (some_non_boolean_variable.someMethod())
```

   In other words, the evaluation of a logic statement can't be "truthy" like you can do
in some languages. In Dart, it must always evaluate to one of these `bool` values.

Lists and Maps

The `List` class in Dart is akin to an array in most languages. An instance of one is a list of
values which are defined with syntax identical to JavaScript:

```
List lst = [ 1, 2, 3 ];
```

Note   Generally, you would write list (and later, set and map) when referring to an instance of the Map, Set, or List classes, and you only capitalize them when referring to the actual class.

You, of course, could also do either of these:

```
var lst1 = [ 1, 2, 3 ];
Object lst2 = [ 1, 2, 3 ];
```

A list uses a zero-based indexing scheme, so `list.length-1` gives you the index of the last element. You can access elements by index:

```
print (lst[1]);
```

A list, being an object, has several methods available on it. I'm not going to go over all of them since this chapter isn't trying to be a reference guide, and especially since most of them can be found in virtually any other language that offers a list-like construct and so you're likely familiar with most of them already, but here's a quick example of a few of them:

```
List lst = [ 8, 3, 12 ];
lst.add(4);
lst.sort((a, b) => a.compareTo(b));
lst.removeLast();
print(lst.indexOf(4));
print(lst);
```

Dart also offers a Set class, which is similar to List, but it's an unordered list, which means you can't retrieve elements by index, you have to use methods contains() and containsAll() instead:

```
Set cookies = Set();
cookies.addAll([ "oatmeal", "chocolate", "rainbow" ]);
cookies.add("oatmeal"); // No harm, no foul
cookies.remove("chocolate");
print(cookies);
print(cookies.contains("oatmeal"));
print(cookies.containsAll([ "chocolate", "rainbow" ]));
```

The call to contains() returns true, while the call to containsAll() returns false since chocolate was remove()'d. Note that add()'ing a value that's already in the set does no harm.

Dart also has a Map class, sometimes called a *dictionary* or a *hash*, or an *object literal* in JavaScript, an instance of which can be created a few ways:

```
var actors = {
  "Ryan Reynolds" : "Deadpool",
  "Hugh Jackman" : "Wolverine"
};
print(actors);

var actresses = Map();
actresses["scarlett johansson"] = "Black Widow";
actresses["Zoe Saldana"] = "Gamora";
print (actresses);

var movies = Map<String, int>();
movies["Iron Man"] = 3;
movies["Thor"] = 3;
print(movies);

print(actors["Ryan Reynolds"]);
print(actresses["Elizabeth Olsen"]);
movies.remove("Thor");
print(movies);
print(actors.keys);
print(actresses.values);

Map sequels = { };
print(sequels.isEmpty);
sequels["The Winter Soldier"] = 2;
sequels["Civil War"] = 3;
sequels.forEach((k, v) {
  print(k + " sequel #" + v.toString());
});
```

The first `actors` map is created using braces and with data defined immediately within it. The second `actresses` map uses the `new` keyword to create a new `Map` instance explicitly. Elements are added to it using bracket notation where the value inside the bracket is the key and the value after the equals is the value to map to that key. The third version shows that you can also define types for the keys and values in a map. That way, if you try to do:

```
Movies[3] = "Iron Man";
```

...you will get a compile error because 3 is an `int`, but the type of the key is defined as `String` (and likewise, the value type is defined as `int`, but we're trying to insert a `String`).

After that, you can see a few critical methods being used. The `remove()` method removes an element from a map. You can get a list of the keys and values by reading the `keys` and `values` attributes (which really means calling a getter method, as you'll see later in the section on classes, even though there's no parenthesis like normally after a method call). The `isEmpty()` method tells you whether the map is empty or not (there's also an `isNotEmpty()` method if you prefer that). Although not shown, a map also provides the `contains()` and `containsAll()` methods, just like a list does. Finally, the `forEach()` method allows you to execute an arbitrary function for each element in the map (the function you supply is passed the key and the value – and there's more to come on functions, so don't worry about the details just yet).

As with lists, there are many more utility methods available on maps, too many to go over here, but we'll likely encounter others as we look at the code of the projects in later chapter.

Finally, one last point related to data types is that there is also a special `dynamic` type that, in effect, turns off Dart's type system. Imagine if you write:

```
Object obj = some_object;
```

Dart knows that you can call some methods on obj like `toString()` and `hashCode()` because they are defined by the `Object` class that all objects extend from. If you try to call `obj.fakeMethod()`, then you'll get a warning because Dart can see, at compile-time, that `fakeMethod()` isn't a method of the `Object` class, or (presumably) of the class that `some_object` is an instance of. But if you write

```
dynamic obj = some_object;
```

Now, if you write `obj.fakeMethod()`, you won't get a warning at compile-time, though you will now get an error at runtime. Think of dynamic as a way of telling Dart: "hey, I'm the one in charge here, trust me, I know what I'm doing!". The dynamic type is typically used with things like return values from interop activities, so you may not encounter it all that much, but it's worth nothing, and it's worth understanding that it's fundamentally different from declaring something of type Object.

When a Single Value Just Won't Do: Enumerations

Need to have an object that contains a fixed number of constant values? Don't wanna have a bunch of variable floating around and don't need a full-blown class? Then an enum (short for *enumeration*) is right for you! Look! Here comes one now!

```
enum SciFiShows { Babylon_5, Stargate_SG1, Star_Trek };
```

And, here's some things you can do with one:

```
main() {
  assert(SciFiShows.Babylon_5.index == 0);
  assert(SciFiShows.Stargate_SG1.index == 1);
  assert(SciFiShows.Star_Trek.index == 2);
  print(SciFiShows.values);
  print(SciFiShows.Stargate_SG1.index);
  var show = SciFiShows.Babylon_5;
  switch (show) {
    case SciFiShows.Babylon_5: print("B5"); break;
    case SciFiShows.Stargate_SG1: print("SG1"); break;
    case SciFiShows.Star_Trek: print("ST"); break;
  }
}
```

Every value in the enum has an implicit `index` getter method, so you can always find the index of a given value (and you'll get a compile error if the value isn't valid in the enum. You can also get a list of all the values in the enum through the `values` property (which too also has an implicit getter). Finally, enum's are especially useful in `switch` statements, and Dart will give you a compile error if you don't have a `case` for all the values in the enum.

What's Your Type: The "as" and "is" Keywords

These two conceptually go together: the is keyword allows you to determine if a reference is of a given type (if it implements a given interface essentially) and as allows you to treat a given type reference as another, assuming it's a superclass. For example:

```
if (shape is Circle) {
  print(circle.circumference);
}
```

This will only print() (which writes content to the console) the circumference if the object reference by shape is of type Circle.

By contrast, you can use as like so:

```
(shape as Circle).circumference = 20;
```

That way, if shape is a Circle, it works as expected, and if shape can be cast to a Circle, then I would work too (perhaps shape is of type Oval, which is a subclass of Circle, for example).

Note, however, that in the example of is, nothing will happen if shape isn't a Circle, but in the as example, an exception will be thrown if shape can't be cast to Circle.

Going with the Flow: Flow Control (and Logic!) Constructs

Dart has several logic and flow control statements and constructs, most of which will be familiar to someone with any programming experience at all.

Looping

Looping in Dart takes on the familiar for, do, and while loop forms:

```
for (var i = 0; i < 10; i++) {
  print(i);
}
```

There is also a `for-in` form, if the target class is iterable:

```
List starfleet = [ "1701", "1234", "1017", "2610", "7410"  ];
main() {
  for (var shipNum in starfleet) {
    print("NCC-" + shipNum);
  }
}
```

A `List` is one such iterable class, so this works well. If you prefer a more functional style, you can use the `forEach` form:

```
main() {
  starfleet.forEach((shipNum) => print("NCC-" + shipNum));
}
```

Note   Don't get hung up on these functions, especially if the syntax looks a little foreign to you. We'll get into functions in just a few sections, and it should all come into focus quickly when we do.

The do and `while` loops offer the typical two forms, `do-while` and `while-do`:

```
while (!isDone()) {
  // Do something
}

do {
  showStatus();
} while (!processDone());
```

Note that as in most other languages, the `continue` keyword is also available in Dart to skip to the next iteration of a loop construct. There is also a `break` keyword to exit from a loop early (which does double duty in the `switch` construct too).

Switch

Dart also offers a `switch` structure, and four keywords work together like in most languages to construct switch statements:

```
switch (someVariable) {
  case 1:
    // Do something
  break;
  case 2:
    // Do something else
  break;
  default:
    // It wasn't 1 or 2
  break;
}
```

The switch statement in Dart can deal with integer or string types, and the compared objects must be of the same types (and no subclasses allowed here!), and the classes must not override the == operator.

If Statements

Finally, because they are essentially flow control elements, yes, your all-time favorite logic statement is present in Dart, and it wouldn't be much use without, would it? Note that in Dart, condition expressions must always evaluate to a boolean value, nothing else is allowed. And yes, you can write else if of course:

```
if (mercury == true || venus == true ||
  earth == true || mars == true
) {
  print ("It's an inner planet");
} else if (jupiter || saturn || uranus || neptune) {
  print ("It's an outer planet");
} else {
  print("Poor Pluto, you are NOT a planet");
}
```

Note that if mercury, venus, earth, and mars were bool types then if (mercury || venus || earth || mars) would also be valid here.

The Big Nothing: void

In most languages, if a function doesn't return anything, you have to slap void in front of it. In Dart, which supports the void keyword, you *can* do that, but you don't *have* to.

In Dart though, void is a bit more… curious.

First, if a function doesn't explicitly return anything, then you can omit a return type entirely; you don't even need to put void in front of it like most languages (although you are free to do so if you prefer). In such cases, an implicit return null; is added to the end of the function. This is the case for all the code samples thus far.

If you do put void in front of a function though, you will then get a compile-time error if you try to return anything. That makes sense. But if you try and return null, that's okay, no error. You can also return a void function (a function that has void before it).

Here's where it gets a little weird though:

```
void func() { }

class MyClass {
  void sayHi() {
    print("Hi");
    dynamic a = 1;
    return a;
  }
}

main() {
  MyClass mc = MyClass();
  var b = mc.sayHi();
  print(b);
}
```

Given that sayHi() is a void function, you'd expect that return a from it would produce an error, right? Well, not so! It will compile. Well, it would compile, except for the print(b); line. That will cause a compile-time error, and the reason is that Dart won't let you use anything returned from a void function (even though you can capture it, since the var b = mc.sayHi(); line compiles and executes without issue – Dart is kind of a tease that way!).

So yeah, void is kind of a weird thing in Dart. My advice is to not use it unless you specifically know that you need to.

But, void isn't just for return types. You can also use void in generic type parameters, where they are treated semantically like Object is:

```
main() {
  List<void> l = [ 1, 2, 3 ]; // Equivalent to List<Object> = [ 1, 2, 3 ];
  print(l);
}
```

Why you might do this is something I'll touch upon on the section on asynchronous code.

Smooth Operators

Dart has a robust set of operators for you to work with, most of which are likely familiar to you, as shown in Table 2-1.

Table 2-1. *Dart operators*

Operator	Meaning
+	Add
-	Subtract
-expr	Prefix unary minus (a.k.a. negation/reverse sign of expression)
*	Multiply
/	Divide
~/	Divide, returning an integer result
%	Get the remainder of an integer division (modulo)
++var	Prefix increment, equivalent to var = var + 1 (expression value is var + 1)
var++	Postfix increment, equivalent to var = var + 1 (expression value is var)
--var	Prefix decrement, equivalent to var = var − 1 (expression value is var − 1)
var--	Postfix decrement, var = var − 1 (expression value is var)

(*continued*)

Table 2-1. (*continued*)

Operator	Meaning
==	Equal
!=	Not equal
>	Greater than
<	Less than
>=	Greater than or equal to
<=	Less than or equal to
=	Assignment
&	Logical AND
|	Logical OR
^	Logical XOR
~expr	Unary bitwise complement (0s become 1s; 1s become 0s)
<<	Shift left
>>	Shift right
a ? b : c	Ternary conditional expression
a ?? b	Binary conditional expression: if a is not null, return a, otherwise return b
..	Cascade notation
()	Function application
[]	List access
.	Member access

A note on the == operator: This is a value check, not an object check. When you need to test if two variables reference the exact same object, use the `identical()` global function.

When using the == operator, as in `if (a == b)`, `true` is returned if they are both `null`, `false` if only one is. When this expression is executed, the `==()` method of the first operand (yes, == is indeed the name of a method!) is executed.

So:

```
if (a == b)
```

...is equivalent to...

```
if (a.==(b))
```

A note on the = operator: There is also a ??= operator which does the assignment only if the operand is null.

Another note on the = operator: There are a host of compound operators that combine an assignment and an operation. These are

```
-=  /=  %=  >>=  ^=  +=  *=  ~/=  <<=  &=  |=
```

A note on the . operator: There is also a conditional version written ?. that allows you to access a member of something where that something could be null.

Take this code, for example:

```
var person = findPerson("Frank Zammetti");
```

If person could be null, then writing print(person?.age) will avoid a null pointer error. The result, in this case, would be null printed, but no error, which is the key point.

A note on the .. operator: This allows you to take code like this:

```
var person = findPerson("Frank Zammetti");
obj.age = 46;
obj.gender = "male";
obj.save();
```

...and instead write it like this...

```
findPerson("Frank Zammetti")
  ..age = 46
  ..gender = "male"
  ..save();
```

Use whichever style is more pleasing to your eyes, Dart doesn't care either way.

Classes can also define custom operators, but that statement doesn't have much value unless we first talk about what classes are all about, so let's do that now, shall we?

Classing the Joint Up: Object Orientation in Dart

Dart is object-oriented, which means we're dealing with classes and objects. Defining a class is as simple as

```
class Hero { }
```

Yep, that's it!

Instance Variables

Now, classes frequently have instance variables (or members, or fields, or properties, all are synonymous) like so:

```
class Hero {
  String firstName;
  String lastName;
}
```

Any instance variable that you don't initialize with a value begins with a value of null. Dart will automatically generate a getter (accessor) method for each variable, and it will also generate a setter (mutator) for any non-final variables.

Instance variables can be marked as static as well, which means you can use them without instantiating the class:

```
class MyClass {
  static String greeting = "Hi";
}

main() {
  print(MyClass.greeting);
}
```

That will print "Hi", all without ever creating an instance of MyClass.

Methods

Classes can also have member functions, called methods:

```
class Hero {
  String firstName;
  String lastName;
  String sayName() {
    return "$lastName, $firstName";
  }
}
```

We're going to look at functions in more detail in the next section, but I'm betting you're already familiar with them generally. If you aren't, then this book probably isn't a good starting point for you since it assumes *some* level of modern programming experience. Right now, understand that the return keywords returns a value from the function (or method, when its part of a class) to the caller.

Now, we have a sayName() method that we could call like so:

```
main() {
  Hero h = new Hero ();
  h.firstName = "Luke";
  h.lastName = "Skywalker";
  print(h.sayName());
}
```

That also demonstrates that setter methods have indeed been created for us, which is why h.firstName = "Luke"; works.

I skipped over something there: as in virtually all object-oriented languages, the new keyword instantiates objects of a given type, as seen in the previous code. However, in Dart, the new keyword is optional. So, in addition to the previous code, you can also write

```
var h = Hero();
```

To be honest, this was, to my brain, one of the weirdest things to get used to about Dart! I'm not sure there's any compelling reason to do one vs. the other, so pretty much just write it the way makes the most sense to you!

Methods can also be marked as static, just like instance variables can be:

```
class MyClass {
  static sayHi() {
    print("Hi");
  }
}

main() {
  MyClass.sayHi();
}
```

As with the static variable example, this again prints "Hi", but this time as a result of calling sayHi() without instantiating MyClass first.

Constructors

Now, classes also frequently have constructors, that is, special function that execute when an instance of them is created. Adding one is simple:

```
class Hero {
  String firstName;
  String lastName;
  Hero(String fn, String ln) {
    firstName = fn;
    lastName = ln;
  }
  String sayName() {
    return "$lastName, $firstName";
  }
}
```

The constructor always has the same name as the class and doesn't have a return type annotation. Now, our test code would look like this:

```
main() {
  Hero h = new Hero("Luke", "Skywalker");
  print(h.sayName());
}
```

However, because a constructor that just sets instance variable values is such a common pattern, Dart has a shortcut constructor form for this:

```dart
class Hero {
  String firstName;
  String lastName;
  Hero(this.firstName, this.lastName);
  String sayName() {
    return "$lastName, $firstName";
  }
}
```

The "this" Reference

The this keyword references the current instance of the class a block of code is executing within (which a construct or not). Typically, you should only use this when there is a naming conflict. For example:

```dart
class Account {
  int balance;
  Account(int balance) {
    this.balance = balance;
  }
}
```

But, philosophical debates about whether you should ever "mask" variable names like this aside (my own personal style says you never do that, I would name that balance argument inBalance or something different than the class-level balance), this allows you to disambiguate such a case and it's necessary specifically in this shortcut constructor form.

Note that if your class doesn't define a constructor, as in the first three versions of Hero mentioned earlier, Dart will generate a default no-argument constructor that just invokes the no-argument constructor of the superclass (which here is Object implicitly). Also, note that subclasses do not inherit constructors.

A constructor can also be marked with the factory keyword. This is used when the constructor might not return an instance of its class. I know, that probably sounds weird because it's an unusual capability of most OOP languages, but it can happen if, for example, you want to return an existing instance of the class from a cache of already constructed objects and not produce a new object, which is what happens by default. A `factory` constructor might also return an instance of a subclass rather than the class itself. A `factory` constructor otherwise works just like any other constructor, and you call them the same too, with the only real difference being that they don't have access to the `this` reference.

Subclassing

I mentioned subclasses here a moment ago, so how do we define those? Well, it's easy:

```
class Hero {
  String firstName;
  String lastName;
  Hero.build(this.firstName, this.lastName);
  String sayName() {
    return "$lastName, $firstName";
  }
}
class UltimateHero extends Hero {
  UltimateHero(fn, ln) : super.build(fn, ln);
  String sayName() {
    return "Jedi $lastName, $firstName";
  }
}
```

The extends keyword, followed by the name of the class we want to subclass, is all it takes.

However, there's a bit more going on here of interest. First is the notion of named constructors. Gaze in awe at that Hero class. See that Hero.build() method? Well, that's a constructor too, but it's what is termed a *named* constructor. The reason this is necessary is because in the UltimateHero class, due to constructors not being inherited, we need to supply one. But, given that it should do the same as what Hero.build() does, there's no point in repeating the code (the DRY – Don't Repeat Yourself – principle). So, how do you call the constructor in the parent class? That's where the : super.build(fn, ln); bit following the UltimateHero(fn, ln) constructor comes in. The super keyword allows you to call methods or access variables in the parent class. But, there's no way to call the constructor *without* it being named. In other words, `super(fn, ln)`, which would work in many other languages, doesn't in Dart. But, what we *can* do is call a named constructor without issue, so that's exactly what we do here, using the syntax from the colon on.

Getters and Setters

Now that you've seen all of that, I want to go back to the notion of getters and setters. You see, you can create your own, aside from the ones implicitly created, to in a sense create new instance variables on-the-fly. For that, Dart offers the `get` and `set` keywords:

```dart
class Hero {
  String firstName;
  String lastName;
  String get fullName => "$lastName, $firstName";
  set fullName(n) => firstName = n;
  Hero(String fn, String ln) {
    firstName = fn;
    lastName = ln;
  }
  String sayName() {
    return "$lastName, $firstName";
  }
}
```

Here, we now have a `fullName` field. When we try to access it, we'll get the same sort of concatenation of `lastName` and `firstName` as `sayName()` provides, but when we try to set it, we'll be overwriting the `firstName` field. So, now we can test it:

```dart
main() {
  Hero h = new Hero("Luke", "Skywalker");
  print(h.sayName());
  print(h.fullName);
  h.fullName = "Anakin";
  print(h.fullName);
}
```

The output here will be

```
Skywalker, Luke
Skywalker, Luke
Skywalker, Anakin
```

Hopefully you can see why!

Interfaces

Dart doesn't distinguish the notion of classes and interfaces like most other object-oriented languages do. Instead, a Dart class also implicitly defines an interface. Therefore, we could re-implement the `UltimateHero` class like so:

```
class UltimateHero implements Hero {
  @override
  String firstName;
  @override
  String lastName;
  UltimateHero(this.firstName, this.lastName);
  String sayName() {
    return "Jedi $lastName, $firstName";
  }
}
```

The `@override` here is a metadata annotation, but we'll get to those later. For now, just understand that it's necessary to indicate to dart that we are overriding the superclass's getter and setter for the two marked fields and without them, we'll get an error. With that change, we also need to change the constructor because now we're not extending the class and so don't have access to the `Hero.build()` constructor (because constructors are never inherited and also implementing an interface means we don't have access to the behaviors of the class that provides the interface, we're just saying that our new class provides that same functionality as contractually obligated by the interface), so it becomes a constructor that mimics what's in Hero instead. The only other change is swapping the `implements` keyword in for `extends` since now we're implementing the interface defined by the `Hero` class rather than extending it.

Tip   Why `implements` vs. `extends` you ask? It's a question many ask in the OOP world. Some people feel that a compositional model, which is what `implements`... err... *implements*... is cleaner. Others think that hierarchies of classes is more proper classical OOP and so prefer `extends`. Whatever your view, understand one key point: they aren't equivalent concepts, and in Dart, as in Java and many other OOP languages, you can only extend a single class directly, but you can implement as many interfaces as you wish. So, if your goal is to build a class that provides an API that mimics multiple classes, then `implements` is what you likely want. Otherwise, you may be on the `extends` road instead.

Abstract Classes

Next, let's quickly touch on `abstract`. This keyword marks an abstract class, like so:

```
abstract class MyAbstractClass {
  someMethod();
}
```

Here, `MyAbstractClass` can't be instantiated and instead must be extended by a concrete class that itself can be instantiated. Methods inside abstract classes can provide an implementation, or they can be themselves be abstract, in which case, they must always be implemented by a subclass. Here, `someMethod()` is considered abstract (because it has no method body), but instead you could also do

```
abstract class MyAbstractClass {
  someMethod() {
    // Do something
  }
}
```

In that case, `someMethod()` has a default implementation and a subclass therefore does not need to provide one if it doesn't want to.

In addition to extending classes, implementing interfaces and abstract classes, Dart also offers the notion of mixins, which is where the `with` keyword comes into play:

```dart
class Person { }

mixin Avenger {
  bool wieldsMjolnir = false;
  bool hasArmor = false;
  bool canShrink = true;
  whichAvenger() {
    if (wieldsMjolnir) {
      print("I'm Thor");
    } else if (hasArmor) {
      print("I'm Iron Man");
    } else {
      print("I'm Ant Man");
    }
  }
}

class Superhero extends Person with Avenger { }

main() {
  Superhero s = new Superhero();
  s.whichAvenger();
}
```

Here, we've got two classes, Person and Superhero, and one mixin, Avenger (which we know based on the mixin keyword that comes before its definition). Notice that Person and Superhero are empty classes, which means that the call to whichAvenger() must be coming from elsewhere, and it is: we've "mixed the Avenger mixin into the Superhero class," so to speak, by specifying with Avenger in the Superhero class definition. Now, whatever is in the Avenger mixin will also be present in Superhero, and our test code works as expected.

Visibility

In Java and many other OOP languages, you typically need to specify what access code has to class members using keywords like public, private, and protected. Dart is different: everything is public unless it begins with an underscore, which marks it as being private to its library, or class.

Operators

As Steve Jobs used to say: "One more thing!"

Of the various operators Dart provides, the following are special (the commas and the period are *not* operators!): <, >, <=, >=, -, +, /, ~/, *, %, |, ^, &, <<, >>, [], []=, ~, ==. How are they special? Well, they're the only ones you can override in a class using the operator keyword:

```
class MyNumber {
  num val;
  num operator + (num n) => val * n;
  MyNumber(v) { this.val = v; }
}

main() {
  MyNumber mn = MyNumber(5);
  print(mn + 2);
}
```

Here, the MyNumber class overrides the + operator. The current value of an instance of this class will be multiplied by a value rather than be added together thanks to the function supplied for the + operator in the override. So, when main() executes, rather than printing 7 as you would normally expect from the + operator, it instead prints 10 since it multiplies the value of mn, 5, by the 2 after the overridden + operator in the print() statement.

The only catch is that if you override the == operator, then you should also override the class's hashCode getter. Otherwise, equivalency can't reliably be determined.

Whew, that was a lot! But it covers probably the majority of what you'll need to know about classes and objects in Dart.

Getting Funky with Functions

In Dart, functions are first-class citizens and have their own type: Function. What that means is that functions can be assigned to variables, can be passed as parameters, and can also be stand-alone entities. There's one key stand-alone function you're already aware of, and that's main().

Functions in Dart have some sweet syntactic sugar too (see what I did there?). They can have named parameters, and they can also have optional parameters. You can have optional parameters whether you use named parameters or purely positional (the typical style of parameter list), but you can't mix the two styles. You can also have default values for parameters. Examine this code:

```
greet(String name) {
  print("Hello, $name");
}

class MyClass {
  greetAgain({ Function f, String n = "human" }) {
    f(n);
  }
}

main() {
  MyClass mc = new MyClass();
  greet("Frank");
  mc.greetAgain( f : greet, n : "Traci" );
  mc.greetAgain( f : greet);
}
```

Here, you can see most of that at work. First, we have a stand-alone greet() function. Then, we have a class with a greetAgain() method. This method accepts a named parameter list, and look, one of those parameters is a Function! Also, see how the n parameter has a default value of human defined? Cool, right? Then, inside the function, we call the function referenced by f, passing it n. In other words, whatever function is passed in as the value of the f parameter, because it's annotated as a Function, we can use that f reference to call it.

Now, in the main() function, we first just call greet(), passing it the name that was passed into it, to have the computer say hello. Then, we call that greetAgain() method of the MyClass instance mc, and this time, we're passing named parameters, and the value of the f parameter is a reference to the greet() function. I show this twice so you can see how it works if you don't pass a name, and it'll just greet a generic human.

Note   In many languages, the data you pass to functions are called arguments. That's the term I grew up with frankly, but the Dart language docs seem to prefer parameters. Truthfully, I may mix those terms sometimes, but they mean the same in this context.

Unfortunately, DartPad does not, as of this writing, allow for importing libraries, which we would need to use the @required annotation that ideally would be before the n parameter in greetAgain(), but not the f parameter. So, because you may want to plug this code in to DartPad and try it, I left that annotation out. Also note that when using positional parameters, you don't use @required, you instead wrap the optional parameters in square brackets.

While most functions have a name, they don't have to, they can also be anonymous. As an example:

```
main() {
  var bands = [ "Dream Theater", "Kamelot", "Periphery" ];
  bands.forEach((band) {
    print("${bands.indexOf(band)}: $band");
  });
}
```

Here, there's a function passed to the forEach() method of the List object bands, but it has no name and as a result, it only exists for the lifetime of the execution of forEach().

An important thing about functions is the scope they introduce. Dart is considered a "lexically scoped" language, which means that the scope of a given thing, a variable mostly, is determined by the structure of the code itself. If it's enclosed in curly braces, then it's within that scope, and that scope extends downward, meaning that if you have nested functions, for example (which is something else you can totally do in Dart!), then the deeper in the nesting you go, those elements still have access to everything above. To demonstrate this, check out this example:

```
bool topLevel = true;

main() {
```

```
  var insideMain = true;

  myFunction() {

    var insideFunction = true;

    nestedFunction() {
      var insideNestedFunction = true;
      assert(topLevel);
      assert(insideMain);
      assert(insideFunction);
      assert(insideNestedFunction);
    }

  }


}
```

The nestedFunction() can use any variable all the way up to the top level.

Dart also supports the concept of closures with functions so that a function will capture, or "close around," its lexical scope, even if the function is used outside of its original scope. In other words, if a function has access to a variable, then the function will, in a sense, "remember" that variable even if the scope the variable is in is no longer "alive", so to speak, when the function executes.

By way of example:

```
remember(int inNumber) {
  return () => print(inNumber);
}

main() {
  var jenny = remember(8675309);
  jenny();
}
```

Here, the call to jenny() print 8675309, even though it wasn't passed to it. This happens because jenny() includes the lexical scope of remember(), and the execution context at the time the reference is captured, which includes the value passed into the call to remember() when getting the reference. It's confusing if you've never encountered it before, I know, but the good news is that you probably won't need to use closures very much in Dart in my experience (as compared to, say JavaScript, where it comes up all the time).

Dart also supports arrow, or lambda, notation for defining functions. So, these are equivalent:

```
talk1() { print("abc"); }
talk2() => print("abc");
```

Tell Me Is It So: Assertions

The assert keyword is like in most other languages and isn't used in production builds. It's used to disrupt normal flow if a given boolean condition is false and throws an AssertionException in that case. For example:

```
assert (firstName == null);
assert (age > 25);
```

Optionally, you can attach a message to the assert like so:

```
assert (firstName != null, "First name was null");
```

Out of Time: Asynchrony

Asychronous (or just async) programming is big business these days! It's everywhere, in all languages, and Dart is no exception. In Dart, two classes are key to asynchrony, Future and Stream, along with two keywords, async and await. Both classes are objects that async functions return when a long-running operation begins, but before it completes, allowing the program to await the result while continuing to do other things, then continue where it left off when the result comes back.

To call a function that returns a Future, you use the await keyword:

```
await someLongRunningFunction();
```

That's all you have to do! Your code will pause at this line until someLongRunningFunction() completes. The program can still do other things rather than being blocked by the long-running operation (for example, if an event handler for a button click fires, which would be blocked if someLongRunningFunction() was synchronous). The async function itself must be marked with the async keyword in front of its body definition and must return a Future:

```
Future someLongRunningFunction() async {
  // Do something that takes a long time
}
```

There's one more key piece of information: the function that calls someLongRunningFunction() must itself be marked as async:

```
MyFunction() async {
  await someLongRunningFunction();
}
```

You can await a function, whether the same or others, as many times as you wish in a single async function and execution will pause on each.

Note   There is also a Future API that allows you to do much the same thing but without using async and await. I'm not covering this just because async/await is generally considered by most to be a more elegant approach, and I certainly echo that sentiment. Feel free to explore that API on your own though if you're curious.

Streams are handled in much the same way, but to read data from the Stream you must use an async for loop:

```
await for (varOrType identifier in expression) {
  // Executes each time the stream emits a value.
}
```

The difference between the two is simply that using a Future means that the return from the long-running function won't occur until that function completes, however long it takes. With a Stream, the function can return data little by little over time, and your code that is awaiting it will execute any time the Stream emits a value. You can break or return from the loop to stop reading form the Stream, and the loop will end when the async function closes the Stream. As before, an await for loop is only allowed inside of an async function.

Ssshhh, Be Quiet: Libraries (and Visibility)

Libraries are used in Dart to make code modular and shareable. A library provides some external API to other code that uses it. It also serves as a method of isolation in that any identifier in a library that starts with an underscore character is visible only inside that library. Interestingly, every single Dart app is automatically a library whether you do anything special or not! Libraries can be packaged up and delivered to others using the Dart SDK's pub tool, which is the package and asset manager

---

Note   I won't be covering the creation of libraries here as it's a bit more advanced and not something we'll need in this book. So, if you're interested in distributing your libraries, then you'll need to consult the Dart documentation. Note that the Dart SDK comes as part of the Flutter SDK, so you have this already.

To use a library, the import keyword comes into play:

```
import "dart:html";
```

Some libraries are provided by your own code, and others are built into Dart, as is this one. For those built-in libraries, the form of the URI, which is what the part of the statement in quotes is, has a particular form: it begins with dart:, which is the scheme identifier portion of the URI.

If the library that you're importing comes from a package, which was touched on briefly in Chapter 1 and which we'll get into in more detail starting with the next chapter, then instead of dart: you would use the package: scheme:

```
import "package:someLib.dart";
```

If the library is part of your code, or perhaps something you copied into your codebase, then the URI is a relative file system path:

```
import "../libs/myLibrary.dart";
```

Sometimes, you may want to import two libraries, but they have conflicting identifiers in them. For example, maybe lib1 has an Account class, and so does lib2, but you need to import both. In that case, the as keyword comes into play:

```
import "libs/lib1.dart";
import "libs/lib2.dart" as lib2;
```

Now, if you want to reference the Account class in lib1, you do

```
Account a = new Account();
```

But if you want the Account object from lib2, you would write

```
lib2.Account = new lib2.Account();
```

With the imports shown here, everything in the library would be imported. You don't have to do that though; you can import just parts of a library too:

```
import "package:lib1.dart" show Account;
import "package:lib2.dart" hide Account;
```

Here, only the Account class from lib1 would be imported, and everything *except* the Account class from lib2 would be imported.

So far, all the imports shown would import the library immediately. But, you can also defer that loading, which helps reduce your app's initial startup time:

```
import "libs/lib1.dart" deferred as lib1;
```

Now, there's a little more work to be done on your part! When you get to the point in your code where you need that library, you must then load it:

```
await lib1.loadLibrary();
```

As you learned in the last section, that code must be in a function marked async.

Note that invoking loadLibrary() on a library multiple times is fine, no harm is done. Also, until the library is loaded, the constants defined in the library, if any, aren't actually constants – they don't exist until it's loaded, so you can't use them.

Deferred loading can also be handy if you want to do A/B testing with your app because you can dynamically load one library vs. another to test the differences.

Let's Be Exceptional: Exception Handling

Exception handling in Dart is simple and looks a lot like Java or JavaScript, or indeed most other languages that deals with exceptions. In contrast to many other languages though, in Dart, you are not required to declare what exceptions a given function must throw, nor must you catch any. In other words, all exceptions in Dart are unchecked.

To begin, you can throw an exception yourself:

```
throw FormatException("This value isn't in the right format");
```

Exceptions are objects, so you need to construct one to throw.

An interesting thing about Dart is that you don't need to throw any specific object or even an object of a particular subtype. You can throw anything as an exception:

```
throw "This value isn't in the right format";
```

That's throwing a string as an exception, and that's perfectly fine in Dart. However, with that said, it's generally considered bad form to throw anything that doesn't extend from the Error or Exception classes that Dart provides, so this "throw anything" is one capability you might want just to forget exists in Dart!

On the flip side, to catch an exception, you write

```
try {
  somethingThatMightThrowAnException();
} on FormatException catch (fe) {
  print(fe);
} on Exception catch (e) {
  Print("Some other Exception: " + e);
} catch (u) {
  print("Unknown exception");
} finally {
  print("All done!");
}
```

A couple of things are noteworthy there. First, you wrap code that might throw an exception (that you want to handle – remember, being unchecked exceptions, you never *need* to handle *any* exceptions) in a try block. Then, you catch one or more exceptions as you see fit. Here, the somethingThatMightThrowAnException() function can throw a FormatException, and we want to handle that explicitly. Then, we'll handle any other object thrown that is a subclass of Exception and display its message. Finally, anything else thrown will be handled as an unknown exception.

Next, notice the syntactic differences there: you can write on <exception_type> catch, or you can just write catch(<object_identifier) where the object identifier is the object that was thrown under whatever name you'd like in the catch block. You can

also just write on if you wish. The difference is what you need to do: if you just want to handle the exception but don't care about the thrown object, you can just write on. If you don't care about the type but do want the thrown object, then just use `catch`. When you care both about the type and also need the thrown object, use `on <exception_type> catch(<object_identifier>)`.

You can also add a `finally` clause to a `try...catch` block. This code will execute whether any sort of exception was thrown or not. This code will execute after any matching `catch` clauses have finished their work.

Finally, you can define your own exception classes just by extending `Exception` or `Error`. You then use them precisely as you do any Dart-provided exception.

I Have the Power: Generators

Sometimes, you have some code that produces some values. Maybe that code relies on some remote system that it needs to call. In that case, you may not want to block the rest of your code from executing while those values are generated. You instead want to generate that list in a "lazy" fashion. Alternatively, you may simply not want or be able to produce the list of values all in one shot. In these situations, a generator is something you'll want to be familiar with

Dart has two types of generators: synchronous, which returns an `Iterable` object, and asynchronous, which returns a `Stream` object. Let's discuss the synchronous type first by way of example:

```
Iterable<int> countTo(int max) sync* {
  int i = 0;
  while (i < max) yield i++;
}

main() {
  Iterable it = countTo(5);
  Iterator i = it.iterator;
  while (i.moveNext()) {
    print(i.current);
  }
}
```

The first thing to note is the sync* marker before the body of the function. This clues Dart into the fact that this is a generator function (and a generator is always a function by the way). The second key point is the use of the yield keyword within the generator. This effectively adds the value to the Iterable that is constructed behind the scenes and returned from the function.

When called, countTo() immediately returns an iterable. Your code can then extract an iterator from that to begin iterating the result list (even though it's not populated yet). Where it gets interesting is that countTo() won't actually execute until the code calling it extracts that iterator and then calls moveNext() on it. When that happens, countTo() will execute until the point it hits the yield statement. The expression i++ is evaluated and is "yielded" back to the caller via the "invisible" iterator. Then, countTo() suspends (since it hasn't met its condition for ending yet), and moveNext() returns true to its caller. Since the code using countTo() is iterating the iterator, we can read the value just yielded via its current property.

Then, countTo() resumes execution the next time moveNext() is called. When the loop ends, the method implicitly executes a return, which causes it to terminate. At that point, moveNext() returns false to its caller, and the while loop ends.

The second type of generator can be demonstrated with this code:

```
Stream<int> countTo(int max) async* {
  int i = 0;
  while (i < max) yield i++;
}

main() async {
  Stream s = countTo(5);
  await for (int i in s) { print(i); }
}
```

The difference here are the use of Stream as a return type and the use of the async* marker instead of *sync before the function body. Another difference is in how we use the countTo() method. Since it's an async method, we need the function it's called in also to be marked with async. Then, the await for is added. This is a form of for loop that is stream-aware. In a sense, because the for loop is awaiting the countTo() function to do its work, that function is effectively "pushing" the value to the for loop via the returned Stream. In this example, it may not seem obvious why you would do this, but imagine if instead of just incrementing i, countTo() instead was calling a remote server to get the next value. Hopefully, then it becomes more obvious what the value of generators is.

77

Metatude: Metadata

Dart also supports the notion of metadata embedded in your code. This is usually called annotations in other languages, and it kinda/sorta is in Dart too (I say it that way because the documentation calls this "metadata annotations," which is a bit verbose, but I suppose it's more accurate).

Dart provides two annotations, one of which you saw earlier: @override. As previously described, this is used to indicate that a class is intentionally overriding a member of its superclass.

The other annotation Dart provides is @deprecated. No, the annotation isn't deprecated, what it marks is, silly! This marks something to indicate that you probably shouldn't be using it anymore and that it might be removed at some point. This is especially common with a class method that will be removed in a future version of your code, but you want to give people using it a bit of time to make the change.

You can also create your own annotations. An annotation is just a class, so this could be an annotation:

```
class MyAnnotation {
  final String note;
  const MyAnnotation(this.note);
}
```

Here, the annotation can take an argument, so we can use it like so:

```
@MyAnnotation("This is my function")
Void myFunction() {
  // Do something
}
```

You can annotate the following language elements: library, class, typedef, type parameter, constructor, factory, function, field, parameter, variable declaration, and import and export directives. The metadata carried by annotations can be retrieved at runtime using Dart's reflection capabilities, but I leave discovering that as an exercise for the reader if and when needed as its generally not needed by most people's application code.

Speaking in General: Generics

Generics are used to inform Dart about the type of something. For example, if you write

```
var ls = List<String>();
```

...then Dart knows that the list ls can only contain Strings. It will enforce that type safety at compile-time.

But that almost seems like they should be called *specifics*, right? You're telling Dart *specifically* what type that List holds. Where the name generics comes into play is when you write something like this:

```
abstract class Things<V> {
  T getByName(String name);
  void setByName(String name, V value);
}
```

Here, we're telling Dart that the Things class can be used for any type, where V is a stand-in for the type (by convention, generic types like this are a single letter, most usually E, K, S, T, or V). Now, with this class serving as an interface, you can go off and implement many different versions of it, all using a different type (maybe Person, Car, Dog, and Planet, all of which could implement this same base interface).

Lists and Maps can be defined generically as shown earlier, and you can use the literal form as well:

```
var brands = <String>[ "Ford", "Pepsi", "Disney" ];
var movieStars = <String, String>{
  "Pitch Black : "Vin Diesel",
  "Captain American" : "Chris Evans",
  "Star Trek" : "William Shatner"
};
```

In Dart, generic types are *reified*, which means that their type is carried with them at runtime, allowing you to test the type of a collection with the is keyword:

```
var veggies = List<String>();
veggies.addAll([ "Peas", "Carrots", "Cauliflower"]);
print(veggies is List<String>);
```

That will print `true`, as you'd expect, thanks to reification. While this seems kind of obvious, it's not the case in every language. Java, for example, uses erasure rather than reification, which means that the type is removed at runtime. So, while you can test that something is a `List`, you can't test that it's a `List<String>` in Java like you can in Dart.

Finally, methods can use generics as well as class definitions:

```dart
class C {
  E showFirst<E>(List<E> lst) {
    E item = lst[0];
    if (item is num) {
      print("It's a number");
    }
    print(item);
    return item;
  }
}

main() async {
  C c = new C();
  c.showFirst(<String>[ "Java", "Dart" ]);
  c.showFirst(<num>[ 42, 66 ]);
}
```

As you can see, we can feed any type to the `showFirst()` method, and it can identify the type using the `is` keyword and act accordingly. That's one of the key benefits of generics: you don't need to write two different versions of `showFirst()`, one to handle strings and one to handle numbers. Instead, a single method can do it just fine. This isn't necessarily the best example since just `print()`'ing item will work regardless of what it is, but if you wanted to do more when it's a number, then this would be ideal.

Summary

In this chapter, you got a look at much of what Dart has to offer. You learned about the basics like data types, operators, comments, logic, and flow control. You also learned some, you might say, mid-level stuff, things like classes, generics, and libraries. Finally, you got an introduction into some slightly more advanced topics such as asynchronous functions, generators, and metadata annotations. From all of this, you should now have a solid foundation of Dart knowledge, plenty with which to start diving into some real Flutter code anyway.

In the next chapter, we'll do a high-level survey of Flutter, focusing primarily on the widgets it offers. We'll start putting some of that Dart knowledge to good use while building directly on top of it a layer of Flutter knowledge so that by the time Chapter 4 rolls around, you'll be well prepared to start building some real projects!

CHAPTER 3

Say Hello to My Little Friend: Flutter, Part I

In the first chapter, you got a brief introduction to Flutter, and in the second, you got some good exposure to Dart. Now, it's time to look at Flutter in a bit more detail.

Given that Flutter is all about the widgets, here we'll look at many of those widgets. But, in direct contravention to what I just said, Flutter is *not*, in fact, *all* about the widgets: there are also APIs, separate from widgets, so we'll also look at some of the APIs that Flutter has to offer our application code (though the APIs will come in Chapter 4, which is effectively the second half of this chapter).

This chapter (along with the next), like the previous one, does not seek to be a deep dive, nor does it attempt to be reference material. With well over 100 widgets available out of the box, and each with numerous options, methods, and events, a single chapter or two to cover them all in depth would take hundreds of pages and would just replicate the documentation found on the flutter.io web site anyway. No, what I'll be doing is pulling out the widgets and APIs I believe most developer will use regularly and discussing those in just enough detail to give you an idea what they're all about. I'll also describe some that demonstrate some concept that you may need or want to know even if it's something I think you may not use all that regularly (and this all applies to the APIs as well).

But, to be sure, there is more available than what you'll find in this chapter and the next, and there's a good chance there will be more by the time this book hits shelves then there even is when I was writing it (and some may be introduced as we build the three apps to follow too). But, this chapter and the next will provide you an excellent survey of what's available and prepare you for the application code to come.

© Frank Zammetti 2019
F. Zammetti, *Practical Flutter*, https://doi.org/10.1007/978-1-4842-4972-7_3

A Buffet of Widgets

We'll begin by looking at the widgets, and as I mentioned earlier, there are well over 100 at the time of this writing. I've attempted to organize them into logical groups to give you some context around them.

Note   Where possible, I've attempted to match up the Material design version (Android style) of widgets with their (iOS style) version widgets. A few are unique to one platform or another or have no direct match, but most do, so you'll see that here. I think that approach will help you conceptualize the cross-platform design goals of both platforms well.

Layout

The layout widgets help you organize your user interface and structure your application in various ways. They, in a sense, allow you to build the skeleton of your app.

MaterialApp, Scaffold, Center, Row, Column, Expanded, Align, and Text

As a general statement, layout in Flutter mainly comes down to a grid structure, which means rows and columns. As such, there is a Row widget and a Column widget. Each can have one or more children, and those children will be laid out horizontally (across the screen) in the case of the Row widget and vertically (down the screen) for a Column widget.

Using them is very simple, as you can see in Listing 3-1.

Listing 3-1. The basics

```
import "package:flutter/material.dart";

void main() => runApp(MyApp());

class MyApp extends StatelessWidget {
```

```
@override
Widget build(BuildContext context) {

  return MaterialApp(title : "Flutter Playground",
    home : Scaffold(
      body : Center(
        child : Row(
          children : [
            Text("Child1"),
            Text("Child2"),
            Text("Child3")
          ]
        )
      )
    )
  );

}

}
```

Figure 3-1 shows the result of running this code.

Figure 3-1. *The basics, in pictures!*

A fair bit is going on here beyond the Row and Column widgets though, so let's break it down.

This is a complete Flutter app, so it begins with the usual import of the material. dart library, which brings in the Material style widgets. Next, we have a main() function that instantiates the MyApp class and passes the instance to the runApp() function that Flutter provides. That gives Flutter the top-level widget it needs to start running the app.

The MyApp class is a StatelessWidget, since for this we do not need any sort of state, and the required build() method produces a single widget of type MaterialApp. This widget implements quite a bit of "plumbing" for us, so it's always a good idea to start with it. You might choose to use the WidgetsApp widget instead, but that will require you to implement a fair bit more code to define at a minimum the routes (read: screens) of your application, so it's generally not something you'll want to do unless you have specific goals that require it. Note that it doesn't matter if you're developing for iOS, you can still use the `MaterialApp` widget as the top-level widget (and in fact, at this time, there is no iOS-specific `CupertinoApp` widget or something like that, which you might expect to find).

The `title` you see here is a property of this widget, and this one is a single-line string of text that is used by the device to identify the app to the user), the `MaterialApp` widget provides quite a few other properties. A few of interest include the `color` property, which defines the primary color used for the application in the OS's interface, and `theme`, which takes as its value a `ThemeData` widget and which further describes the colors used for the app.

The `MaterialApp` widget also requires a `home` property, and the value of it must be a widget, and this is the top of the widget tree for the main screen of your app (or, at least, the screen that the user starts at, main or not). Most commonly, you'll specify a scaffolding widget for this. There are a couple of scaffolding widgets, but they all serve the same purpose: they implement the basic layout structure of a screen in your app. Like `MaterialApp`, the basic `Scaffold` widget takes care of many common app UI elements for you like the top-level navigation bar, drawers (those little elements that slide out from the side of the screen to show options) and bottom sheets (like drawers, but they slide up from the bottom). The other kinds of scaffolding widgets are the `CupertinoPageScaffold`, which is specific to iOS and which provides basic iOS page layout structure including a top navigation bar and content over a background, and `CupertinoTabScaffold`, which is like `CupertinoPageScaffold` except that it includes a tabbed navigation bar at the bottom.

Note   To use the Cupertino widgets, you would need to add an import `"package:flutter/cupertino.dart"`; to the app. Then, if you wanted, you could change `Scaffold` to `CupertinoPageScaffold`, which would then require you to change `home` to `child`, since that's what the `CupertinoPageScaffold` widget requires. Also note that there is no limitation to using Cupertino widgets on an iOS device, or vice versa. Recall that Flutter renders the UI itself rather than relying on the OS, and that allows you to easily run one type of UI on the "wrong" platform, so to speak, if you wish!

The `Scaffold` widget provides a number of properties, including `floatingActionButton`, which allows your app to support a Floating Action Button, or FAB (which is a widget that will be covered later); `drawer`, which allows your app to have a sliding drawer for hidden functionality; `bottomNavigationBar`, which allows your app to have a navigation bar at the bottom; and `backgroundColor`, which enables you to define the background color of the page.

Whichever scaffolding widget you use, it will require a child widget. With the `Scaffold` widget, you specify that via the `body` property. Here, I want all my widgets to be vertically centered, so the `Center` widget is used. This widget will center all its children within itself, but the critical thing is that by default, a `Center` widget will be as big as possible, meaning it will fill whatever space its parent widget allows. In this case, the parent widget is the `Scaffold`, which automatically has available the full size of the screen, so essentially the `Center` widget will fill the entire screen.

The child of the `Center` is a single `Row` widget, which means that the `Row` will be centered within the `Center` and thus centered on the screen. The `Row` widget has a property `children`, which allows us to specify an array of widgets that will be laid out across the `Row`. Here, three children are defined: three `Text` widgets. A `Text` widget displays a string of text in a single style. Some interesting properties that `Text` supports are `overflow`, which tells Flutter what to do when the text overflows the bounds of its container (specifying `overflow : TextOverflow.ellipsis`, for example, causes ... to be appended to the end); `textAlign`, which lets you determine how text should be aligned horizontally; and `textScaleFactor`, which tells Flutter the number of font pixels for each logical pixel unit and thereby scale the text.

One thing to notice if you try this sample (you HAVE tried this sample, right?!) is that all the `Text` widgets are scrunched up on the left. What if we want them horizontally centered? In that case, we need to tell the `Row` to center them, and to do that, we add `mainAxisAlignment : MainAxisAlignment.center` to the `Row`'s constructor call (it's just another property, just like `children` is).

Now, within the `Row`, its children must fit within the horizontal space it fills. It's actually considered an error to have children that need more space than the `Row` can provide, and a `Row` will never scroll. But, what if in our example here we want the second `Text` to fill any available space? Well, then we can do this:

```
Expanded(child : Text("Child2") )
```

The Expanded causes its child to fill all available space. Now, after the first and third Text widgets are rendered (using the space they require, but no more, since we haven't attempted to specify a width for either), then whatever remains will be filled by that second Text widget.

One other widget to mention here is the Align widget. Like the Center widget, Align is generally used when you have only one child, and it serves a similar purpose to Center but has more flexibility in that it's not just for centering content. This widget aligns its child within itself and can also optionally size itself based on the child's size. The key to using it is the alignment property. If you set that to Alignment.center, then congratulations, you've just created a Center widget! The value of this property is an Alignment class instance, but Alignment.center is a static instance which has x and y values of 0 and 0. The x and y values are how you specify the alignment, with 0, 0 being the center of the rectangular area that the Align widget takes up. If you have values of −1 and −1, then that represents the top left of the rectangle, and 1, 1 is the bottom right (starting to see how this works?)

Finally, we have the Column widget, and I've left it for last because virtually everything discussed for the Row widget also applies to the Column widget. The obvious difference is that its children are laid out going down the screen. Otherwise, you use it the same, and most everything mentioned about Row applies to Column as well, just going in a vertical direction. You can, of course, nest Row widgets within Column widgets, and vice versa, allowing you to create arbitrarily complex grid structures, and really, that's what a great deal of Flutter UI development boils down to!

Container, Padding, Transform

The Container widget is, along with Row and Column (and ignoring the application and page-level widgets) probably one of the most-used widgets Flutter offers for laying out your UI. It's a bit of a jack-of-all-trades in that it combines what a number of other widgets provide into one sleek package.

For example, what do you do if you want to put some padding around the second Text widget in the previous example? Well, one easy answer is to wrap it in a Padding widget:

```
Padding(padding : EdgeInsets.all(20.0), child : Text("Child2") )
```

That puts 20 pixels around the Text (above, below, left, and right, which is what EdgeInsets.all(20.0) says). You can use only() instead of all() to specify the left, top, right, and bottom values separately, or you can use symmetric() to specify a vertical and horizontal value that will be applied to the top and bottom and/or left and right equally.

What if you want to scale that Text to 200%? That's where the Transform widget comes into play:

```
Transform.scale(scale : 2, child : Text("Child2") )
```

The scale() static method returns a new Transform widget with a scale factor of 2, which means twice as large as normal.

Now, what does any of this have to do with Container, you ask? Well, what it has to do with it is that Container combines all this functionality, and more! For example, we can mimic a Center widget by replacing it with this Container:

```
Container(alignment : Alignment.center, child...
```

And, we can scale the Text with it too:

```
Container(transform : Matrix4.identity()..scale(2.0), child :
Text("Child2") )
```

The syntax is a little more complex because now we have to use matrix math to scale the child widget manually, something the Transform widget does for us automatically (a good reason to use it!), and that's largely true of any of the other widgets that Container subsumes, but you *can* accomplish the same goals with Container as with those other widgets, that's the point.

Likewise, if you want to add padding:

```
Container(padding : EdgeInsets.all(20.0), child : Text("Child2") )
```

Flutter developers often use Container and little else, and that's entirely viable. However, I would suggest that if for no other reason than a somewhat cleaner API that you should look to the purpose-built widgets first and use Container only as a fallback or unless you have specific goals it meets best.

ConstrainedBox, FittedBox, RotatedBox, SizedBox

Flutter offers several "box" components that act a lot like Row and Column and Container, but which provide various positioning, sizing, and other manipulations on its single child.

The first is ConstrainedBox, which is used to impose additional restraints on its child. For example, let's say you want to make the second Text widget in the previous example be forced to a minimum width, you can wrap it in a ConstrainedBox and define that constraint on it:

```
ConstrainedBox(constraints : BoxConstraints(minWidth : 200.0), child :
Text("Child2"))
```

The BoxConstraints class offers some properties for defining a constraint, with minWidth, minHeight, maxWidth, and maxHeight being probably the most commonly used.

Next up is the FittedBox, which scales and positions its child within itself according to a fit property. This can be useful because if you noticed when we did the scale example before, sometimes the text wasn't scaled and repositioned as we expect. This widget can solve that problem for us, and it works great in conjunction with the ConstrainedBox widget:

```
ConstrainedBox(constraints : BoxConstraints(minWidth: 200.0), child :
FittedBox(fit: BoxFit.fill, child : Text("Child2") ) )
```

This scales the Text widget, but in contrast to the previous scale example, this also repositions the Text, so it remains centered, and it scales it up to be a minimum width of 200 pixels in width, so it scales the height to maintain the aspect ratio automatically. If you try this and compare it to the previous scale example you'll see, I think, that the scaling here is better and probably more like what you expect.

Similarly, the RotatedBox gives us a way to rotate its child that might be in a form that is more rational to you:

```
RotatedBox(quarterTurns : 3, child : Text("Child2") )
```

The quarterTurns property is the number of clockwise quarter turns to rotate the child by. So, if you need quarter turns, this widget is perfect, but if you need arbitrary degrees then you'll need to deal with Transform.

Finally, the `SizedBox` widget forces its child to have a specific width and height:

```
SizedBox(width : 200, height : 400, child : Text("Child2") )
```

Here, if you try it, you'll notice that the result is the `Text` widget seeming to "float" up and left of its usual position. That's because the `Text` itself is sized to 200 pixels by 400 pixels, but that doesn't imply a scale of any sort. The actual text is by default left aligned and top aligned inside the `Text` widget, so giving it this size results in this "floating" into the upper-left corner of the `Text`, which takes up the 200x400 pixels specified. What this widget does to its child will be dependent on what its child does in response to defining its width and height (assuming the child supports those properties at all).

Divider

The `Divider` widget is a straightforward one that displays a one device pixel thick horizontal line, with a little bit of padding on either side. Simply add them between the `Text` items in the previous example:

```
Text("Child1"),
Divider(),
Text("Child2"),
Divider(),
Text("Child3")
```

...and, well, you'll see nothing! That's because a `Divider` can only be horizontal, but when the layout is in a `Row`, they won't display. So, just change the `Row` to a `Column`, and now you'll see some beautiful lines between the `Text` widgets!

Card

A `Card` widget is a Material design widget that is essentially just a box with rounded corners and a slight drop shadow around content. Typically, it's used to show some related information in a logical grouping. Coding one is simple, as Listing 3-2 shows.

Listing 3-2. The Divider in action

```
import "package:flutter/material.dart";

void main() => runApp(MyApp());
class MyApp extends StatelessWidget {

  @override
  Widget build(BuildContext context) {

    return MaterialApp(title : "Flutter Playground",
      home : Scaffold(
        body : Center(
          child : Card(
            child : Column(mainAxisSize: MainAxisSize.min,
              children : [
                Text("Child1"),
                Divider(),
                Text("Child2"),
                Divider(),
                Text("Child3")
              ]
            )
          )
        )
      )
    );

  }

}
```

You can replace the return statement in the example we've been hacking at all along to try it out, or just gaze longingly at Figure 3-2.

Figure 3-2. *The Card widget*

The Card widget doesn't have a ton of properties, but some of the most interesting include color, which allows you to set the background color of the card; elevation, which will enable you to set the size of the shadow; and shape, which allows you to alter the rounded corners of the Card (to make them more or less rounded).

Drawer

The Drawer widget is most usually given as the value to the drawer property of a Scaffold widget, although it doesn't have to be. This widget is a Material design panel that slides in horizontally from the left to provide a way for the user to activate app functionality or navigate through the app and which is hidden until called upon. Another widget, AppBar, goes typically along with a Drawer because it automatically provides an appropriate IconButton (a widget that is a button the user can click which shows just an icon on it) to show and hide the Drawer (which can also be done via a swipe in or out from the edge).

The coding for a Drawer is easy, if it's within a Scaffold, as Listing 3-3 demonstrates.

Listing 3-3. The Drawer widget in "action"

```
import "package:flutter/material.dart";

void main() => runApp(MyApp());

class MyApp extends StatelessWidget {

  @override
  Widget build(BuildContext context) {

    return MaterialApp(title : "Flutter Playground",
      home : Scaffold(
        appBar : AppBar(
          title : Text("Flutter Playground!")
        ),
        drawer : Drawer(
          child : Column(
            children : [
              Text("Item 1"),
              Divider(),
              Text("Item 2"),
              Divider(),
              Text("Item 3")
            ]
          )
        ),
```

```
      body : Center(
        child : Row(
          children : [
            Text("Child1"),
            Text("Child2"),
            Text("Child3")
          ]
        )
      )
    );

  }


}
```

Here, you can see the AppBar as well as the Drawer. The actual contents of the Drawer are entirely up to you, though a ListView (another widget we'll look at later) is typical, often with the first child being a DrawerHeader widget, which provides a common way to display user account status information. But again, using those are optional, as you can see in the sample code. Aside from the child widget, the Drawer widget also has an elevation property, like the same-named property of the Card widget. Figure 3-3 shows what this looks like both before the user clicks the "hamburger" icon to show the Drawer and after when it's showing.

Figure 3-3. *The Drawer widget, before and after expansion*

And, for the most part, that's about all there is to the Drawer widget! It's an essential and common widget, but it's also effortless to use thanks to Flutter!

Note   The CupertinoNavigationBar widget is the rough equivalent to the AppBar widget, which is customarily used for Material (Android) apps.

Navigation

Navigation widgets allow the user to move through your app in some fashion, or your app to move them between different parts of the app automatically (different screens, for example).

First, let's talk about the `Navigator` widget. Since in most cases you'll start your app with a `WidgetsApp` or a `MaterialApp`, you'll automatically get a `Navigator` widget (you can also create one explicitly, but that's less typical). This widget manages a set of child widgets as a stack. In other words, one such child is visible at a time, with the rest "beneath" it. These children are the various screens of your apps, which are called *routes* in Flutter. The `Navigator` provides methods such as `push()` and `pop()` to add and remove routes.

You've seen the use of `MaterialApp` a couple of times now, and you've seen the home property of it used. Well, guess what? The value of that property is the first route in your app! You were using a `Navigator` without even knowing it!

You can explicitly add routes to the `Navigator` with `push()` as mentioned. For example:

```
Navigator.push(context, MaterialPageRoute<void>(
  builder : (BuildContext context) {
    return Scaffold(
      body : Center(child : Text("My new page"))
    );
  }
));
```

You always add a `MaterialPageRoute` widget when calling `push()`, and this requires the use of a `builder` function, a pattern you'll see plenty in Flutter. This is needed because when a route is navigated to, it will be built and re-built many times and that will occur in different contexts depending on when it occurs. Therefore, hardcoding the children would result, potentially, in your code executing in the wrong context. The builder pattern avoids this problem.

When you `push()` a new route onto a `Navigator` stack, it becomes visible immediately. To go back to the previous route, you `pop()` it off the stack, passing the current build context:

```
Navigator.pop(context);
```

The first, "default" route is named / and subsequent routes can be added with a name, which allows you to then navigate to them by name. To do so, you add a routes property to the `MaterialApp` like so:

```
routes : <String, WidgetBuilder> {
  "/announcements" : (BuildContext bc) => Page(title : "P1"),
```

98

```
      "/birthdays" : (BuildContext bc) => Page(title : "P2"),
      "/data" : (BuildContext bc) => Page(title : "Pe"),
}
```

Now, you can navigate to a route by name:

```
Navigator.pushNamed(context, "/birthdays");
```

You can also nest `Navigator` widgets. In other words, one route in a `Navigator` can itself have a `Navigator`. This allows the user to take "sub-journeys," so to speak, through your app.

BottomNavigationBar

Sometimes, a `Navigator` isn't the best choice for navigating between parts of your app. One significant consideration with it is that there is no user-facing interface to it, it's entirely programmatic. Fortunately, Flutter offers a few visual navigation widgets too, one of which is the `BottomNavigationBar`. This widget provides a bar at the bottom of the screen with icons and/or text that the user can click to move between parts of your app.

In fact, this widget doesn't really *do* any navigation itself, making its name a bit of a misnomer. The navigation part is up to your code, and really you don't *have* to use it for navigation even! However, it normally is used to navigate, after a fashion, here's one way to do so, Listing 3-4.

Listing 3-4. The BottomNavigationBar

```
import "package:flutter/material.dart";

void main() => runApp(MyApp());

class MyApp extends StatefulWidget {
 MyApp({Key key}) : super(key : key);
 @override
 _MyApp createState() => _MyApp();
}

class _MyApp extends State {

 var _currentPage = 0;
```

```
var _pages = [
  Text("Page 1 - Announcements"),
  Text("Page 2 - Birthdays"),
  Text("Page 3 - Data")
];

  @override
  Widget build(BuildContext context) {

    return MaterialApp(title : "Flutter Playground",
      home : Scaffold(
        body : Center(child : _pages.elementAt(_currentPage)),
        bottomNavigationBar : BottomNavigationBar(
          items : [
            BottomNavigationBarItem(
              icon : Icon(Icons.announcement),
              title : Text("Announcements")
            ),
            BottomNavigationBarItem(
              icon : Icon(Icons.cake),
              title : Text("Birthdays")
            ),
            BottomNavigationBarItem(
              icon : Icon(Icons.cloud),
              title : Text("Data")
            ),
          ],
          currentIndex : _currentPage,
          fixedColor : Colors.red,
          onTap : (int inIndex) {
            setState(() { _currentPage = inIndex; });
          }
        )
      )
    );
  }
}
```

Figure 3-4 shows you what this code produces.

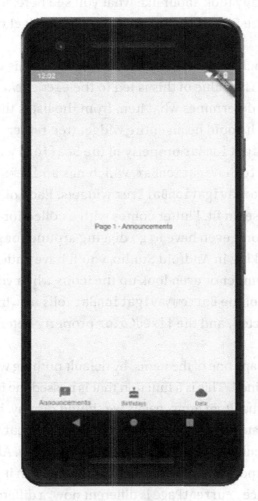

Figure 3-4. *The BottomNavigationBar widget*

Here, we start by creating a stateful widget. This is necessary because the top-level widget is built once unless it has state that changes, which is precisely what we need to happen when the user clicks one of the items on the bar. Hence, we have to make this a stateful widget to provide that state. You'll recall the pattern of needing to create *two* classes when dealing with state: a class extending from `StatefulWidget` and one extending from `State`. Although it may seem weird (it does to me anyway!), the class that actually is your widget is the one extending from `State`, *not* the one extending from `StatefulWidget`. Whether you find this weird or not, the key is to recognize the pattern. For the most part, the `StatefulWidget` class is basically boilerplate and will usually look about like what you see here, and the `State` class looks more or less like the `StatelessWidget`-extending widget classes you've seen a bunch of times now.

Getting into the actual `State` widget class, the state for this widget is the private `_currentPage` variable. The value of this is fed to the `elementAt()` method of the private `_pages` list. This determines what item from the list is the contents inside the `Center` widget (which could be an entire widget tree rather than a single `Text` widget). The `bottomNavigationBar` property of the `Scaffold` widget takes as its value an instance of `BottomNavigationBar`, which has an `items` property. This property is a list of `BottomNavigationBarItem` widgets. Each of those can have an `icon` and a `title` as we seem fit. Flutter comes with a collection of icons thanks to the `Icons` class, so we don't even have to go digging around for graphics if we don't want to! And, when working in Android Studio, you'll have code completion, so you don't even have to remember or even look up the icons when you need them! The `currentIndex` property of the `BottomNavigationBar` tells us which of the items on the bar is currently selected, and the `fixedColor` property determines what color to make that selected item.

Now, when the user taps one of the items, by default nothing will happen. To fix that, the `onTap` property is defined. This is a function that is passed the index of the tapped item. So, now we know what item from `_pages` we should display, but how does the value of `_currentPage` get updated? That's where the call to the `setState()` method, supplied by virtue of this class extending the `State` class, comes into play. All we need to do is call this method and do the updates to the `_currentPage` variable in it. This triggers Flutter to rebuild the widget. Since `_currentPage` is different now, a different element from `_pages` will be displayed. The result for the user is that they appear to have navigated to a new page.

TabBar (CupertinoTabBar) and TabBarView (CupertinoTabView)

Another ubiquitous navigation element is the `TabBar`, and its iOS equivalent `CupertinoTabBar`. Going along with these is the `TabBarView` and `CupertinoTabView` widgets, respectively (note that I'll be talking about `TabBar` and `TabBarView` only from here on out, but it all applies to `CupertinoTabBar` and `CupertinoTabView` as well).

A TabBarView is essentially a stack of screens (or *views*, if you will) where only one is visible at a time, and the user can move between them. The way one becomes visible is by user interaction with a TabBar. They can click the icon for one of the tabs or swipe between them. There is usually some sort of animation between the views, a slide for example.

Let's look at an example and then discuss it, that example being Listing 3-5, and which you can see in Figure 3-5.

Listing 3-5. The TabBar widget

```
import "package:flutter/material.dart";

void main() => runApp(MyApp());

class MyApp extends StatelessWidget {

  @override
  Widget build(BuildContext context) {

    return MaterialApp(
      home : DefaultTabController(
        length : 3,
        child : Scaffold(
          appBar : AppBar(title : Text("Flutter Playground"),
            bottom : TabBar(
              tabs : [
                Tab(icon : Icon(Icons.announcement)),
                Tab(icon : Icon(Icons.cake)),
                Tab(icon : Icon(Icons.cloud))
              ]
            )
          ),
          body : TabBarView(
            children : [
              Center(child : Text("Announcements")),
              Center(child : Text("Birthdays")),
              Center(child : Text("Data"))
            ]
          )
        )
```

```
      )
    );
  }

}
```

Behind the scenes, a TabController widget will be responsible for keeping track of what tab is current and the content of each. You can create one manually, but that requires extra work on your part, so most of the time you'll just use the DefaultTabController widget as the value of the home property of a MaterialApp widget, which takes care of all the details for you.

Figure 3-5. *The TabBar widget*

However, you do it, you have to tell the `TabController` how many tabs there are via the `length` property. After that, you need to describe each tab for the `TabController`, and that's done by giving it an array of `tabs` where each item is a `Tab` widget. Here, we just specify an icon for each.

Once the tabs themselves are defined, we then must tell the `TabController` what the content for each tab is, and that's done by providing a `TabBarView` widget as the value of the `body` property. Each element in the `children` list can be as complex a widget tree as you need. Here, it's just some `Center` widgets with `Text` widgets in them.

With all of that done, the interaction of moving between the views is automatic from our perspective, and the user can navigate between them freely.

Stepper

The last navigation widget I want to discuss is the `Stepper` widget. This is used to walk the user through a defined sequence of events. Conceptually, think about what happens when you go to buy something on Amazon or another eCommerce retailer. First, you must enter your shipping information, then click a button to continue. Then you enter payment information and then click a button to continue. Finally, maybe you must decide if you need gift wrapping and other services. You click a button one last time, and your order is placed. That's a sequence of three steps, and a Stepper provides that same functionality in a Flutter app.

Look at this example code, Listing 3-6.

Listing 3-6. Stepping with the Stepper widget

```
import "package:flutter/material.dart";

void main() => runApp(MyApp());

class MyApp extends StatefulWidget {
 MyApp({Key key}) : super(key : key);
 @override
 _MyApp createState() => _MyApp();
}
```

```
class _MyApp extends State {

  var _currentStep = 0;

  @override
  Widget build(BuildContext context) {
    return MaterialApp(title : "Flutter Playground",
      home : Scaffold(
        appBar : AppBar(title : Text("Flutter Playground")),
        body : Stepper(
          type : StepperType.vertical,
            currentStep : _currentStep,
          onStepContinue : _currentStep < 2 ?
            () => setState(() => _currentStep += 1) : null,
          onStepCancel : _currentStep > 0 ?
            () => setState(() => _currentStep -= 1) : null,
          steps : [
            Step(
              title : Text("Get Ready"), isActive : true,
              content : Text("Let's begin...")
            ),
            Step(
              title : Text("Get Set"), isActive : true,
              content : Text("Ok, just a little more...")
            ),
            Step(
              title : Text("Go!"), isActive : true,
              content : Text("And, we're done!")
            )
          ]
        )
      )
    );
  }
}
```

Figure 3-6 shows what this looks like on the big screen.

Figure 3-6. *Walking a mile in Stepper's shoes (okay, that one was a stretch, I admit!)*

Most of it should look familiar by now, until we get to the Stepper widget as the body of the Scaffold widget. You first need to tell it whether you want your steps to be displayed vertically or horizontally via the type property. You also need to tell it what step the user is currently on, and that's done here by virtue of the _currentStep variable. This is a stateful widget since the value of that variable is what determines what step is displayed, which is what state is all about in Flutter.

We also must provide some code to the `Stepper` for when the user clicks the Continue and Cancel buttons, which will be presented by the `Stepper`. Here, the value of `_currentStep` is incremented when Continue is clicked as long as we're not on the final step, and decremented when Cancel is clicked as long as we're not on the first step. This allows the user to go backward and forwards through the sequence at will.

Next, we need to define the `steps` of the sequence; each one is a `Step` widget. This widget takes some title text to display next to the circle for the step and an `isActive` property that will grey the step out when set to `false` (note that it does not do anything but alter the styling of the step's circle – your code has to do something in order to skip it or whatever is appropriate when inactive). After that, we define the `content`, which can be as complex of a widget tree as you need.

Each `Step` can also have a `subtitle` if you wish, and each has a `state` property that determines the styling of the component and whether the step is interactive. Again, your code must provide the functionality to back this up though. Note too that the Stepper widget provides an `onStepTapped` property that is a function you provide that is called when the user taps one of the step circles. Obviously, you'll generally provide code to jump to the selected step directly.

Input

Input widgets are used to obtain user input in some fashion (he said, obviously!). Flutter comes with a range of such widgets, some perhaps a bit unexpected.

Form

In Flutter, user input begins with a `Form` widget. Well, actually, that's not true: the `Form` widget is actually optional. But, since it does offer some utility and is therefore used frequently around user input, let's talk about it as if it was required!

`Form` is a container for form fields, and I mean that literally: there is a `FormField` widget that wraps all input fields and which are then made children of the `Form` widget. The reason you might choose to use a `Form` widget is that it provides you some common functionality including saving the form data, resetting it and validating it. Without `Form`, you would be left to implement any of that yourself that you need entirely, so why not use the plumbing `Form` provides?

Let's look at a `Form` example, a typical login form, which will also demonstrate some other user input-related ideas. Listing 3-7 shows the Form, along with a bit more.

Listing 3-7. The Form widget, and its cohorts

```
import "package:flutter/material.dart";

void main() => runApp(MyApp());

class MyApp extends StatefulWidget {
  MyApp({Key key}) : super(key : key);
  @override
  _MyApp createState() => _MyApp();
}

class LoginData {
  String username = "";
  String password = "";
}

class _MyApp extends State {

  LoginData _loginData = new LoginData();
  GlobalKey<FormState> _formKey = new GlobalKey<FormState>();

  @override
  Widget build(BuildContext inContext) {
    return MaterialApp(home : Scaffold(
      body : Container(
        padding : EdgeInsets.all(50.0),
        child : Form(
          key : this._formKey,
          child : Column(
            children : [
              TextFormField(
                keyboardType :
                  TextInputType.emailAddress,
                validator : (String inValue) {
                  if (inValue.length == 0) {
                    return "Please enter username";
                  }
```

109

```
          return null;
        },
        onSaved: (String inValue) {
          this._loginData.username = inValue;
        },
        decoration : InputDecoration(
          hintText : "none@none.com",
          labelText : "Username (eMail address)"
        )
      ),
      TextFormField(
        obscureText : true,
        validator : (String inValue) {
          if (inValue.length < 10) {
            return "Password must be >=10 in length";
          }
          return null;
        },
        onSaved : (String inValue) {
          this._loginData.password = inValue;
        },
        decoration : InputDecoration(
          hintText : "Password",
          labelText : "Password"
        )
      ),
      RaisedButton(
        child : Text("Log In!"),
        onPressed : () {
          if (_formKey.currentState.validate()) {
            _formKey.currentState.save();
            print("Username: ${_loginData.username}");
            print("Password: ${_loginData.password}");
          }
        }
      )
```

```
          ]
        )
      )
    )
  ));
  }
}
```

Peek at Figure 3-7 to see the result of executing this code. It shouldn't be all that surprising, but it's good to see that the code does what your mind envisions it does.

Figure 3-7. *The gatekeeper to your app, courtesy of the Form widget (and friends!)*

After the usual `import` and `main()` function, we're dealing with a `StatefulWidget`, so we have the usual class definition for that. But, before we get to the `State` class that you know goes along with it, we have one small class: `LoginData`. An instance of this class will wind up storing the username and password entered by the user. This is a typical pattern when dealing with Flutter forms and is nice because it consolidates all the input in one object, making it easier to work with.

After that comes the `_MyApp State` class. This is like any other `State` class you've seen before, but in this one, we have a few new things. First, we have that instance of `LoginData` I mentioned. After that is an instance of the `GlobalKey` class. A `GlobalKey` is a key that is unique across the entire app. This usually comes into play as the value of the key property of a widget, which determines how a widget replaces another in the widget tree. If the `runtimeType` and `key` properties of the two widgets are equal, then the new widget replaces the old widget by updating the underlying element. Otherwise, the old element is removed from the tree, the new widget is inflated into an element, and the new element is inserted into the tree. Using a `GlobalKey` as the widget's key (as opposed to a `LocalKey`, which is another type that only ensures uniqueness under a given parent) allows the element to be moved around the widget tree without losing state. When a new widget is found (meaning that its `key` and `runtimeType` don't match a previous widget in the same location in the tree) but there was a widget with that same `GlobalKey` elsewhere in the tree in the previous frame, then that widget's element is moved to the new location.

As an aside, the key property is extremely powerful because it gives us a way to directly "reach out and touch" widgets, something you frankly should rarely do. But, when you need to, this is one way how. For example, add a new variable to the `_MyApp` class like so:

```
GlobalKey _btnKey = new GlobalKey();
```

Then, to the `RaisedButton`, add a key property referencing it:

```
key : _btnKey,
```

Finally, in the `onPressed` handler of the button, do this:

```
print(((
  _btnKey.currentWidget as RaisedButton).child as Text).data
);
```

The result will be that the label of the text will be written to the console. For that to work, we have to cast `_btnKey.currentWidget` to `RaisedButton` using the as keyword since the type of `currentWidget` is `Widget`, and the cast the `child` property of that to `Text`, and then the `data` property is the text of the button. In this way, you can access any property of any widget or execute methods directly on a widget, as long as it has a key (whether a `GlobalKey` or a `LocalKey`). I said you really shouldn't ever do this and that's because it's in a sense anathema to the reactive nature of Flutter. Instead, it's usually the case that you'll use state to drive these sorts of interactions. But, it's a good trick to have in your back pocket if it ever comes up, and if nothing else, it helps you understand some of the internals of Flutter just a little bit.

After that comes the usual `build()` method. It starts like any other you've seen, but now we have a `Form` widget in the tree. Usually, a widget that is the only child of another widget does not need an explicit key, which is why up until this point I haven't shown the key property, but here the key property of the `Form` widget is a reference to `_formKey` as discussed earlier.

As you can see, the `Form` widget has a `child` property, so if we want to have multiple fields in the form, which we do, then we'll need some sort of container component, so I went with `Column` here.

The children of the `Column`, three of them, are the username entry field, password entry field, and the Log In button. The first two use `TextFormField` widgets. This is a widget that effectively combines two others: `FormField`, which you'll recall I previously said must wrap all fields in a `Form`, and `TextField`, which is a widget for getting user text input (there is a corresponding `CupertinoTextField` as well). The username is a `TextFormField`; since the username is actually the user's eMail address (a common but not especially good security practice), we want the keyboard displayed to be more oriented toward entering eMail addresses. The `keyboardType` property allows us to do this. The `TextInputType` class has several constants for various keyboard types, `emailAddress` being the one applicable here.

This widget also has a `validator` property, which defines a function that will perform validation on the field when the Log In button is clicked. This function can do anything you wish, but in the end, it must either return a string that is an error message to display in red below the field or null if the value is valid.

Note that the data itself in the field is never saved anywhere; it only exists transiently in the `Form`. That's not of much use though, so to address that, we need to implement a callback function for the `onSaved` property. This function will fire when the `save()` method of the `Form` is called, which will happen later, as you'll see (and, it's not actually a

113

method on the Form itself, but that too you'll see shortly). The onSaved handler function just stores the inValue passed into the _loginData variable's username field.

Although optional, the decoration property is an instance of InputDecoration and is commonly used to declare some hintText (shown in the field when nothing has yet been entered) and a label for the field via the labelText property, which gets shown above the field.

The password field is just like the username field except that, being a password, what the user enters shouldn't be shown on the screen, so the obscureText property is set to true to accomplish that. Otherwise, we have another validator function doing much the same as for password and an onSaved handler again to store the data, plus a decoration instance of InputDecoration once more.

Finally, we come to the Log In button. In it, we do a couple of things. First, the validate() method is called, which we can do through the _formKey variable. This provides us a reference to the widget, and within that widget is the currentState property that contains the values currently entered on the form. That's the object the validate() method is actually on, and since each field has a validator function attached, validate() knows how to call each of them and either display the error fields or else return true if the form is valid according to the validators on all its fields. In that case, we call save() on the currentState, which results in all the onSaved handlers firing and thus the form data is stored in _loginData. Finally, we print that information to the console to ensure everything worked as expected.

Checkbox

Yeah, you know what a Checkbox is! It's a little box that you... wait for it... check! Or uncheck... but it's called a Checkbox, not an UnCheckbox, but I guess that's a philosophical discussion for another day. Either way, Flutter has them, and they're a piece of cake to use.

Note Listing 3-8 demonstrates Checkbox, as well as Switch, Slider and Radio, and Figure 3-8 shows it. Please refer to these in the coming sections.

Listing 3-8. Checkbox, along with Switch, Slider, and Radio

```
import "package:flutter/material.dart";

void main() => runApp(MyApp());
```

```
class MyApp extends StatefulWidget {
  MyApp({Key key}) : super(key : key);
  @override
  _MyApp createState() => _MyApp();
}

class _MyApp extends State {

  GlobalKey<FormState> _formKey = new GlobalKey<FormState>();
  var _checkboxValue = false;
  var _switchValue = false;
  var _sliderValue = .3;
  var _radioValue = 1;

  @override
  Widget build(BuildContext inContext) {
    return MaterialApp(home : Scaffold(
      body : Container(
        padding : EdgeInsets.all(50.0),
        child : Form(
          key : this._formKey,
          child : Column(
            children : [
              Checkbox(
                value : _checkboxValue,
                onChanged : (bool inValue) {
                  setState(() { _checkboxValue = inValue; });
                }
              ),
              Switch(
                value : _switchValue,
                onChanged : (bool inValue) {
                  setState(() { _switchValue = inValue; });
                }
              ),
              Slider(
                min : 0, max : 20,
```

```
            value : _sliderValue,
            onChanged : (inValue) {
              setState(() => _sliderValue = inValue);
            }
          ),
          Row(children : [
            Radio(value : 1, groupValue : _radioValue,
              onChanged : (int inValue) {
                setState(() { _radioValue = inValue; });
              }
            ),
            Text("Option 1")
          ]),
          Row(children : [
            Radio(value : 2, groupValue : _radioValue,
              onChanged : (int inValue) {
                setState(() { _radioValue = inValue; });
              }
            ),
            Text("Option 2")
          ]),
          Row(children : [
            Radio(value : 3, groupValue : _radioValue,
              onChanged : (int inValue) {
                setState(() { _radioValue = inValue; });
              }
            ),
            Text("Option 3")
          ])
        ]
      )
    )
  )
));
  }
}
```

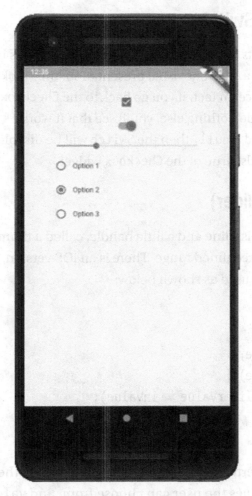

Figure 3-8. *A gaggle of input widgets (Checkbox, Switch, Slider and Radio)*

Yep, that's it! As long as your `StatefulWidget` has a `checkboxValue` variable, then you're good to go. Alternatively, you can supply an `onChanged` callback handler function to do something else when the `Checkbox` is checked or unchecked. Also, `Checkbox` supports a `tristate` flag (`true` or `false`, `false` by default) that allows for three values: checked, unchecked, and null. The latter will display as a dash in the `Checkbox`.

One thing to note is that the `Checkbox` widget does not intrinsically have a text label, something that is common with such components. To achieve that, you'll need to build it yourself, usually by placing a `Checkbox` and a `Text` widget in a `Row` container (assuming you want the label next to the `Checkbox`, otherwise use `Column` or some other layout structure).

117

Switch (CupertinoSwitch)

The Switch widget, and its iOS counterpart CupertinoSwitch, is in most regards just like a Checkbox, but with a different visual presentation: they look like little switches you might find on a tech device. In fact, if you go back to the Checkbox snippet and change Checkbox to Switch and do nothing else, you'll see that it works!

Note that if onChanged is null, then the Switch will be disabled and not respond to user interaction. This is also true of the Checkbox widget.

Slider (CupertinoSlider)

A Slider is a widget that is a line and a little handle, called a thumb, that the user frags to select a value from a predefined range. There is an iOS version, CupertinoSlider, that works the same. Either is used as shown below:

```
Slider(
  min : 0, max : 20,
  value : _sliderValue,
  onChanged : (inValue) {
    setState(() => _sliderValue = inValue);
  }
)
```

The important properties are min and max, which define the lower and upper limits of the range of values the user can choose from, and value, which is its current value. As a member of a StatefulWidget, the value of this should be a variable in the State object. Finally, onChanged is required to set the value in State when the thumb is moved.

There are also properties like activeColor and inactiveColor for adjusting the color of the portion of the slider track that is active and inactive, respectively. You can also determine the number of divisions within the range (when null, the default, the Slider will automatically produce divisions that are a continuous and discrete set of values within the min to max range). There are also event handler hooks for when the user begins moving the thumb (onChangeStart) and when they lift their thumb (onChangeEnd).

Radio

It's a little funny to think about, but I'm a bit older than I'd like to admit these days, old enough that I remember those days of car radios that had a row of buttons, one per stored radio station, and when you would press one, the others would pop back out, and the one you pressed would now be the current station. I say it's funny because I bet a lot of younger people reading this have never seen such a thing, yet here we have a widget, called Radio no less, that implements that metaphor, a metaphor many younger people don't know!

But I digress, and hey, you kids get off my lawn!

The Radio widget is a lot like CheckBox or Switch except that unlike those, it never exists on its own. A Radio widget always has one or more sister Radio widgets hanging out around it, and they are mutually exclusive: selecting any one Radio causes the other in its group to be de-selected. As such, code like the following is common:

```
Column(children : [
  Row(children : [
    Radio(value : 1, groupValue : _radioValue,
      onChanged : (int inValue) {
        setState(() { _radioValue = inValue; });
      }
    ),
    Text("Option 1")
  ]),
  Row(children : [
    Radio(value : 2, groupValue : _radioValue,
      onChanged : (int inValue) {
        setState(() { _radioValue = inValue; });
      }
    ),
    Text("Option 2")
  ]),
```

```
Row(children : [
  Radio(value : 3, groupValue : _radioValue,
    onChanged : (int inValue) {
      setState(() { _radioValue = inValue; });
    }
  ),
  Text("Option 3")
])
])
```

Here, three Radio widgets are present, each with an associated Text to label it. Notice how all of them have the same groupValue property value? That's by design: by virtue of them all having the same variable reference, they become part of the same group, which conveys to them the mutual exclusivity I mentioned. Each has a discrete value though, so when the first Radio is selected, its value is transferred to _radioValue by virtue of the setState() call in its onChanged handler. The code using these Radio widgets can then examine the value to determine which was selected.

Date and Time Pickers (CupertinoDatePicker, CupertinoTimerPicker)

Choosing a date or time in an app is a common activity, so naturally, Flutter provides widgets for that. More precisely, it provides functions for you to call to show UI components for this purpose, at least on Android. For that platform, we have the showDatePicker() and showTimePicker() functions, as shown in Listing 3-9.

Listing 3-9. Picking a date and a time (but not a nose)

```
import "package:flutter/material.dart";

void main() => runApp(MyApp());

class MyApp extends StatelessWidget {
  @override
  Widget build(BuildContext context) {
    return MaterialApp(home : Scaffold(body : Home()));
  }
}
```

```dart
class Home extends StatelessWidget  {

  Future<void> _selectDate(inContext) async {
    DateTime selectedDate = await showDatePicker(
      context : inContext,
      initialDate : DateTime.now(),
      firstDate : DateTime(2017),
      lastDate : DateTime(2021)
    );
    print(selectedDate);
  }

  Future<void> _selectTime(inContext) async {
    TimeOfDay selectedTime = await showTimePicker(
      context : inContext,
      initialTime : TimeOfDay.now(),
    );
    print(selectedTime);
  }

  @override
  Widget build(BuildContext inContext) {
    return Scaffold(
      body : Column(
        children : [
          Container(height : 50),
          RaisedButton(
            child : Text("Test DatePicker"),
            onPressed : () => _selectDate(inContext)
          ),
          RaisedButton(
            child : Text("Test TimePicker"),
            onPressed : () => _selectTime(inContext)
          )
        ]
      )
```

```
    );
  }
}
```

Both of these functions are asynchronous, so we'll need some `async` functions to make use of them, namely, the `_selectDate()` and `_selectTime()` methods, which are called from the two buttons in the main layout.

Figure 3-9. *Date picker and time picker*

As you can see (in the code, as well as in Figure 3-9), they make use of the `showDatePicker()` and `showTimePicker()`, respectively. The former requires the build context, the `initialDate` that's selected by default, and the `firstDate` and `lastDate` that the picker will allow to be chosen, here just specified as years. A `DateTime` object is returned and is displayed. For `showTimePicker()`, only the build context and the `initialTime` are necessary.

There is a `CupertinoDatePicker` and a `CupertinoTimerPicker` widgets for the iOS side, and they are implemented as conventional widgets, so no functions to call for them.

Note that there are three other pickers available on Android: `DayPicker` for picking from the days of a month, `MonthPicker` for choosing from the months of the year, and `YearPicker` for selecting from a year of lists.

Dismissible

The `Dismissible` widget is an element that the user can get rid of by flinging it in a given direction. The widget has a `direction` property that specifies which direction it can be dragged in. When the user drags it, the child of it slides out of view, and if the optional `resizeDirection` property isn't `null`, the `Dismissible` animates its height or width, whichever is perpendicular to the dismiss direction, to zero.

Here's an example:

```
Dismissible(
  key : GlobalKey(),
  onDismissed : (direction) { print("Goodbye!"); },
  child : Container(
    color : Colors.yellow, width : 100, height : 50,
    child : Text("Swipe me")
  )
)
```

If you wish, you can implement a "leave-behind," which is what happens if the `background` property is specified. In that case, the widget it describes is stacked behind the `Dismissible`'s `child` and is shown when the child is dragged away.

The `onDismissed` callback function will be called when the size has collapsed to zero when `resizeDuration` is specified, or immediately after the slide animation if it's not. A key also must be defined for this to work; in this example, it's not used though so I just use a `GlobalKey` instance to fulfill that requirement.

Dialogs, Popups, and Messages

There are ways to interact with the user, to show them something, that is, in a sense "out of band," meaning content that isn't directly part of the screen they are currently looking at. Broadly, those are dialogs (typically, where we request some information), popups (usually, where we show some information that needs more immediate attention) and messages (typically, how we show quick, transient pieces of information to the user).

Tooltip

The Tooltip widget is handy for showing a description of some other widget when you perform some appropriate action (most commonly long-pressing a button). To apply one, you wrap the target widget in a Tooltip, like so:

```
Tooltip(
  message : "Tapping me will destroy the universe. Ouch!",
  child : RaisedButton(
    child : Text("Do Not Tap!"),
    onPressed : () { print("BOOM!"); }
  )
)
```

In fact, some widgets have a tooltip property that automatically wraps the widget in a Tooltip, but you can do so manually if not.

Usually, a Tooltip is displayed below the widget it wraps, but you can set its preferBelow property to false to reverse that (and it will automatically do so if there isn't enough room to display it below). You can also adjust the verticalOffset property to determine the distance between the Tooltip and its target widget.

SimpleDialog (CupertinoDialog)

A SimpleDialog is a popup element that offers the user a choice between several options. The SimpleDialog can optionally have some title text which is displayed above the options. Most of the time, the choices are rendered using the SimpleDialogOption widget. An instance of SimpleDialog is normally passed to the showDialog() function for display, as you can see in Listing 3-10.

Listing 3-10. A SimpleDialog

```
import "package:flutter/material.dart";

void main() => runApp(MyApp());

class MyApp extends StatelessWidget {
  @override
  Widget build(BuildContext context) {
    return MaterialApp(home : Scaffold(body : Home()));
  }
}

class Home extends StatelessWidget {

  @override
  Widget build(BuildContext inContext) {

    Future _showIt() async {
      switch (await showDialog(
        context : inContext,
        builder : (BuildContext inContext) {
          return SimpleDialog(
            title : Text("What's your favorite food?"),
            children : [
              SimpleDialogOption(
                onPressed : () {
                  Navigator.pop(inContext, "brocolli");
                },
                child : Text("Brocolli")
              ),
              SimpleDialogOption(
                onPressed : () {
                  Navigator.pop(inContext, "steak");
                },
                child : Text("Steak")
              )
            ]
```

```
        );
      }
  )) {
    case "brocolli": print("Brocolli"); break;
    case "steak": print("Steak"); break;
  }
}

  return Scaffold(
    body : Center(
      child : RaisedButton(
        child : Text("Show it"),
        onPressed : _showIt
      )
    )
  );

}

}
```

What this looks like in practice can be glimpsed in Figure 3-10.

Figure 3-10. *It doesn't get much simpler than SimpleDialog (it's in the name after all!)*

When the RaisedButton is tapped, it calls the _timeForADialog() function. This function awaits the return value from showDialog() as the value of the switch statement. When the user then clicks one of the options, first the dialog must be hidden, which is what the Navigator.pop() call does. The dialog is on the top of the navigation stack at that point, hence pop()'ing it off hides it. The second argument to pop() is the value to return, which the two case statements then handle to print() the result to the console.

There is a CupertinoDialog widget, and corresponding CupertinoDialogAction widget, for providing the same sort of dialog on iOS, and you would use them the same way.

Note   The structure here is a little different than what you've seen before. The reason is that if you try to call showDialog() from the RaisedButton's onPressed handler directly, which is what you'd likely think to do first, you'll find that you get an error talking about needing a MaterialLocalization. The problem is that showDialog() must be called in a build context that has a MaterialApp as an ancestor, which by default includes a MaterialLocalization widget, which is involved with localizing apps. The build context inside the RaisedButton's onPressed handler though has no such ancestor (even if the build() method returned MaterialApp as the top-level widget, that represents a different build context than the build context passed into build() itself). So, the solution is to create a top-level MaterialApp widget and then make the home property point to another widget, a Scaffold in this case, which itself has the Home widget as a child (the Scaffold is optional here, but it's necessary for some other examples that will build on this in this section). That way, the build context for the top-level widget is the one that applies to the showDialog() call, which does have MaterialApp as an ancestor, and thus the error is avoided. Although I haven't done it for most code samples, what you see here is a bit more typical structure, but it hasn't mattered until now, so I chose to keep the code more straightforward to this point (and I'll continue to do so except where it matters, as it does here).

AlertDialog (CupertinoAlertDialog)

The AlertDialog is much like the SimpleDialog except that it is meant for urgent situations that require their immediate attention and typically don't require more than a binary choice of some sort (or no choice at all). Building on the SimpleDialog example code, all we need to change is the _showIt() function:

```
_showIt() {
  return showDialog(
    context : inContext,
    barrierDismissible : false,
    builder : (BuildContext context) {
```

```
    return AlertDialog(
      title : Text("We come in peace..."),
      content : Center(child :
        Text("...shoot to kill shoot to kill shoot to kill")
      ),
      actions : [
        FlatButton(
          child : Text("Beam me up, Scotty!"),
          onPressed : () { Navigator.of(context).pop(); }
        )
      ]
    );
  }
);
}
```

As before, showDialog() is used, but this time the builder() function returns an AlertDialog. The content property is how we tell AlertDialog what to display, and then the actions property allows us to provide an array of elements for the user to click, just one FlatButton in this case. Like with SimpleDialog, we need to pop() the dialog off the navigator stack, and there's nothing to return this time, so no second argument is needed. The barrierDismissable property set to false ensures that the user must click the FlatButton; the dialog cannot be dismissed by clicking elsewhere on the screen as the SimpleDialog could be. This is appropriate for an informational popup meant to alert the user to something important (Captain Kirk's hypocrisy may or may not qualify in this instance!)

Note that there is an iOS version of this dialog, aptly named CupertinoAlertDialog, and you use it the same way.

SnackBar

A SnackBar is a lightweight message component that shows a transient message at the bottom of the screen for some period of time, and optionally with a single action, the user can tap, most usually to dismiss the SnackBar. Building on the same sample as for the SimpleDialog and AlertDialog, we'll change the _showIt() function as shown here:

```
_showIt() {
  Scaffold.of(inContext).showSnackBar(
    SnackBar(
      backgroundColor : Colors.red,
      duration : Duration(seconds : 5),
      content : Text("I like pie!"),
      action : SnackBarAction(
        label : "Chow down",
        onPressed: () {
          print("Gettin' fat!");
        }
      )
    )
  );
}
```

Figure 3-11 shows you the result.

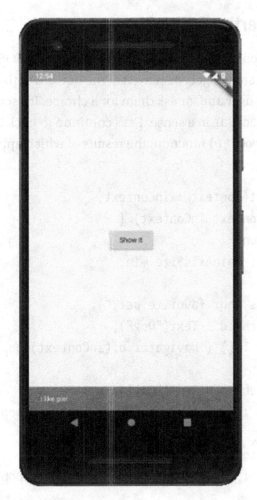

Figure 3-11. *The SnackBar widget (on the bottom)*

We have to use the `Scaffold.of(inContext)` call to get a reference to the `Scaffold` that is the parent to the widget calling this function. That `Scaffold` has a `showSnackBar()` method, which is what we call. We can optionally set the `backgroundColor` as well as the `duration`, the latter needing an instance of the `Duration` class (which can accept values in many forms such as hours, minutes, and seconds). The `content` is the text to show on the `SnackBar`. The `action` property is optional but if present shows a clickable bit of text. Usually, you would hide the `SnackBar` here when tapped, but nothing says you must, as shown. If you don't, then the `SnackBar` will automatically disappear after the specified duration (or the default duration if not specified).

BottomSheet (CupertinoActionSheet)

Bottom sheets, as provided by the BottomSheet widget (and its iOS counterpart
CupertinoActionSheet) are widgets displayed at the bottom of the screen to show
additional content to the user and/or ask them for a choice. It's sort of a cross between
a SimpleDialog and a SnackBar in a sense. Let's continue to hack the previous example
and again change the _showIt() function, the results of which appear in Figure 3-12.

```
_showIt() {
  showModalBottomSheet(context : inContext,
    builder : (BuildContext inContext) {
      return new Column(
        mainAxisSize : MainAxisSize.min,
        children : [
          Text("What's your favorite pet?"),
          FlatButton(child : Text("Dog"),
            onPressed : () { Navigator.of(inContext).pop(); },
          ),
          FlatButton(child : Text("Cat"),
            onPressed : () { Navigator.of(inContext).pop(); },
          ),
          FlatButton(child : Text("Ferret"),
            onPressed : () { Navigator.of(inContext).pop(); }
          )
        ]
      );
    }
  );
}
```

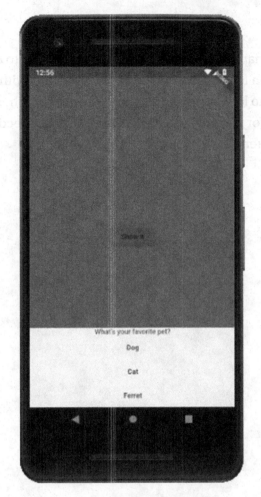

Figure 3-12. *A BottomSheet... not a top or side sheet, but a BottomSheet!*

There's actually two variations of BottomSheet, one shown via a call to showModalBottomSheet() and another shown by calling the showBottomSheet() of the Scaffold that the widget showing the sheet descends from. The difference is that the former prevents the user from interacting with other parts of the app until the sheet is hidden (what is termed being "model"), while the other is called "persistent" because it remains, unless and until dismissed, but doesn't disallow interactions with other parts of the app. In either case, the BottomSheet is constructed in the same fundamental way. What content you show on it is up to you, as is whether it's interactive or not. In this example, I've got a Text heading with three FlatButton widgets below it. Tapping any of them results in the BottomSheet being hidden via the Navigator.of(inContext).pop() call you've seen a few times now.

133

Summary

Whew, that was a long chapter! I think this is an excellent place to take a little break. In this chapter, you began to see the widgets that Flutter ships with, at a high level, but there's still plenty more to look at, including more widgets and then some APIs.

So, grab a snack, go for a stretch, maybe a bio break if you need to, and then meet me right back here for Chapter 4!

CHAPTER 4

Say Hello to My Little Friend: Flutter, Part II

In the last chapter, you began your exploration of the widgets Flutter ships with. Now, in this chapter, we'll play the back nine, to use some golf lingo (I'm not a golfer – I consider golf a nice walk interrupted by a game – but it's a good phrase none the less) and continue looking at the widgets, followed by a brief dive into some APIs that Flutter provides.

Styling Widgets

Flutter has a rich system for styling widgets in various ways, and being widget-oriented at its core, you do this, largely at least, through widgets that are specifically designed to style other widgets. It's like widget inception up in here!

Note that for the next four sections, Listing 4-1, while not printed here, is the full working example and is included in the code bundle, and Figure 4-1 here is the result of running it, so please refer to this screenshot as you read the next four sections to give it all context.

© Frank Zammetti 2019

F. Zammetti, *Practical Flutter*, https://doi.org/10.1007/978-1-4842-4972-7_4

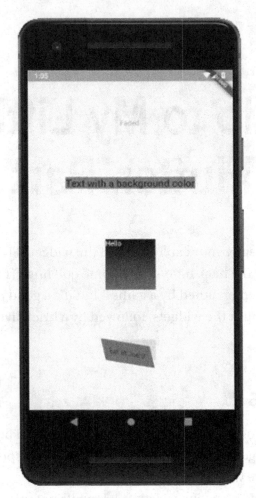

Figure 4-1. *Demonstration of the following four sections (trust me, it's better in color!)*

Theme and ThemeData

The Theme widget applies a theme to its child widgets. This includes colors and typographic settings.

When we looked at the MaterialApp widget, you saw that it has a theme property that can be used to declare the theme to apply for the entire application. Where the Theme widget comes into play is typically when you want to override that application-level theme for just some subset of widgets. Alternatively, you could just wrap the entire application's widget tree in a Theme widget and apply the theme that way, but that's not usually done in favor of the theme property of MaterialApp.

There are two choices when dealing with the Theme widget: extending the parent theme or building a new one. Extending the parent theme (which means whatever theme is nearest when traversing up the widget tree) is good when you only want to change a subset of elements. To do this is easy:

```
Theme(
  data : Theme.of(context).copyWith(accentColor : Colors.red),
  child : /* Your widget tree to be styled with this theme */
)
```

The Theme.of() method is basically how you say "hey, Flutter, what's the nearest theme to this widget?" Whatever parent widget has a theme is the theme it will find (and remember: even if you don't explicitly define a theme anywhere there's a default theme automatically that will be found). This method returns a ThemeData object, which has a copyWith() method. This method returns a new ThemeData object but with whatever properties you pass to it overriding what was in it before. Here, we're making the accentColor property of the new ThemeData use Colors.red, overriding whatever it was before. Now, all widgets underneath this Theme widget will have a red accent color regardless of what any other widgets in the app have.

To create a whole new Theme is arguably even easier:

```
Theme(
  data : ThemeData( accentColor : Colors.red ),
  child : /* Your widget tree to be styled with this theme */
);
```

No need to get the parent ThemeData; you just create a new instance and define the properties you want. There are many properties supported by ThemeData, far too many to list here, so you'll need to refer to the Flutter documentation to see which you want to define.

Now, once you have the Theme widget defined, you still must make use of it in individual widgets. But, with the Theme in place, it makes it easy:

```
Theme (
  data : ThemeData( accentColor : Colors.red ),
  child : Container(
    color : Theme.of(context).accentColor,
    child : Text(
```

137

```
        "Text with a background color,"
        style : Theme.of(context).textTheme.title,
      )
    )
)
```

Remember the key point: since the `Container` here is wrapped in a `Theme`, `Theme.of(context)` will return that theme's `ThemeData`; if the `Container` was not wrapped in a `Theme`, then the application-level `ThemeData` for the `Theme` specified in the `theme` property of the `MaterialApp` widget would be used; if no `theme` was specified on the `MaterialApp`, then a default `Theme` and `ThemeData` would be built under the covers and used by default.

Opacity

The `Opacity` widget is a simple one: it makes its child transparent by a specified amount. As a simple example, just replace the second `Text` in the example from earlier with this:

```
Opacity(opacity: .25, child : Text("Faded") )
```

When you rerun it, you'll see that the text is now semi-transparent (or to state it another way: 25% opaque). There's not much more to it than this!

DecoratedBox

The `DecoratedBox` widget is exactly what it says: a box, which is decorated! More conceptually, it paints a decoration onto another box-like container widget that is a child of the `DecoratedBox`. Going along with `DecoratedBox`, nearly always, is the `BoxDecoration` widget, which defines the decoration you want.

Let's look at an example:

```
DecoratedBox(
  decoration : BoxDecoration(
    gradient : LinearGradient(
      begin : Alignment.topCenter,
      end : Alignment.bottomCenter,
      colors : [ Color(0xFF000000), Color(0xFFFF0000) ],
```

```
      tileMode : TileMode.repeated
    )
  ),
  child : Container(width : 100, height : 100,
    child : Text("Hello",
      style : TextStyle(color : Colors.white)
    )
  )
)
```

Here, we wrap a `DecoratedBox` around a `Container` that is parent to a `Text` widget. On its own, the `DecoratedBox` won't display anything; that's where its child comes in. We need to give it a box to decorate, and that's what the `Container` is for. The `Text` inside it is just an added bonus to show that it's the `Container` being decorated and not the `Text` itself.

Now, *how* it's being decorated is where the `decoration` property comes into play, and its value is an instance of `BoxDecoration`. The `BoxDecoration` widget provides a way to decorate with colors, or with images (to have a background image applied to the `Container` behind the `Text`, for example) or play with the borders (rounded corners, for example) and apply shadows and gradients, the latter of which is shown here. The `LinearGradient` is one of several gradient classes (in addition to `RadialGradient` and `SweepGradient`) that take a position in the box to begin and end the gradient (conveniently specified with the `Alignment` class constants) and the colors to use and how to repeat the gradient if needed based on the size of the box.

`DecoratedBox`, combined with `BoxDecoration`, is a handy and flexible way to add styling to any container element as your needs require.

Transform

The `Transform` widget applies some sort of geometric transformation on its child element. Virtually any kind of transformation can be coded with this. As an example:

```
Center(
  child : Container(
    color : Colors.yellow,
    child : Transform(
      alignment : Alignment.bottomLeft,
```

```
        transform : Matrix4.skewY(0.4)..rotateZ(-3 / 12.0),
        child : Container(
          padding : const EdgeInsets.all(12.0),
          color : Colors.red,
          child : Text("Eat at Joe's!")
        )
      )
    )
  )
```

That rotates and skews a red box with a yellow background that has some text in it while keeping the bottom left corner of the box pinned to its original location. It may not be an especially useful example, but it begins to hint at the sort of power this widget provides if you are familiar with matrix transformations.

In addition to this constructor, there is also `Transform.rotate()`, `Transform.scale()`, and `Transform.translate()` which each returns a `Transform` widget specifically configured for the three most common types of transformations, namely, rotations, scaling, and translations. These are considerably easier to use since they don't require you to know matrix operations (they take a simple subset of arguments that is less math-y, if you will), so if you need one of these common transformation types, I highly recommend using them instead of the `Transform()` constructor.

Animations and Transitions

Animations in a user interface are big business these days! Users expect their apps to move visually and to do so in a visually appealing way. Flutter provides some animation widgets for just this purpose. Given that by their nature it wouldn't make much sense to show screenshots of any of this, I haven't done so. But, I think this would be an excellent opportunity for you to fire up Android Studio, create a basic project, and then work on running this code. You'll have to do some work to create a basic app, but it should be an excellent exercise to test your understanding to this point as well as showing you what this all does.

AnimatedContainer

For relatively simple animations, the AnimatedContainer widget is perfect. It gradually changes its values over a defined period of time. It does this automatically – you just tell it what the starting values are, then change to the new values and it will animate (or tween) between them as required.

As a simple example:

```
class _MyApp extends State {

  var _color = Colors.yellow;
  var _height = 200.0;
  var _width = 200.0;

  @override
  Widget build(BuildContext context) {
    return MaterialApp(home : Scaffold(
      body : Center(child : Column(
        mainAxisAlignment : MainAxisAlignment.center,
        children : [
          AnimatedContainer(
            duration : Duration(seconds : 1),
            color : _color, width : _width, height : _height
          ),
          RaisedButton(
            child : Text("Animate!"),
            onPressed : () {
              _color = Colors.red;
              _height = 400.0;
              _width = 400.0;
              setState(() {});
            }
          )
        ]
      ))
    ));
  }
}
```

Here, we've got an `AnimatedContainer` with its `duration` property set to one second so that's how long the animation will take. We set the initial `color`, `width`, and `height` properties to the values of the variables defined in the `State`. Then, when the user clicks the `RaisedButton`, the values of all three variables are changed and `setState()` is called, which triggers the rebuild, but now Flutter will do so over one second of time, gradually making the `AnimatedContainer` bigger and gradually changing it to red.

You'll also find a `DecoratedBoxTransition` which can be used to animate the various properties of a `DecoratedBox`, so it's conceptually pretty similar to `AnimatedContainer`, but for a specific target widget.

AnimatedCrossFade

The `AnimatedCrossFade` widget is a widget specifically designed to cross-fade between two elements. A cross-fade is when one element fades out while another fades in at the same location. It's simple to use:

```
class _MyApp extends State {

  var _showFirst = true;

  @override
  Widget build(BuildContext context) {
    return MaterialApp(home : Scaffold(
      body : Center(child : Column(
        mainAxisAlignment : MainAxisAlignment.center,
        children : [
          AnimatedCrossFade(
            duration : Duration(seconds : 2),
            firstChild : FlutterLogo(
              style : FlutterLogoStyle.horizontal,
              size : 100.0
            ),
            secondChild : FlutterLogo(
              style : FlutterLogoStyle.stacked,
              size : 100.0
            ),
```

```
          crossFadeState : _showFirst ?
            CrossFadeState.showFirst :
            CrossFadeState.showSecond,
        ),
      RaisedButton(
        child : Text("Cross-Fade!"),
        onPressed : () {
          _showFirst = false;
          setState(() {});
        }
      )
    ]
  ))
 ));
 }
}
```

First, this is the first time you've seen the `FlutterLogo` widget. As I'm sure you can guess, this is one that displays the Flutter widget with various stylings. You don't need to add it as a resource or anything like that, it's just there automatically for you to use.

Now, here, we embed two of them inside an `AnimatedCrossFade` widget by setting the `firstChild` and `secondChild` properties to instances of `FlutterLogo`. Like `AnimatedContainer`, this widget has a `duration` property too, which is set to two seconds here.

The `crossFadeState` property is what matters most: it tells the widget which of the two widgets to show. When set to the value of `CrossFadeState.showFirst`, it shows the first. Otherwise, it shows the second when the value is `CrossFadeState.showSecond`. This is based on the value of the boolean `_showFirst` variable, which starts out `true`, so the first image appears but then gets set to `false` when the `RaisedButton` is clicked, and voila, we have ourselves a cross-fade!

Note that there is also a `FadeTransition` that animates the opacity of an element. You could build your own `AnimatedCrossFade` with two `FadeTransition` widgets working simultaneously if you wanted (which, while I haven't checked, I'd be willing to bet is exactly how `AnimatedCrossFade` is implemented).

AnimatedDefaultTextStyle

For animating text, AnimatedDefaultTextStyle is a good choice. It works very similarly to AnimatedContainer and AnimatedCrossFade:

```
class _MyApp extends State {

  var _color = Colors.red;
  var _fontSize = 20.0;

  @override
  Widget build(BuildContext context) {
    return MaterialApp(home : Scaffold(
      body : Center(child : Column(
        mainAxisAlignment : MainAxisAlignment.center,
        children : [
          AnimatedDefaultTextStyle(
            duration : const Duration(seconds : 1),
            style : TextStyle(
              color : _color, fontSize : _fontSize
            ),
            child : Text("I am some text")
          ),
          RaisedButton(
            child : Text("Enhance! Enhance! Enhance!"),
            onPressed : () {
              _color = Colors.blue;
              _fontSize = 40.0;
              setState(() {});
            }
          )
        ]
      ))
    ));
  }
}
```

Here, the Text that is the child of the `AnimatedDefaultTextStyle` is enlarged 100% and its color changed over the course of one second. By this point I'm going to assume that not much needs to be explained here given how similar these last three widgets have been.

A Few Others: AnimatedOpacity, AnimatedPositioned, PositionedTransition, SlideTransition, AnimatedSize, ScaleTransition, SizeTransition, and RotationTransition

I'm going to save some space here and just mention without showing examples that in addition to the widgets you've seen in this section, there are a few others, as you can see in the heading. These can be used just like the others to animate the opacity of an element, or the position of an element, the size of an element, or the rotation of an element.

Note that the `AnimatedOpacity` widget should be used sparingly because opacity animation is a relatively expensive operation (this would apply to the `AnimatedCrossFade` and `FadeTransition` widgets too).

Also note that the `AnimatedPositioned` widget only works if the child is an element of a `Stack`, which is a widget we never discussed explicitly. In brief, it allows you to display several children overlapped over one another (whether they are the same size or not, meaning that if a larger element is beneath a smaller one then the larger element can "peek out" from behind the smaller one on top, at least partially). You'll definitely be seeing the stack again in later chapters, but understand that it's not the same as the navigator stack that you saw earlier. They are two separate concepts. The `Stack` widget is just a container for other elements that can be on top of each other.

An interesting note about the `*Transition` widgets is that they all support physics, which allows you to have animations that aren't purely linear. This is true to varying degrees for the `Animated*` widgets, but the support for it in the `*Transition` widgets tends to be a bit more robust, which means you can get more exciting animations.

Drag and Drop

Although somewhat less common on mobile devices, the drag-and-drop interaction is common on desktops, and either way, Flutter does support it. It does so via two main widgets: Draggable and DragTarget. Using them is not too tough:

```
class MyApp extends StatelessWidget {

  @override
  Widget build(BuildContext context) {
    return MaterialApp(home : Scaffold(
      body : Center(child : Column(mainAxisAlignment :
        MainAxisAlignment.center,
        children : [
          DragTarget(
            builder : (BuildContext context,
              List<String> accepted,
              List<dynamic> rejected) {
              return new Container(width : 200, height : 200,
                color : Colors.lightBlue);
            },
            onAccept : (data) => print(data)
          ),
          Container(height : 50),
          Draggable(
            data : "I was dragged",
            child : Container(width : 100, height : 100,
              color : Colors.red),
            feedback : Container(width : 100, height : 100,
              color : Colors.yellow)
          )
        ]
      ))
    ));
  }
}
```

First, we have a `DragTarget`, which of course is where the thing being dragged can be dropped. We need to specify the data type that this target will accept, and in this case, it's a plain old `String`. The `builder()` function returns a `Container`, but it can return anything we want to make a drop target.

Next, a second `Container` is added to the `Column` layout, just to give us a little bit of space between the `DragTarget` and the `Draggable`, which is next. The primary things we need to supply here are the `data` property, which is any arbitrary data you want to provide to the `DragTarget`, and then the `feedback` property, which is a widget that the user will physically (err, virtually? Physically-virtually? What's the right verb?!) drag.

You see, the way it works is that the original widget, which is specified via the `child` attribute, never moves. Instead, when the user begins to move the `child` `Container`, the widget determined by `feedback` is rendered and begins to be draggable. When it's dropped onto a `DragTarget`, the `onAccept` handler function on the `DragTarget` fires and receives the `data` property value of the `Draggable`.

There are a host of other callbacks that can be triggered in various situations on both widgets, but probably the most useful is the `onDragComplete` handler, which is a function that fires when the `Draggable` is dropped on a `DragTarget`. This is usually the place where you'd hide the original child widget or do whatever else makes sense.

Finally, there is a `LongPressDraggable` widget that can be used in place of `Draggable`. The difference is that this one makes the `child` draggable from a long press instead. It's a minor interaction difference that merely depends on your use case.

Data Views

It is a typical pattern in any app, mobile or otherwise, to show the user lists of data in some form. Flutter provides a handful of widgets specifically for that purpose (though you can always build your own if you want with various scrolling components, but that will usually not be necessary given the widgets here).

Table

The `Table` widget is perhaps the simplest of what I term "data views," that is, widgets used to display a collection of data. If you're familiar with an HTML table, then you already have a basic idea what the `Table` widget is all about: displaying elements in an organization of rows and columns. Look at the sample code in Listing 4-2 and the result in Figure 4-2.

Listing 4-2. Setting the table with the Table widget

```
import "package:flutter/material.dart";

void main() => runApp(MyApp());

class MyApp extends StatelessWidget  {

  Widget build(BuildContext inContext) {
    return MaterialApp(home : Scaffold(
      body : Column(children : [
        Container(height : 100),
        Table(
          border : TableBorder(
            top : BorderSide(width : 2),
            bottom : BorderSide(width : 2),
            left : BorderSide(width : 2),
            right : BorderSide(width : 2)
          ),
          children : [
            TableRow(
              children : [
                Center(child : Padding(
                  padding : EdgeInsets.all(10),
                  child : Text("1"))
                ),
                Center(child : Padding(
                  padding :  EdgeInsets.all(10),
                  child : Text("2"))
                ),
                Center(child : Padding(
                  padding :  EdgeInsets.all(10),
                  child : Text("3"))
                )
              ]
            )
          ]
        )
      ]
```

```
      )
    ])
  ));
  }

}
```

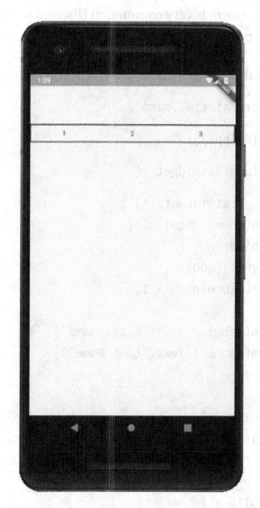

Figure 4-2. *It's not much to look at, but it's just a basic Table example after all!*

It's straightforward, right? You can optionally define the border of the Table, but by default, it will have none. Then, you just need to supply some rows via children, which can be any widget or widget tree you like but it must at the top be an instance of TableRow, and the children of each is a cell, or column, in the row. Every row in a Table must have the same number of children. You can manually set the widths of the columns with the columnWidths property, and you can adjust the vertical alignment of content in each cell with the defaultVerticalAlignment property.

DataTable

Displaying data in a tabular form is very common in UIs, and so Flutter provides the DataTable widget for this purpose, as shown in Listing 4-3.

Listing 4-3. The DataTable widget

```dart
import "package:flutter/material.dart";

void main() => runApp(MyApp());

class MyApp extends StatelessWidget  {

  Widget build(BuildContext inContext) {
    return MaterialApp(home : Scaffold(
      body : Column(children : [
        Container(height : 100),
        DataTable(sortColumnIndex : 1,
          columns : [
            DataColumn(label : Text("First Name")),
            DataColumn(label : Text("Last Name"))
          ],
          rows : [
            DataRow(cells : [
              DataCell(Text("Leia")),
              DataCell(Text("Organa"), showEditIcon : true)
            ]),
            DataRow(cells : [
              DataCell(Text("Luke")),
              DataCell(Text("Skywalker"))
            ]),
```

```
        DataRow(cells : [
          DataCell(Text("Han")),
          DataCell(Text("Solo"))
        ])
      ]
    )
  ])
));
}

}
```

In simplest terms, a `DataTable` requires that you tell it what the `columns` in the table are and then of course what the data `rows` to display are. Each column is defined via a `DataColumn` instance while each row is defined with a `DataRow` instance which contains a collection of `cells` whose members are `DataCell` instances. Although not required, you can supply the `sortColumnIndex` property to indicate which column the data is currently sorted by. Note that this is just a visual indicator though – your code is responsible for physically sorting the data (you most of the time won't supply the data inline as in this example; you'll instead have some function that produces the list, and that's the natural place to sort the data as well). You can see most of this in Figure 4-3.

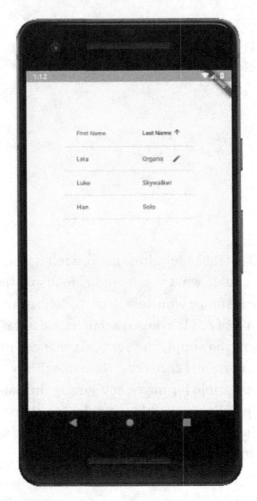

Figure 4-3. *Are you team Star Wars or Star Trek? Oh yeah, and that's a DataTable!*

A `DataColumn` can supply a tooltip property to show some descriptive text when the column is long-pressed, and a `DataCell` can include a `showEditIcon` property that, when `true`, shows a little pencil icon to indicate the cell can be edited. The actual editing must be supplied by your code, however.

Note that a DataTable is a somewhat expensive widget computationally owing to the layout process it must implement. Therefore, if you have a lot of data to display it is recommended that you use the `PaginatedeDataTable` widget instead. It works much like `DataTable` does, but it splits the data into pages that the user can move between. That way, it only has to lay one page at a time, which is less expensive.

GridView

The GridView widget displays a two-dimensional grid of widgets. It can scroll in either direction according to the scrollDirection property (defaulting to Axis.vertical) and which provides several layouts, the most common being the one generated by the GridView.count() constructor as Listing 4-4 shows.

Listing 4-4. A GridView full of fluttering Flutter logos (okay, they're not fluttering)

```
import "package:flutter/material.dart";

void main() => runApp(MyApp());

class MyApp extends StatelessWidget  {

  @override
  Widget build(BuildContext inContext) {
    return MaterialApp(home : Scaffold(
      body : GridView.count(
        padding : EdgeInsets.all(4.0),
        crossAxisCount : 4, childAspectRatio : 1.0,
        mainAxisSpacing : 4.0, crossAxisSpacing : 4.0,
        children: [
          GridTile(child : new FlutterLogo()),
          GridTile(child : new FlutterLogo()),
          GridTile(child : new FlutterLogo()),
          GridTile(child : new FlutterLogo()),
          GridTile(child : new FlutterLogo()),
          GridTile(child : new FlutterLogo()),
          GridTile(child : new FlutterLogo()),
          GridTile(child : new FlutterLogo()),
          GridTile(child : new FlutterLogo())
        ]
      )
    ));
  }
}
```

153

This produces a layout, shown in Figure 4-4, with a fixed number of elements (called tiles) in the cross axis. Others include `GridView.extent()`, which produces a layout with tiles that have a maximum cross-axis extent. You can also use the `GridView.builder()` constructor if you have an "infinite" number of tiles to display.

Figure 4-4. *It's not much to look at, I admit, but it demonstrates GridView well enough*

Note that `GridView` is very much like `ListView`, which in a sense is a purely linear `GridView` (we'll be looking at `ListView` shortly).

ListView and ListTile

The ListView widget is probably the most important of the data view widgets. Certainly, I would say it's likely to be the one you'll use most often when you have a scrolling list of items to display. In its simplest form, coding it looks like Listing 4-5.

Listing 4-5. Coding a simple static ListView

```
import "package:flutter/material.dart";

void main() => runApp(MyApp());

class MyApp extends StatelessWidget  {

  @override
  Widget build(BuildContext inContext) {
    return MaterialApp(home : Scaffold(
      body : ListView(children : [
        ListTile(leading: Icon(Icons.gif), title: Text("1")),
        ListTile(leading: Icon(Icons.book), title: Text("2")),
        ListTile(leading: Icon(Icons.call), title: Text("3")),
        ListTile(leading: Icon(Icons.dns), title: Text("4")),
        ListTile(leading: Icon(Icons.cake), title: Text("5")),
        ListTile(leading: Icon(Icons.pets), title: Text("6")),
        ListTile(leading: Icon(Icons.poll), title: Text("7")),
        ListTile(leading: Icon(Icons.face), title: Text("8")),
        ListTile(leading: Icon(Icons.home), title: Text("9")),
        ListTile(leading: Icon(Icons.adb), title: Text("10")),
        ListTile(leading: Icon(Icons.dvr), title: Text("11")),
        ListTile(leading: Icon(Icons.hd), title: Text("12")),
        ListTile(leading: Icon(Icons.toc), title: Text("3")),
        ListTile(leading: Icon(Icons.tv), title: Text("14")),
        ListTile(leading: Icon(Icons.help), title: Text("15"))
      ])
    ));
  }
}
```

The children of ListView can be anything you like, but frequently you will use a ListTile widget (several of them, to be more precise). ListTile is a widget that is a single fixed-height row that contains some text and a leading or trailing icon. ListTile can show up to three lines of text, including a subtitle. In the example, the leading property is used to show an Icon before the text, which you can see in Figure 4-5.

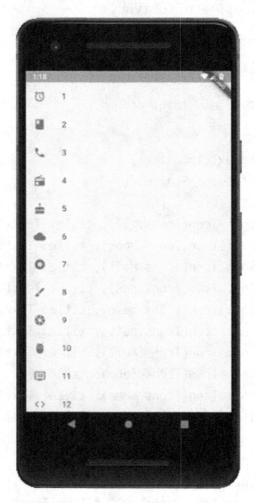

Figure 4-5. *The ListView widget, in conjunction with ListTile*

The ListView can scroll vertically or horizontally depending on the setting of its scrollDirection property. You can even adjust the way the ListView handles scrolling by adjusting the physics property, which is an instance of ScrollPhysics.

ListView supplies a couple of different constructors, with the default one shown in the example. There is also a ListView.builder() constructor that uses a builder function to render the rows. ListView.separated() is also available, and this will provide you a ListView with items separated by list separators you define. The ListView.custom() constructor allows you more flexibility in setting the child model to make the ListView look and work in pretty much any way you want.

There is also the PageView widget, which is a ListView that supports pagination. This is a good choice if you have many items that you want to ensure are displayed with good performance, but more importantly, that is logical to break into groupings in some way where each grouping becomes a page.

Miscellaneous

Some widgets defy categorization. Well, not for long, because now we have a miscellaneous category just for them!

CircularProgressIndicator (CupertinoActivityIndicator) and LinearProgressIndicator

What do you show your users while some long-running activity is ongoing? Maybe it's a call to a remote server that is responding a bit slowly. There are many choices, but CircularProgressIndicator is one of the best. It's just an animated circle, but it gets the job done and is very easy to use:

```
CircularProgressIndicator()
```

Yep, in simplest terms, that's all it takes! Flutter handles everything else for you. Now, there are of course some options that will be of interest to you. First, strokeWidth allows you to determine how thick the circle is. The backgroundColor property lets you set a different color behind the indicator. Finally, valueColor allows you to define the color of the circle itself. Unfortunately, it's not as simple as setting a color from the Colors class. No, you have to provide an instance of the Animation class or one of its descendants. Almost always, it will be the AlwaysStoppedAnimation class, which has a constructor that accepts a color, so it winds up not being *that* much more difficult.

For iOS, there is a corresponding `CupertinoActivityIndicator` which looks and works much the same. To use it, you'll need to import `package:flutter/cupertino.dart`, which is true of all the Cupertino widgets. Plus, it doesn't have quite the same degree of flexibility: it only has a `radius` property to define how big it is – no color options are present.

Finally, if you're not into curves, there is a `LinearProgressIndicator` that shows progress as a colored line:

```
LinearProgressIndicator(value : .25, backgroundColor : Colors.yellow)
```

Here, `value` is a number between zero and one that determines how much progress has been made and hence how much of the bar is colored. The `backgroundColor` is the color of the portion of the bar corresponding to remaining progress while the value of `valueColor` (which like `CircularProgressIndicator` takes an instance of an `Animation` as a value) is the portion that has completed. So, in the example, 75% of the bar would be colored yellow while 25% of it would be colored whatever the default color of the theme is since there is no `valueColor` specified.

Icon

The `Icon` widget is just about as simple as a Flutter widget gets: it provides a means to show a Material icon on the screen. To use it, all you do is this:

```
Icon(Icons.radio)
```

The `Icons` class contains a list of Material icons for your use, quite a lot of them in fact. However, you can also add your own. As it happens, these are implemented via fonts, and you can add custom fonts if you want other icons (the popular Font Awesome icon collection, for example).

To do this requires us to jump into the `pubspec.yaml` file, which was briefly mentioned in Chapter 1. In short, this file provides configuration information that Flutter uses to build and run your app. It lists things like dependencies your project has, its name, what version of Flutter it requires, and more. Depending on your needs, you may never have to touch it after the new project wizard creates it. And, what it creates will look something like this:

```
name: flutter_playground
description: flutter playground

version: 1.0.0+1
```

```
environment:
  sdk: ">=2.0.0-dev.68.0 <3.0.0"

dependencies:
  flutter:
    sdk: flutter

  cupertino_icons: ^0.1.2

dev_dependencies:
  flutter_test:
    sdk: flutter

flutter:

  uses-material-design: true
```

This is the pubspec.yaml that was generated for the Flutter Playground app I generated while writing this chapter (which is nothing but the basic Flutter Application project). Note that I've removed the comments here, but there are quite a few that explains what most of this is and even gives you hints about some of the other things you can do, including adding new fonts for icons! It explains that you can add a True Type Font (TTF) file to your project and then add a section under the flutter heading here to reference it. For example, to add Font Awesome, you might do:

```
flutter:
  fonts:
    - family: FontAwesome
      fonts:
        - asset: fonts/font-awesome-400.ttf
```

Once you do that, you can create an instance of IconData that specifies the code point, which is a reference number for the icon you want in the font you added (which you can find on the Font Awesome web site fontawesome.com) and the font family it belongs to, like so:

```
Icon(IconData(0xf556, fontFamily : "FontAwesome"))
```

That's not too tough. But, there's an even easier way for at least some fonts, Font Awesome, for example, which is perhaps the most popular font-based collections of icons out there and so has a little better support in Flutter. Here, you can add a plugin that will make things even easier. A plugin is something that extends Dart and/or Flutter. Usually, it's some Dart code that you can then import into your project as needed. To use a plugin, you just need to add a single line to `pubspec.yaml` under the `dependencies` heading:

```
dependencies:
  font_awesome_flutter: ^8.4.0
```

That specifies that we want version 8.4.0 of the `font_awesome_flutter` plugin or higher, if a higher version is available (if you aren't familiar with semantic versioning, then a quick Google search will get you up to speed in no time – it's pretty simple, so if it's new to you, don't worry because it's easy to pick up but is also beyond the scope of this book). Information on this plugin can be found at `https://pub.dartlang.org/packages,` and you can find many other useful plugins in this repository, all which get added the same way. This won't be the last plugin we see used in this book.

You'll then need to tell Android Studio to get dependencies, which it will automatically show a prompt bar for above the editor when it recognizes that `pubspec.yaml` has changed. Click Packages Get and the dependencies will be downloaded. This includes the necessary TTF file and some extra code.

That extra code can now be used in your code once you add an import:

```
import "package:font_awesome_flutter/font_awesome_flutter.dart";
```

The benefit to doing this is that instead of having to deal with finding the code point, you instead can now just write:

```
Icon(FontAwesomeIcons.angry)
```

It makes it just as easy as using the built-in Material icons, but now you have way more icons to choose from thanks to Font Awesome and this plugin!

We'll look at `pubspec.yaml` as necessary as we forge on, but this serves as a good first introduction to it showing you some of the options it provides you and your Flutter projects.

Image

Along the same lines as the Icon widget is the Image widget, which as I'm sure you can guess is used to display an image of some sort. This widget offers several different constructors, each for fetching an image from a different location. I'm only going to talk about two of them though because they are the most common in my experience: Image.asset() to load an image from the app itself and Image.network() to load it from a network location.

First, Image.asset() allows us to load an image that is included in the app bundle itself:

```
Image.asset("img/ron.jpg")
```

That seems easy, right? But, there's one part missing: we must tell Flutter about our image, which is called an asset. To do so, we have to dive back into pubspec.yaml and add a new section under the flutter heading:

```
assets:
  - img/ron.jpg
```

Every asset you want to include must be declared in this section. Otherwise, the Flutter SDK won't know to include it. You could also do - img/ to include everything under the img directory. But, note that only files directly under img/ would be included – anything in subdirectories of img/ would *not* be (you would have to add an entry for each subdirectory).

It's a bit of a tangential point, but note that assets aren't just about images – you can include text assets as well, things like JSON files. You can load those using the rootBundle object, which is available throughout your application's code. For example, to load a settings.json file:

```
String settings = await rootBundleloadString("textAssets/settings.json");
```

Also tangential but worth knowing: When a build is done, the Flutter SDK creates a special archive that goes along with your app called the asset bundle. You can read from this at runtime, as shown by the settings.json example (and, obviously, Image.asset() is doing so under the covers).

Note   There is a fair bit more to asset bundling in Flutter than I'm covering here, things like variant assets, resolution-aware image assets, and the `AssetBundle` object that provides access to bundled resources (that's the class that `rootBundle` is an instance of, and it offers other facilities, as most classes do). However, for our purposes in this book, we won't need much more than what you see here, so if you think you need those other capabilities, then you'll have to explore them on `flutter.io`.

Lastly, loading an image from the network is even easier since there aren't even any assets to declare:

```
Image.network("http://zammetti.com/booksarticles/img/darkness.png")
```

Yep, that's it! Assuming the device has connectivity, the image will be loaded and displayed just as if it were bundled with the application (albeit perhaps a little slower, given intrinsic network latency).

Chip

A `Chip` is small visual elements that are typically meant to display attributes of things, or small text, or to represent entities like users or quick actions the user can take.

A typical usage is to show a small element representing the current user, perhaps next to their name on a details page. A simple example might be what's shown in Listing 4-6 and shown in Figure 4-6.

Listing 4-6. A simple Chip

```
import "package:flutter/material.dart";

void main() => runApp(MyApp());

class MyApp extends StatelessWidget  {

  @override
  Widget build(BuildContext inContext) {
    return MaterialApp(home : Scaffold(
      body : Center(child :
```

```
    Chip(
      avatar : CircleAvatar(
        backgroundImage : AssetImage("img/ron.jpg")
      ),
      backgroundColor : Colors.grey.shade300,
      label : Text("Frank Zammetti")
    )
  )
));
}
}
```

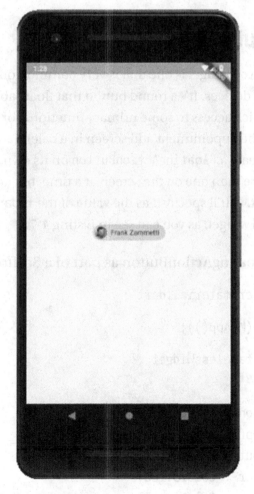

Figure 4-6. *A Chip off the old Flutter block*

The `avatar` property is optional and usually shows either an image or the initials of the user. This property takes a value that is itself a `Widget`, so in theory, you could put anything you want here. In this case, I'm using a `CircleAvatar` widget, which is common for this use case. It can show images or text (typically a person's initials when the `Chip` represents a person) or can itself contain child widgets. In this case, I've used the same image as for the previous `Image` example to show a little picture of me. The `backgroundColor` property, of course, is the color of the chip, and the `label` property is the text to display next to the avatar image (or alone, if no avatar property is specified).

If you add an `onDeleted` property, then the `Chip` will include a delete button for deleting the entity it represents. You'll need to provide a function to implement the delete though as this is purely a visual addition to the `Chip`.

FloatingActionButton

The `FloatingActionButton` widget is one that is very common on Android devices, somewhat less so on iOS devices. It's a round button that floats above the main content and provides the user quick access to some primary function. For example, it might be the button that triggers the appointment add screen in a calendar app.

It's rare that you'll create a `FloatingActionButton` on its own, although you can. It's also unusual to have more than one on the screen at a time, but again, you technically can. More times than not, you'll specify it as the value of the `floatingActionButton` property of the `Scaffold` widget, as you can see in Listing 4-7.

Listing 4-7. A basic FloatingActionButton as part of a Scaffold

```
import "package:flutter/material.dart";

void main() => runApp(MyApp());

class MyApp extends StatelessWidget  {

  @override
  Widget build(BuildContext inContext) {
    return MaterialApp(home : Scaffold(
      floatingActionButton : FloatingActionButton(
        backgroundColor : Colors.red,
        foregroundColor : Colors.yellow,
```

```
      child : Icon(Icons.add),
      onPressed : () { print("Ouch! Stop it!"); }
    ),
    body : Center(child : Text("Click it!"))
  ));
}
}
```

Usually, the child of the FloatingActionButton will be an Icon, as you can see in Figure 4-7, though there's nothing that says it must be.

Figure 4-7. *A FloatingActionButton doing its, uh, floating thing*

The backgroundColor property makes the button itself whatever color you like, and foregroundColor makes the icon or text on the button the specified color. The onPressed property is optional and if not specified will make the button disabled and unresponsive to touch. That isn't usually much good though so you'll need to define a function to implement whatever the functionality for the button should be.

You can also adjust the shadow via the elevation property, and you can even make the button square by setting the shape property to an instance of a RoundedRectangleBorder widget, among other tweaks its properties allow for.

PopupMenuButton

The PopupMenuButton widget implements the common "three-dot" menu paradigm to display a popup menu providing options to a user. This widget can be placed anywhere you deem appropriate and will show up as three vertical dots. The widget has an onSelected property that is a callback function you provide which receives the value associated with the selected option. You can then implement whatever functionality is appropriate. Here's an example, Listing 4-8.

Listing 4-8. A PopupMenuButton, and its menu

```
import "package:flutter/material.dart";

void main() => runApp(MyApp());

class MyApp extends StatelessWidget  {

  @override
  Widget build(BuildContext inContext) {
    return MaterialApp(home : Scaffold(
      body : Center(child :
        PopupMenuButton(
          onSelected : (String result) { print(result); },
          itemBuilder : (BuildContext context) =>
            <PopupMenuEntry<String>>[
              PopupMenuItem(
                value : "copy", child : Text("Copy")
              ),
```

```
        PopupMenuItem(
          value : "cut", child : Text("Cut")
        ),
        PopupMenuItem(
          value : "paste", child : Text("Paste")
        )
      ]
    )
  )
));
  }
}
```

I'm gonna go out on a limb here and say you probably know what this looks like without seeing a screenshot! The PopupMenuButton widget uses the builder pattern previously discussed to construct a list of PopupMenuItem widgets. These widgets can have any child you deem appropriate, but most commonly it's just a Text widget. You associate a value with each item, and then your onSelected function is passed that value and is responsible for what each does (here it's just print()'d to the console).

Some of the other properties supported included the ability to pre-select an item with the initialValue property, the ability to react to the user canceling without selecting an item by supplying a function to the onCanceled property, and adjusting the shadow with the elevation property and play with the padding via the padding property.

Wither APIs?

In addition to the wide variety of widgets, Flutter also offers some APIs for your use, packaged into libraries. They fall into three rough categories: core Flutter framework libraries, Dart libraries, and other/support libraries. We'll look at each group here, although because of what's covered, the latter two groups will wind up being combined.

Note that, as with the widgets, this is intended as a very brief, high-level look at what's available. There are more APIs than will be shown here, and for most of these, there won't be any sample code or in-depth details, just a basic "here's something that might be of interest to you," and as before, I'll try and point out the things that I believe *will* be of interest to most developers. You definitely should though spend some time on `flutter.io` to see all that's available though, and you'll need to reference that online documentation to get all the details you need to put most of this to proper use, but after this section, you should have at least some idea what's available and what to look up, and that's the goal here!

Core Flutter Framework Libraries

The core Flutter framework libraries provide most of the basic functionality of Flutter. Much of this is used internally by the widgets themselves, and so you may find that you don't have cause to use all that much of this directly. Indeed, some of it you will though of course, so let's have a look.

Note that you must import these to use them, and the `import` syntax to use is `package:flutter/<library-name>.dart`.

animation

The animation library provides a variety of functions for implementing various animations in Flutter apps. Some of the interesting members of note include

- `Animation` – This class contains basic information about an animation, things like whether it's running and allowing you to hook event listener functions to it.

- `AnimationController` – This class allows you to control an animation, things like starting and stopping, resetting, and repeating an animation.

- `Curve` – This class contains data defining an easing curve, which allows you to have animations that aren't strictly linear in appearance. There are numerous subclasses of `Curve` including `Cubic`, `ElasticInOutCurve`, `Interval`, and `Sawtooth` that define common easings.

- `Tween` – Like `Curve`, this class contains data defining a particular type of tween operation, and like `Curve`, it has many subclasses for common tweens such as `ColorTween` (tween between two colors),

TextStyleTween (for animating between two text styles such as going from regular text to bold text), and RectTween (interpolation between two rectangles, perhaps to animate the size of a rectangle).

foundation

This library contains foundational Flutter classes, functions, and more. All other layers of Flutter will use this library. Some of its contents include

- Key – You've seen this class before in its GlobalKey and LocalKey subclasses.

- kReleaseMode – A constant that if true if the application is compiled in release mode.

- required – A constant that is used to mark a parameter in a method or function as being required. Yes, you can use this on your own classes!

- debugPrintStack – A function that dumps the current stack to the console.

- debugWordWrap – A function to wrap a given string to a given length.

- TargetPlatform – An enum that provides values corresponding to the various supported platforms (android, fuscia, and iOS at the time of this writing).

gestures

The gestures library contains code for recognizing different user gestures common on touch-oriented devices, things like double-taps, swiping movements plus drag-and-drop operations. Here you'll find things like

- DoubleTapGestureRecognizer – A class that knows how to detect a double-tap

- PanGestureRecognizer – A class that recognizes drag movements in both horizontal and vertical directions

- ScaleGestureRecognizer – A class to recognize pinch gestures typically used for zooming in and out

painting

The painting library includes a variety of classes that wrap the Flutter engine's painting API, which handles the basic and core painting operations that everything else depends on, for performing more specialized painting tasks like painting scaled images, borders around boxes, and interpolating between shadows. Some of the things you'll find here, many of which should look familiar to you already just from the sample code you've looked a thus far, include

- `Alignment` – A class that defines a point inside a rectangle

- `AssetImage` – A class that fetches an image from an `AssetBundle` and determines the appropriate image based on context

- `Border` – A class defining the border of a box

- `Gradient` – A class for showing a 2D color gradient

- `TextDecoration` – A class used to show a linear decoration (read: a line) above or below some text

- `debugDisableShadows` – A property you can set to `true` to turn all shadows into solid color blocks for troubleshooting purposes

- `BorderStyle` – An enum with values for defining the style of line to draw as the border of a box (`none`, `solid`, or a `List` of `values`)

- `TextAlign` – An enum with values for defining how text will horizontally align, whether `center`, `end`, `justify`, `left`, or `start`

services

This library contains functionality for dealing with the underlying device platform in relatively low-level ways. Some of what you'll find here includes:

- `AssetBundle` – A class that consists of a collection of resources used by the application (we talked about this briefly before). Things like images and even data files can be asses in an `AssetBundle`.

- `ByteData` – A class that represents a fixed-length, random-access sequence of bytes that also provides random and unaligned access to the fixed-width integers and floating-point numbers represented by those bytes.

170

- `Clipboard` – A class that contains utility methods for working with the system clipboard (`getData()` and `setData()` methods). This makes use of the `ClipboardData` class to hold the data being put on or taken from the `Clipboard`.

- `HapticFeedback` – A class that provides access to the device's haptic engine. Methods like `heavyImpact()` to produce a haptic collision response corresponding to a heavy mass and `mediumImpact()` and `lightImpact()` for medium and light masses respectively can be found here.

- `SystemSound` – A class that provides a `play()` method that accepts a `SystemSoundType` instance to let your app play one of the sounds from the system's library of short system sounds as specified by the `SystemSoundType`.

- `DeviceOrientation` – An enum with values such as `landscapeLeft` and `portraitDown` that can be used to determine and change device orientation.

widgets

There is also a widgets library, and if you guess that it contains all the Flutter widgets, you would pretty much be right! Given that, there's not much point going over it here since you have seen most of its contents already and will continue to see its contents thanks to writing Flutter code in later chapters. But, if you ever are wondering where the widgets live, the answer is in this library, and you can naturally get to the documentation of widgets through the documentation for this library (though since there's separate documentation for widgets explicitly, there's not much point to going that route – but you *can*).

Dart Libraries

The Dart libraries are provided by Dart itself. To import these, you use the import form `dart:<library-name>.dart`.

core

Technically, there is a library called core that contains built-in types, collections, and other basic functionality every Dart program need (or, at least, has access to). As such, and in contrast with all the other Dart libraries, you *do not* need to import this library explicitly. It's effectively done automatically for you by virtue of, you know, *writing a Dart program*! As such, I'm going to skip going over anything here because much of it you've either seen already or will see, so no point being redundant I figure.

ui

Although these are Dart libraries, given that Google runs the show with both Flutter *and* Dart, you will sometimes find some cross-pollinization, so to speak, and this library is one such instance. This library contains built-in types and core primitives for Flutter applications. However, given that what this library contains exposes the lower-level services that Flutter frameworks use to bootstrap applications, things like classes for driving the input, graphics, text, layout, and rendering subsystems of the framework, you are unlikely to use too much here directly in your application code, and in places where you *do* need to use it, I think it's better to see it in a specific context. Therefore, I won't go into details of the contents of this library here.

async

This library provides support for asynchronous programming. While there are several classes and functions, I think it's fair to say that the following two are the real stars of the show:

- Future – This is a class that represents a computation whose return value might not be available yet. You'll find that many methods across Flutter and Dart return a Future. The Future has a then() method, which is a function you provide that will execute when the Future finally returns its value. You'll be seeing plenty of this class in the code to come.

- Stream – A class that provides asynchronous access to a stream of data. The Stream class has a listen() method, which is a function you provide that will execute every time more data is available in the Stream.

Seriously, I think it's fair to say that if you know nothing else about this library, then you will know almost all you'll ever need, with few exceptions!

collection

The core library already contains some collections-related functionality, but the collection library supplements that with things like

- DoubleLinkedQueue – A Queue class (which, hey, is another class in this library!) based on a double-linked list implementation.

- HashSet – An unordered hash table-based Set implementation class.

- SplayTreeMap – A Map class that stores objects that can be ordered relative to each other.

- UnmodifiableListView – A class with a name that's a mouthful but which provides a simple use: it's a view of another List that can't be modified.

convert

In this library, you'll find utilities for encoding and decoding between different data representations including the common JSON and UTF-8 formats. Some of the most common things you'll use here are

- JsonCodec – A class that encodes and decodes JSON string and objects. The methods json.encode() and json.decode() are your main entry points (note that json is an instance of JsonCodec that is always automatically available to your code if you've imported this library).

- Utf8Codec – A class which you'll also find an automatic instance of named uft8. It too has an encode() and decode() method that you can use to convert between Unicode strings and their corresponding byte values.

- AsciiCodec – A class which, through its automatic ascii instance, lets you encode strings as ASCII bytes via its encode() method and decode ASCII bytes to strings via decode().

- Base64Codec – A class used to encode and decode things in base64, again with an encode() and decode() method and available via the top-level base64 instance (are you starting to see a pattern?!).

173

Note that in addition to the `json` and `base64` instances, because JSON and base64 encoding/decoding is so common, you'll also find top-level functions `base64Encode()`, `base64Decode()`, `jsonEncode()` and `jsonDecode()`.

io

The io library provides various facilities for dealing with file, socket, network, and other input/output functionality. Probably the most important components are

- `File` – A class representing a file on the file system. You can `copy()`, `create()`, check the `length()` of, `openRead()`, `openWrite()`, and `rename()` files, among many operations available on it.

- `Directory` – A class representing a directory on the file system. You can `create()`, `list()` the subdirectories of, `rename()`, and `delete()` directories, among many operations available on it.

- `HttpClient` – A class that can be used to fetch content from a remote server via HTTP. Going along with this is the `Cookie` class for dealing with HTTP cookies, `HttpClientBasicCredentials` for supporting BASIC Auth, `HttpHeaders` for working with HTTP headers, and even `HttpServer` if you need your app to act as an HTTP server!

- `Socket` – A class for performing low-level communications over a TCP socket.

- `exit()` – A top-level function for exiting the Dart VM process with a given error code. You probably don't want to do this in a mobile app, but if you're writing a generic Dart program, then you might want to know about this.

There is definitely more available in this library, a lot of other classes related to HTTP communications specifically to name some, but I suspect this is the stuff you'll use most.

math

All programming languages have math functions (well, I'm sure you could find *at least one* that *doesn't*, but that's just weird!), and Dart is no exception thanks to the math library. Here you'll discover mathematical constants and functions, including random number generation. Some highlights for you:

- Random – A class for generating random numbers, including cryptographically secure random numbers via its `secure()` method.

- `pi` – The venerable constant you know and love and, uh, eat a lot of I guess? I do!

- `cos()` – A function for getting the cosine of a value by converting radians to a double first. Most of the other trigonometry functions you know and love (or hate, depending on how your schooling went!) are here too: `acos()`, `asin()`, `atan()`, `sin()`, and so on.

- `max()` – Returns the larger of two numbers.

- `min()` – Returns the smaller of two numbers.

- `sqrt()` – Returns the square root of a number.

Other (Support) Libraries

Finally, we have just a couple of other/support libraries. There are, of course, more than just two, but they get pretty special-purpose pretty fast, so I think just talking about these few will mostly be sufficient.

crypto

If cryptography if your game, then the crypto library is just the thing for you! Need to hash a value? Well, here you go:

- MD5 – A class for generating MD5 hashes. You don't even have to instantiate one because this library gives you an `md5` instance automatically. At this point, you probably shouldn't be using MD5 except for backward-compatibility though.

- Sha1 – Ah, a better class for hashing than MD5, complete with its own `sha1` instance.

- Sha256 – Oh, but Sha1 not good enough for ya? Okay, fine, you can haz Sha256 instead! And yes, there's a `sha256` instance ready and waiting for ya.

collection

Wait, we already saw a collection library, didn't we?! Indeed, we did! But I guess Google figured you didn't get your fill of collections just yet, so there's another one! In it, you'll find even more collections, like

- `CanonocalizedMap` – A map class whose keys are converted to canonical values of a specified type. This can be useful for when you want case-insensitive keys in your map and where null is not allowed.

- `DelegatingSet` – A set class that delegates all operations to a base set. Handy for when you want to hide non-set methods of a `Set` object.

- `UnionSet` – A set class that provides a view of the union of a set of `Set` instances (wow, set-Inception right there!).

- `binarySearch()` – A top-level function that finds a value in a `List`, if any.

- `compareNatural()` – A top-level function to compare two strings according to natural sort ordering.

- `mergeMaps()` – A top-level function that merges two `Map` instances and returns a new `Map`.

- `shuffle()` – A top-level function that shuffles a `List` randomly.

convert

And, just like collection, if you thought you had enough ways to convert from one thing to another, Google disagrees apparently because there is yet another convert library! It has some interesting bits at least:

- `HexCodec` – A class for all your byte arrays to and from hexadecimal string conversion needs! This library gives you a `hex` instance to use right off the bat, and it's got the typical `encode()` and `decode()` methods as you've I'm sure come to expect.

- `PercentCodec` – This is a bit of an oddly named class because what it means by "percent" is "URL-encoded." As with `HexCodec`, you'll find a `percent` instance all set for you.

Summary

In this chapter, along with the previous chapter, we took a plane ride at 30,000 feet and looked at the beautiful Flutter landscape below! In the process, you got a good picture of many of (most, even!) the widgets Flutter ships with. You also looked at some of the APIs Flutter offers out of the box, all of which provide you the foundation you need, along with the previous two chapters, to start building some Flutter apps!

And, in the next chapter, that's precisely what we're going to do! The first app to build won't be anything too technically challenging, but it will serve as an excellent first foray into the world of Flutter coding.

Let's get to hacking some code, shall we?

CHAPTER 5

FlutterBook, Part I

Okay my friend, now it's time for some fun! We've slogged through the preliminaries, you've got a good foundation of knowledge about Dart and Flutter, so now it's time to put it to good use and start building some real apps! Over the next five chapters, we'll create three apps together, beginning with FlutterBook.

In the process, you'll get some real experience with Flutter, just the thing you need to reach the next level of your Flutter journey.

So, without further ado, let's get to it, beginning with talking about something that seems like it might be kind of relevant in this endeavor: discussing what, exactly, it is that we're going to build!

What Are We Building?

The term PIM was made popular back in the days of the original PalmPilot devices, though it existed before then. PIM stands for "Personal Information Manager" (or "Management," depending on who you ask) and is basically a fancy way to say an application (or device, in the case of the PalmPilot) that stores some basic information that most busy, modern people need to know, and allows it to be consumed easily. Before the electronics age, you might have a little notepad with tabs for various bits of information, but it all amounts to about the same thing either way. What data constitutes a PIM can vary, but for most people, there are four primary pieces of information: appointments, contacts, notes, and tasks. There can be others, and there can even be some overlap between those four, but those are generally considered to be the basics, and they are precisely what FlutterBook will contain.

This application will present four "entities," which is the term I'll use to apply generically to appointments, contacts, notes, and tasks. It will provide a way for the user to enter items of each type, store them on the device, and present a way for them to be viewed, edited, and deleted. As we build the app, we'll do so in a roughly modular way

© Frank Zammetti 2019
F. Zammetti, *Practical Flutter*, https://doi.org/10.1007/978-1-4842-4972-7_5

so that later, if you want, you can add other modules to deal with other types of data (hey now, that sounds like a suggested exercise to me!). For example, maybe bookmarks are something you'd like in your PIM too, or maybe recipes if you're a chef. The point is, you'll be able to add them without much difficulty because we'll design the code to be reasonably modular and easy to extend.

But, it's all well and good to talk about what it is, but seeing it is better, no? I think so, and that's why I've provided Figure 5-1 for you to look at.

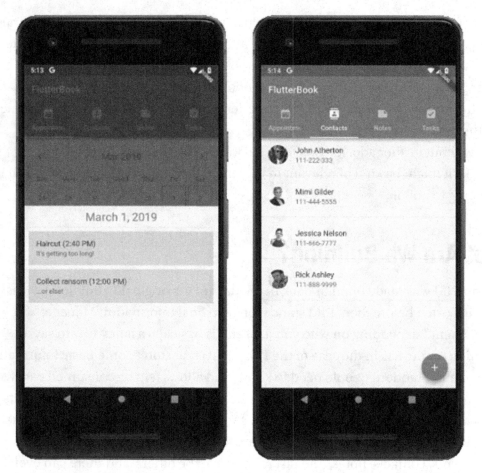

Figure 5-1. *FlutterBook, the Appointments and Contacts entity list screens*

As you can see, along the top are tabs that the user can click on to move between the four entity types (ostensibly, they can swipe to perform this navigation too, but swipe is a little problematic owing to the functionality provided on the screens, but we'll talk about that later).

Each entity will have two screens to work with: a list screen and an entry screen. Here, you can see the list screens, although for the appointments on the left the term "list" is a bit of a misnomer because what you'll actually see is a giant calendar that the user can interact with (you can see it peeking out from behind the day details, which appears by virtue of me having clicked the first date, so you can see the appointments for that day). For contacts though, it really is a list.

For notes and tasks, there is a similar pattern at play, as Figure 5-2 show.

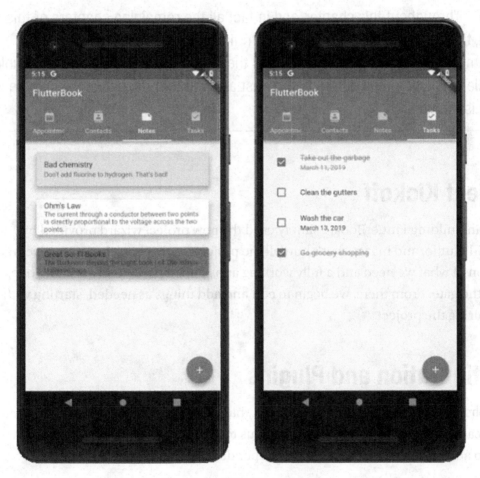

Figure 5-2. *FlutterBook, the Notes and Tasks entity list screens*

Each list screen is a little different in nature, owing to each entity type being a bit different: appointments make sense to be in a calendar, while contacts should show an avatar image, notes look (roughly) like sticky notes by using Cards, and the tasks list allows the user to check off completed tasks. It all also provides for a good variety of Flutter things to look at for your learning experience!

The entry screens we'll get into as we look at each entity type, but this begins to give you an idea of what this thing looks like.

Note   Throughout this chapter, and in fact all the remaining chapters of this book, the code has been condensed by removing comments and `print()` statements and some spacing here and there, so what you'll see in the download bundle will look a little different. But, rest assured that the actual executable code is identical.

Project Kickoff

To begin building FlutterBook, I simply used the new project wizard provided by Android Studio, and in fact, that's how all the projects in this book began. It gives us the skeleton of what we need and a fully working app, if not a particularly exciting one, right out of the gate. From there, we begin to edit and add things as needed, starting with configuring the project.

Configuration and Plugins

The `pubspec.yaml` file, shown in Listing 5-1, has most of what we need automatically, but because this project is going to require us to dip into Flutter plugins a little bit, we'll need to add a few, as you can see in the dependencies section:

Listing 5-1. The pubspec.yaml file

```
name: flutter_book
description: flutter_book
version: 1.0.0+1
```

```
environment:
  sdk: ">=2.1.0 <3.0.0"

dependencies:
  flutter:
    sdk: flutter
  scoped_model: 1.0.1
  sqflite: 1.1.2
  path_provider: 0.5.0+1
  flutter_slidable: 0.4.9
  intl: 0.15.7
  image_picker: 0.4.12+1
  flutter_calendar_carousel: 1.3.15+3
  cupertino_icons: ^0.1.2

dev_dependencies:
  flutter_test:
    sdk: flutter

flutter:
  uses-material-design: true
```

Caution   Remember that YAML files are indentation-sensitive! For example, if one of these dependencies isn't properly indented ("properly" here being two spaces from its parent), then you'll run into problems. Note here that the child of flutter is sdk, but scoped_model is a child of dependencies, not flutter, therefore scoped_model should be two spaces to the right of dependencies, not two spaces to the right of flutter lined up with sdk. It's an easy mistake to make (just ask my awesome technical reviewer!), especially if you're new to YAML structure.

There are quite a few plugins here, and you will, of course, learn a little about them as they are encountered in the code, but just to give you a basic overview, they are

- `scoped_model` – This will provide us a very nice way to manage state throughout the app.

- `sqflite` – Since data storage is a requirement of this app, we have to choose how to do so, and I decided to go with the popular SQLite database, which this plugin provides us access to (and no, the name is not a typo!).

- `path_provider` – For the contacts, we'll have to store the avatar image, if any, for the contact, and SQLite turns out to not be the best place to do that. Instead, we'll use the file system. Each app gets its own documents directory where we can store arbitrary files, and this plugin helps us get to that.

- `flutter_slidable` – For contacts, notes, and tasks, the user can slide them on the list screen to reveal a delete button. This is a widget that gives us that capability.

- `intl` – We'll need some date and time formatting functions from this since some of our entities deal with dates and times.

- `image_picker` – This plugin provides the infrastructure the app will need to let the user add avatar images for contacts from either their gallery or by taking a picture with the camera of their device.

- `flutter_calendar_carousel` – This widget provides the calendar and functionality for the appointments list screen.

Everything else in this file should look familiar to you by now and aside from the dependencies listed here is what the new project wizard created for us.

UI Structure

The basic structure of this app's UI is shown in Figure 5-3.

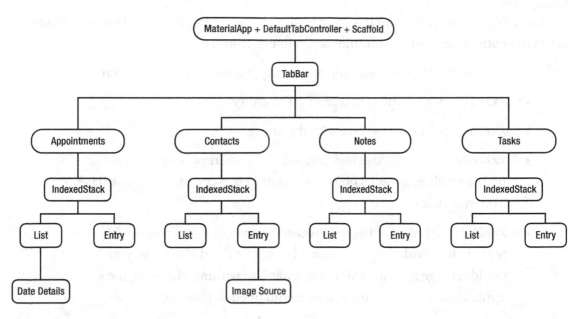

Figure 5-3. *The basic UI structure*

While this doesn't show every last detail, it gives you a high-level picture of things. At the top, the main widget, is a `MaterialApp`, with a `DefaultTabController` under it with a `Scaffold` right below it. Under that is a `TabBar`. Under the `TabBar` are four main screens, one for each of the four entities. Each of those has two "sub-screens," if you will: the list and the entry screens, and these are children of an `IndexedStack`. This allows the code to show either of the two screens just by changing the index of the stack. Under the list screen for appointments is a `BottomSheet` that shows the details for a selected date, and under the entry screen for contacts is a dialog shown for the user to select an image source (camera or gallery).

The details of the list and entry screens for each type are, of course, more complicated than this, but we'll look at those later when the time is right. Before then though, let's talk about the basic structure of the app from a code standpoint.

App Code Structure

As far as the directory structure of the app goes, it's 100% standard, nothing new to see here. All the code for the app lives in the `lib` directory like always, although this time, given the number of files and the desire to make it at least somewhat modular, each entity type gets its own directory. So, the `lib/contacts` directory contains the files related to contacts, `lib/notes` the files related to notes, and so on.

In each of them, you'll find the same basic set of files, and in all the following cases, xxx is the entity name, so Appointments, Contacts, Notes, or Tasks:

- xxx.dart – These files are the main entry point to each of these screens.

- xxxList.dart – The list screen for the entity.

- xxxEntry – The entry screen for the entity.

- xxxModel.dart – These files contain a class to represent each entity type, as well as a model object as required by scoped_model (we'll get into that later).

- xxxDBWorker.dart – These files contain the code that works with SQLite. It provides an abstraction layer over the database so you could change the data storage mechanism without changing the application code, just these files would need to change.

The Starting Line

Now it's time to start looking at code! As per the usual, it all starts in the main.dart file in the root of the project:

```
import "dart:io";
import "package:flutter/material.dart";
import "package:path_provider/path_provider.dart";
import "appointments/Appointments.dart";
import "contacts/Contacts.dart";
import "notes/Notes.dart";
import "tasks/Tasks.dart";
import "utils.dart" as utils;

void main() {

  startMeUp() async {
    Directory docsDir =
      await getApplicationDocumentsDirectory();
    utils.docsDir = docsDir;
    runApp(FlutterBook());
  }
```

```
    startMeUp();

}
```

Let's stop here and discuss this preceding bit (I will typically break up these listing to present them in more digestible chunks – especially for the longer ones, it's an important thing to help you understand what's going on).

First, we have some imports. You already know that `material.dart` is the code of Material Flutter classes. We need the `io` library and the `path_provider` plugin for getting the application's documents directory (we'll come back to this shortly). The rest are application code. The four screen files are imported, and then `utils.dart` is brought in. We'll be looking at that in the next section, but in short, it contains some functions and variables that are global concerns throughout the code and so live in this file.

After that comes the usual `main()` function where execution begins. Here, there's a bit of trick in that we need to retrieve the app's documents directory. The `getApplicationDocumentsDirectory()` function is provided by the `path_provider. dart` import for this purpose. It returns a `Directory` object, which is provided by the Dart `io` library imported. In addition to this function, this plugin also supplies a `getExternalStorageDirectory()`, which is only available on Android (and then only some devices), so you should usually check the OS type before making this call. This provides a path to top-level storage on an external storage device (SD card usually) where the app can read and write data. Finally, there is a `getTemporaryDirectory()` function. This returns path the temporary directory for the app (where you typically write short-lived, transient data, in contrast to `getApplicationDocumentsDirectory()`, which provides durable storage).

There's a problem here though: we have to ensure that no other code executes until this code completes because otherwise, we'll throw exceptions due to the databases not being available. As you'll see later, each of the four databases, one for each entity, is a separate SQLite file stored in the app's documents directory, so if that code gets called before docDir is determined, which it would be because the screens would load when the main widget is created, we'd have issues. So, to accomplish that, I create a function inside `main()` (yes, you can do that in Dart!) and ensure it's an `async` function because we'll `await` the call to `getApplicationDocumentsDirectory()`. Once that returns the `Directory`, that gets stored in `utils.docsDir` (so that we only have to get a reference to this directory once) and then call the usual `runApp()`, passing it a new instance of the `FlutterBook` class.

> **Note**   This isn't necessarily the best way to do things because it means that the
> UI won't be built until `getApplicationDocumentsDirectory()` resolves.
> That's usually not a good thing to do in terms of user experience, but given that
> this isn't going to take too long, not even noticeable, I'd expect, this was the
> easiest way to do things.

After that, the main widget is created, which is where that `FlutterBook` class comes
into play, as you can see here:

```
class FlutterBook extends StatelessWidget {

  Widget build(BuildContext inContext) {

    return MaterialApp(
      home : DefaultTabController(
        length : 4,
        child : Scaffold(
          appBar : AppBar(
            title : Text("FlutterBook"),
            bottom : TabBar(
              tabs : [
                Tab(icon : Icon(Icons.date_range),
                  text : "Appointments"),
                Tab(icon : Icon(Icons.contacts),
                  text : "Contacts"),
                Tab(icon : Icon(Icons.note),
                  text : "Notes"),
                Tab(icon : Icon(Icons.assignment_turned_in),
                  text : "Tasks")
              ]
            )
          ),
```

CHAPTER 5   FLUTTERBOOK, PART I

```
        body : TabBarView(
          children : [
            Appointments(), Contacts(), Notes(), Tasks()
          ]
        )
      )
    )
  );

  }

}
```

First, we have that `MaterialApp` I mentioned earlier, with a `DefaultTabController` as its home screen. `DefaultTabController` is a type of `TabController`, which is responsible for coordinating tab selection in a `TabBar`, which you can see is the `bottom` child of the `AppBar` under the `Scaffold`. The controller takes care of switching between the children, which are defined by the `tabs` property of the `TabBar`. Each entry in `tabs` is a `Tab` object, which can have an `icon` and/or a `text` label, and I opted to show both. With this setup, you don't have to do anything else to enable navigation; these widgets take care of it for you.

Finally, the `body` of the `Scaffold` must be a `TabBarView`, so that it can be appropriately displayed by the `TabBar` and managed properly by `DefaultTabController`. The `children` of it are the four screens, one for each entity (and obviously those are where most of the action is, and we'll get to that action in short order, but we have some other things to look at first, starting with `utils.dart`).

Some Global Utilities

The `utils.dart` file contains those global utility-type bits I spoke of earlier, so let's take a look at it now:

```
import "dart:io";
import "package:flutter/material.dart";
import "package:path_provider/path_provider.dart";
```

```
import "package:intl/intl.dart";
import "BaseModel.dart";

Directory docsDir;
```

As you saw when we looked at main.dart, the docDir is the app's documents directory, which was captured in main() there.

The next thing we find in this file is the selectDate() function:

```
Future selectDate(
  BuildContext inContext, BaseModel inModel,
  String inDateString
) async {

  DateTime initialDate = DateTime.now();

  if (inDateString != null) {
    List dateParts = inDateString.split(",");
    initialDate = DateTime(
      int.parse(dateParts[0]),
      int.parse(dateParts[1]),
      int.parse(dateParts[2])
    );
  }

  DateTime picked = await showDatePicker(
    context : inContext, initialDate : initialDate,
    firstDate : DateTime(1900), lastDate : DateTime(2100)
  );

  if (picked != null) {
    inModel.setChosenDate(
      DateFormat.yMMMMd("en_US").format(picked.toLocal())
    );
    return "${picked.year},${picked.month},${picked.day}";
  }

}
```

This function will be a little hard to explain fully at this point because it depends on a few things you haven't seen yet, but let's go as far as we can, and you can come back to it later where you have that other information.

Firstly, this is used to select a date on the appointments, contacts, and tasks entry screens (the date of an appointment, the birthday of a contact or the due date of a task). As such, it must be generic and work with all three entity types (and perhaps others later). So, what gets passed to it is the BuildContext of the entry screen it's called from, along with something called a BaseModel and a date in string form. The BaseModel is that thing we haven't gotten to yet, so, for now, it's enough to say that it's ultimately where the selected date will go and leave it at that. The date passed in, which is optional, will be in the form yyyy,mm,dd if supplied, and this is a common form throughout the code. The reason is that when storing a date to SQLite, there is no date data type available, so saving it as a string makes sense. I chose this format because it makes it easy to construct a DateTime object since its constructor takes precisely those pieces of information in just that order, something you can see here. If a date is passed in, the split() function is used to tokenize it, then the DateTime is constructed, passing each of the parsed tokens to it, so the year, followed by the month, followed by the day, exactly as it appears in string form.

The initialDate is what day will be selected when the popup calendar is shown, which is applicable when editing an entity only (when creating, there will be no initialDate specified so that the calendar will select the current day).

Then, a call to showDatePicker() is called, something you saw in the previous two chapters. This displays a popup calendar for the user, and it returns a DateTime instance. Note that the range of selectable years is from 1900 to 2100. Logically, it would make more sense to limit it based on entity type (vis a vis, there's no point creating an appointment for a date in the past), and that's where firstDate and lastDate comes into play. But, just to keep the volume of code down, I didn't implement this logic and instead picked a range that would, nominally at least, work for all the entity types.

Once showDatePicker() comes back (it's asynchronous after all, as we can tell by the await in the call to it), we see if they picked something. The returned value will be null if the user clicks Cancel. Otherwise, we'll have a DateTime object for the selected date. Now, as I alluded to earlier, we have to store that date in the BaseModel instance that was passed in, so a call to the setChosenDate() function accomplishes that. The value passed needs to be in a human-readable form, and what toString() of a DateTime object provides by default arguably isn't, so now we use some functionality from the `intl.dart` file imported. Specifically, the `DateFormat.yMMMMd.format()` function provides a string in the form "MONTH dd, yyyy" where MONTH is the full month name (January, February, March, etc.) This plugin contains a wealth of date and time formatting code, as well as other general internationalization and localization functionality. For more info, see here: `https://pub.dartlang.org/packages/intl` (I'll rarely describe these modules in their entirety as there's typically way too much to go into detail on, so we'll discuss just what's needed by the code here – the `path_provider` was an exception because it doesn't offer all that much, even though what it offers is rather necessary!)

However, we're not done yet! The code that called this function needs that date back, so it is returned. The form it's returned in is the same form that may have been passed in, namely `yyyy,mm,dd`.

Like I said, this function will make a little more sense once you know about the models and later when you see it used, which you, in fact, won't until the next chapter, so let's not dwell on it and instead look at the models a bit, which gets into the topic of state management.

On State Management

The concept of state and state management – that is, where the data that your widgets produce and consume and how your code interacts with it – is a topic that, surprisingly, is mostly left to developers to figure out. Flutter, at least at the time of this writing, doesn't say anything definitive on the topic (rumor has it that is changing and before long Flutter maybe have a canonically "correct" state management approach, but it was not yet the case when this book went to print).

Oh, of course, you've got the notion of stateful widgets that was explored in previous chapters (and which you'll undoubtedly see again before this book is over). That indeed is a form of state. But really, it's only one *kind* of state: local state. In other words, it's state that is local to a given component. For that, stateful widgets tend to be quite sufficient.

But there is another kind of state, a state which you might consider "global." To put it another way, its state that is needed outside the widget and, in many cases, beyond the lifetime of a given widget. Maybe widgets that are children of another need its parents' state. Or, maybe vice versa, the parent of a given widget (and maybe not the *direct* parent) needs access to its child's state. The former case isn't too tough, but the latter can be surprisingly frustrating in Flutter. Or, perhaps the widget that needs to see the state of another isn't even in the same widget tree (not directly anyway). These situations can get tricky to deal with if all you have to work with are stateful widgets and the setState() paradigm that provides.

As I said, Flutter doesn't specify a definitive answer here. There are numerous state management solutions available to you in a Flutter app beyond setState(), just to name a few: BLoC, Redux, and scoped_model. There's probably a dozen more out there at least, all with pros and cons. So, which state management approach you use will be dependent on many factors including, but not limited to, your goals for the project, the specific state interactions you need and, at the end of the day, your simple personal preferences on how you like to structure your code.

In this project, and in fact for the rest of this book, I'm going to focus on one specific approach from that list: scoped_model. The reason for this decision comes down to just my belief that scoped_model is perhaps the most straightforward option available because that simplicity tends to make for simpler application code, and I like that! Simple is solid, as the saying goes! Honestly, when looking at all the options, scoped_model just makes the most sense to my brain, so that's the one I'm going with. You of course absolutely should explore the options and see what suits your mental model. If it winds up being scoped_model, then great! If not, no problem, we can still be friends, but at least after reading this book, you'll have a good understanding of at least this one option so as to be able to do a meaningful comparison to the others.

So, what is scoped_model all about? Well, it's just three simple classes that, when used in conjunction with three simple steps on your part, provides a model – that is, a store of data – for a widget tree.

The first class required that you create a model class, which will extend from the scoped_model Model class, and here is where you will place your data-handling logic and, naturally, your data variables. Note that you may not have any need for any real logic, and that's perfectly okay (though a little atypical). The whole purpose of putting the code in this model class is ultimately so that you can call the notifyListeners() method of the base Model class (which can only be called from a subclass of Model). This is the secret sauce! Calling this method informs any widget that has been "hooked up" to the model class that the model has changed and they should, if necessary, re-paint themselves.

The second step is hooking `scoped_model` up to your widget tree. This part is super-easy: just wrap a widget in the second class you must know about: `ScopedModel`. For example, if your top-most widget is a `Column`, then you might do:

```
return ScopedModel<your-model-class-here>(
  child : Column(...)
)
```

Actually, you don't have to wrap the top-most widget in the tree, though that is most common because it means that any widget in the tree can have access to your model. But, if only a subset of widgets needs access to the model, then you can instead choose a widget that is a parent to those, even if not the top-most widget, and wrap that in `ScopedModel`. In either case, you must tell `ScopedModel` the type via the generic declaration `<your-model-class-here>` (that's the class that extends from the `scoped_model` base `Model` class).

Finally, for any widgets underneath the one wrapped in `ScopedModel` that you want to access the model, wrap that widget in the third class to be aware of: `ScopedModelDescendent` (and again specifying the type). As with `ScopedModel`, you don't need to wrap every single widget separately; just wrapping one will cover all its children too. Any widgets wrapped with this class will rebuild when the model changes (assuming Flutter's diff algorithm determines it to be necessary of course). The syntax for `ScopedModelDescendent` is a little different then `ScopedModel` though because the builder pattern is required:

```
return ScopedModel<your-model-class-here>(
  child :
    ScopedModelDescendent<your-model-class-here>(
      builder : (BuildContext inContext, Widget inChild,
        <your-model-class-here> inModel) {
          return Column(...);
      }
  );
)
```

Now, within the `Column`, if you have a `Text` that you want to display the value from the model with, you can do:

```
Text(inModel.myVariable)
```

And voila, you've got yourself a store of data that is the state of your app, ready to be used and that will rebuild your UI when the data changes, all without using stateful widgets (that's right, you can do all of this with stateless widgets!) and in a more global way.

The final piece of the puzzle is changing the state, and to understand, let's look at an actual model class, the `BaseModel.dart` file from FlutterBook. Before we start that exploration though, let me say that each type of entity FlutterBook deals with has its own model class. You don't *have* to do it that way – you could have a single model class that holds the data for all four entity types. But I feel that keeping them separate is more logical. But, the fact is that they all have a few bits of commonality between them, so rather than duplicate code, I instead created a `BaseModel` class, and this is what extends from the `scoped_model` base `Model` class. Then, the model classes for the individual entity types extends from this `BaseModel` class, which obviously means they extend from the `scoped_model` Model class as well, just as we need in the end.

```
import "package:scoped_model/scoped_model.dart";
```

Obviously, `scoped_model` won't be of much use to us unless we import it, so that's imported first. Then, the BaseModel class begins:

```
class BaseModel extends Model {
```

Ah, see, it really does extend from the `Model` class that `scoped_model` provides!

```
int stackIndex = 0;
List entityList = [ ];
var entityBeingEdited;
String chosenDate;
```

These are the four pieces of information that all (or at least most, in the case of `chosenDate`, have in common). Remember earlier how I said that each of the four entity's screens is in actuality two screens, list, and entry, both children of an `IndexedStack`? Well, which is showing depends on the setting of the `stackIndex` variable here. Also, since all four entity types have some sort of list of entities, the `enityList` will contain them. The `entityBeingEdited` will be a reference to the entity that the user selects when they want to edit an existing entity. This is how the data for the entity is transferred from the list screen to the entry screen. Finally, the `chosenDate` variable will store a date chosen by the user when editing an entry. You'll see why this is needed shortly, but for now, let's continue with this class.

```
void setChosenDate(String inDate) {
  chosenDate = inDate;
  notifyListeners();
}
```

When the user chooses a date, they'll do so via a popup, but then the selected date has to get back into the model. A call to this method will do that. As you can see, the last thing it does is calls notifyListeners(). This is key because this is what updates the screen to show the date that was selected. Without this, the data would be saved in the model, but the user wouldn't know it by looking at the screen because the widgets wrapped by ScopedModel (and ScopedModelDescendent) wouldn't have known to re-paint themselves otherwise.

```
void loadData(String inEntityType, dynamic inDatabase) async {
  entityList = await inDatabase.getAll();
  notifyListeners();
}
```

The loadData() method will be called whenever an entity is added or removed from entityList (code which you'll see soon). This makes use of the xxxDBWorker class, the one that knows how to talk to SQLite. Once again, we'll be getting to this soon, but for now, just note that the result of the call to the getAll() method replaces entityList, and then notifyListeners() is again called so that the list of entities re-paints itself. Seeing the pattern yet?

Finally, we have the setStackIndex() method:

```
void setStackIndex(int inStackIndex) {
  stackIndex = inStackIndex;
  notifyListeners();
}
```

This is the method that will be called whenever we want to navigate the user between the list and entry screens for a given entity.

I realize that you don't yet have the full context in which this code is used, but you will before long! For now, the basic concepts of scoped_model are what's important, and hopefully, that's starting to make some sense. It will, I expect, make complete sense once we see the code for an entity, and that's exactly what we're looking at right now!

Starting with an Easy One: Notes

Of the four entity types, I think the code for notes is probably the simplest, so that's probably a good place to start. We begin that exploration with the code that defines the main, top-level screen, for this entity type.

The Starting Point: Notes.dart

As you'll recall each of the four entities has a master screen that is the main content of its tab. The Notes.dart file contains the code for that screen, and it begins, as most Dart source files do, with some imports:

```
import "package:flutter/material.dart";
import "package:scoped_model/scoped_model.dart";
import "NotesDBWorker.dart";
import "NotesList.dart";
import "NotesEntry.dart";
import "NotesModel.dart" show NotesModel, notesModel;
```

Aside from the usual suspects like material.dart, we have scoped_model.dart coming in. As you'll see the entire widget tree for this screen will have access to the model for notes. We also need to bring in the NotesDBWorker.dart file so that we can load the notes data, as you'll see next. Then, we need the source files for the two sub-screens: NotesList.dart and NotesEntry.dart. Finally, we need the model for notes in NotesModel.dart. We'll get to all of those in turn, but marching on with this source file we have:

```
class Notes extends StatelessWidget {
```

Ah, it's the beginning of a widget! Most importantly, note that it's a stateless widget. Remember: using scoped_model means you're dealing with state, but that doesn't imply you have to have stateful widgets. Stateful widgets are effectively another approach to state, an approach we're not using in this app (in this source file or any other).

After that, we find a constructor:

```
Notes() {
  notesModel.loadData("notes", NotesDBWorker.db);
}
```

Recall that the BaseModel has a loadData() method and it was written generically so it would work with any entity type. However, the only reason it can be written generically like that is that the constructor here calls it and provides the entity-specification information it needs, namely the entity type and a reference to the database for this entity type (the database stuff is coming up!). The result of this call is that entityList in the model will have a list of notes loaded into it from the SQLite database and so when the list screen is built, they will be displayed. Technically, since this data load is asynchronous, the list screen can and usually is built before the data is available, but due to it being wrapped in scoped_model and loadData() calling notifyListeners() when the data is loaded, the screen gets notified when the data is available and re-paints to show the data, all of which happens quickly.

```
Widget build(BuildContext inContext) {

  return ScopedModel<NotesModel>(
    model : notesModel,
    child : ScopedModelDescendant<NotesModel>(
      builder : (BuildContext inContext, Widget inChild,
        NotesModel inModel
      ) {
        return IndexedStack(
          index : inModel.stackIndex,
          children : [ NotesList(), NotesEntry() ]
        );
      }
    )
  );

}
```

Finally, the widget is returned from the build() method, which you of course know must be present given that this entire source file is defining a widget. You can see the ScopedModel at the top, with a ScopedModelDescendent underneath it, as discussed earlier. An IndexedStack is used to contain the two screens, which are defined in separate source files that we'll look at soon. Notice that the index value of the IndexedStack is a reference to the stackIndex field in the NotesModel instance.

That's how we can display one screen vs. the other: set the value of stackIndex to 0, and NotesList is shown; set it to 1 to display NotesEntry (assuming, of course, that notifyListeners() is called after that change, which it is, as you saw in BaseModel).

The Model: NotesModel.dart

The model class for this entity is found in NotesModel.dart. The model for this entity type isn't just the model class though; it's also a class representing a note.

But, before any of that, we start with

```
import "../BaseModel.dart";
```

As you know, this class will extend BaseModel, which itself extends Model from scoped_model, so it must be imported.

Next, we have a class definition:

```
class Note {

  int id;
  String title;
  String content;
  String color;

  String toString() {
    return "{ id=$id, title=$title, "
      "content=$content, color=$color }";
  }

}
```

Instances of this class represent notes. Each note has four pieces of information: a unique id, a title, content (which is the note text itself), and a color for the background of the Card on the list screen for a note, so each of those is represented by a member variable here. While not required, I also added a toString() method, which overrides the default implementation provided by the Object class, which is the parent of all classes in Dart. That default implementation isn't beneficial: it just says what type the object it's called on is. This version instead shows the details of the note, which is very handy when debugging when you want to print() a note object to the console.

Next up is the model class itself:

```
class NotesModel extends BaseModel {

  String color;

  void setColor(String inColor) {
    color = inColor;
    notifyListeners();
  }

}
```

Yep, that's it! Most of what this class needs are provided by BaseModel, so it's just that color that is an issue. At the risk of jumping the gun a bit: this is needed because when the user selects a color block on the entry screen, just changing the values in a Note instance wouldn't reflect in the model and the screen wouldn't know to change. We instead need a direct member of the model class for this to occur. Don't worry; I don't expect that you'll totally understand this part just yet! Once we get to the edit screen, it should start to make sense quickly.

But, there's one more line in this file, and it's rather important:

```
NotesModel notesModel = NotesModel();
```

We have a class definition before this, but we don't have an instance of NotesModel yet. That's what we get from this line. The file is only ever parsed once, no matter how many times it's imported, or where it's imported, so this ensures we only ever have a single instance of NotesModel, which it happens is exactly all we need!

The Database Layer: NotesDBWorker.dart

The next file to look at is NotesDBWorker.dart, which contains all the code for working with SQLite. First up are some imports:

```
import "package:path/path.dart";
import "package:sqflite/sqflite.dart";
import "../utils.dart" as utils;
import "NotesModel.dart";
```

There's probably not too much surprising there. The `path.dart` module contains functions for working with paths on a file system in an ostensibly cross-platform manner. Things like getting the platform separator character, normalizing paths, getting file extensions from a path, and so on. Most of the typical path operations you'd expect are here, but we'll just need one, which will turn up shortly.

Before that though, the `NotesDBWorker` class itself begins:

```
class NotesDBWorker {

  NotesDBWorker._();
  static final NotesDBWorker db = NotesDBWorker._();
```

The first step is ensuring there is only ever a single instance of this class, so we're going to implement a singleton pattern. That begins with creating a private constructor, as seen on the first line. On the second line, the constructor is called, and the instance of the class stored statically in db.

Next, we need to have an instance of the Database class, which is the key class when dealing with SQLite via the `sqflite` plugin:

```
Database _db;


Future get database async {

  if (_db == null) {
    _db = await init();
  }
  return _db;

}
```

When the database getter is called, we see if there is already an instance in _db. If so, it's returned, but if not, then the init() method is called. Doing this ensures that the single instance of `NotesDBWorker` only ever has one `Database` object in it, which is exactly what we want to ensure no data integrity issues.

Now, speaking of that `init()` method:

```
Future<Database> init() async {

  String path = join(utils.docsDir.path, "notes.db");
  Database db = await openDatabase(
    path, version : 1, onOpen : (db) { },
    onCreate : (Database inDB, int inVersion) async {
      await inDB.execute(
        "CREATE TABLE IF NOT EXISTS notes ("
          "id INTEGER PRIMARY KEY,"
          "title TEXT,"
          "content TEXT,"
          "color TEXT"
        ")"
      );
    }
  );
  return db;

}
```

The key task here is to make sure the notes database exists in SQLite. The database will be stored as a file in the app's documents directory, so we need a path to that. Here, the one function from the path module we need is used: the `join()` method, which concatenates the documents directory path to the name of the file, notes.db (we're free to call it whatever we want, but I dare say that name is logical).

Once that's done, we need to create a Database object from that path, which is where the `openDatabase()` function comes in. We feed it the path, plus a `version` (which allows you to do schema updates if need be) plus a callback function to call when the database is opened (which here is empty since there's nothing to do in this situation). We also give it a function to call when the database is created, which is where we create the table we need for notes, assuming it doesn't already exist. The `execute()` method of the created `Database` object is how we do that, and it simply takes the SQL to execute. Once that's done, the `Database` instance is returned, which you'll recall gets stored in _db in the `database` getter. After that, we're ready to perform database operations!

But, before we get to those operations, there are two helper functions we have to create. The problem, so to speak, is that SQLite and `sqflite` don't know anything about our Note class, all they know are basic Dart maps. So, we need to provide some functions that can convert from a map to a Note and vice-versa. They're nothing fancy though, as you can see:

```
Note noteFromMap(Map inMap) {

  Note note = Note();
  note.id = inMap["id"];
  note.title = inMap["title"];
  note.content = inMap["content"];
  note.color = inMap["color"];
  return note;

}

Map<String, dynamic> noteToMap(Note inNote) {

  Map<String, dynamic> map = Map<String, dynamic>();
  map["id"] = inNote.id;
  map["title"] = inNote.title;
  map["content"] = inNote.content;
  map["color"] = inNote.color;
  return map;

}
```

Yep, quite simple, and I'd bet entirely apparent to you by now, so let's get to more exciting stuff: creating a note in the database!

Note   This is also why, as much as I wanted to, I couldn't have a single DBWorker for all entities. Aside from the actual SQL statements being different, which I could have dealt with by just using some switch statements, there doesn't at present appear to be something akin to Java's reflection capabilities in Dart. From my reading, that's something that's coming, but when I wrote this code, it wasn't possible, so without winding up with something very convoluted, there didn't seem to be a way to do this dynamically. I like Dart, but sometimes I miss the freewheeling, reckless abandon of JavaScript!

```
Future create(Note inNote) async {

  Database db = await database;
  var val = await db.rawQuery(
    "SELECT MAX(id) + 1 AS id FROM notes"
  );
  int id = val.first["id"];
  if (id == null) { id = 1; }

  return await db.rawInsert(
    "INSERT INTO notes (id, title, content, color) "
    "VALUES (?, ?, ?, ?)",
    [ id, inNote.title, inNote.content, inNote.color ]
  );

}
```

Creating a note is a three-step process. First, we need to get a reference to the Database object, so we await that (remember: the getter function will be called to satisfy this). Second, we need to come up with a unique ID for the note. To do this, we query the existing notes and just increment whatever the highest ID we find is. If this is the first note though, we'll get null back, so we explicitly deal with that situation (in practice, null for an ID actually does work, but it strikes me as bad form if nothing else, so this check ensures we always have a valid numeric ID).

Once that's done, the third step is to call the rawInsert() method of the Database object referenced by db is called and a simple SQL query executed to insert the values, which are naturally taken from the Note object passed in as inNote. As you can see, we return the Future that rawInsert() returns, so the caller of create() can await this result, but that's the only information we need this method to return, so we're done!

Note   If you look up the API for the Database object, you'll see that in addition to the rawInsert() method, there is also an insert() method, and a similar split for other operations. Why use one vs. the other? In truth, I have no good reason to give you in this case! The insert() method is essentially an abstraction that saves you from having to write SQL yourself, which you have to do for rawInsert(). Personally, I'm comfortable with SQL and actually prefer writing it myself most of the time, but if you prefer something a little higher level, then you may prefer `insert()` to `rawInsert()` and, at least in this app, there's not really any good reason to prefer one vs. the other, and aside from avoiding writing SQL I'm not sure there is in general either.

Next, we need the ability to get a specified note. In case it's not obvious by now, we're just implementing CRUD operations, that is, Create, Read (or "get"), Update, and Delete.

```
Future<Note> get(int inID) async {

  Database db = await database;
  var rec = await db.query(
    "notes", where : "id = ?", whereArgs : [ inID ]
  );
  return noteFromMap(rec.first);

}
```

The caller passes in the ID they want to retrieve, and the query() method of the Database instance is called. This takes the name of the table to query, and a where clause (there are multiple forms this method can take, this is just one) plus the values for that where clause. Here, we just need to query the id field. The result of this call will be a map, so we need that noteFromMap() function now to return a Note object.

Going along with this is the ability to retrieve all notes in one call, specifically to populate the list screen, which the getAll() method does:

```
Future<List> getAll() async {

  Database db = await database;
  var recs = await db.query("notes");
  var list = recs.isNotEmpty ?
  recs.map((m) => noteFromMap(m)).toList() : [ ];
  return list;

}
```

Here, the query() method just needs the name of the table, and it will dutifully retrieve all the records in it. If we got no records back then an empty list is returned, but if we did get records then we map() the returned list and for each, call noteFromMap(), and finally convert the resultant map to a list to return to the caller.

Updating a note is next:

```
Future update(Note inNote) async {

  Database db = await database;
  return await db.update("notes", noteToMap(inNote),
    where : "id = ?", whereArgs : [ inNote.id ]
  );
}
```

Well, that's not too tough, is it? The update() method takes the name of the table, the map that contains the values to update (which we get by calling noteToMap() to convert the inNote Note object to a map) and the where clause to identify the record by ID to be updated. This method knows how to take the elements of the map and convert them to column names – well, there's no real conversion necessary as it assumes the columns are named after the items in the map, but you knew what I mean!

The final method to look at is, of course, delete():

```
Future delete(int inID) async {

  Database db = await database;
  return await db.delete(
    "notes", where : "id = ?", whereArgs : [ inID ]
  );

}
```

Yep, that's all there is to it! By this point, I would bet (and hope!) that an explanation isn't necessary. So, let's get to some screen code, starting with the list screen.

The List Screen: NotesList.dart

The list screen for notes begins with a set of imports:

```
import "package:flutter/material.dart";
import "package:scoped_model/scoped_model.dart";
```

```
import "package:flutter_slidable/flutter_slidable.dart";
import "NotesDBWorker.dart";
import "NotesModel.dart" show Note, NotesModel, notesModel;

class NotesList extends StatelessWidget {
```

The only thing new here, or unexpected, is that `flutter_slidable.dart` import; otherwise, we've got the usual suspects as far as imports go and a perfectly typical widget class beginning. Let's skip that one import for the moment until we encounter it and instead start looking at the ubiquitous `build()` method:

```
Widget build(BuildContext inContext) {

  return ScopedModel<NotesModel>(
    model : notesModel,
    child : ScopedModelDescendant<NotesModel>(
      builder : (BuildContext inContext, Widget inChild,
        NotesModel inModel
      ) {
        return Scaffold(
```

As you're now very familiar with, we have a `ScopedModel` that references the `notesModel` instance. This has a `ScopedModelDescendent` as a `child` so that all the children in this widget true can access the model. The `builder()` function is provided, and we begin to build our widget, which starts with a `Scaffold`, as is most common for a screen in a Flutter app.

```
floatingActionButton : FloatingActionButton(
  child : Icon(Icons.add, color : Colors.white),
  onPressed : () {
    notesModel.entityBeingEdited = Note();
    notesModel.setColor(null);
    notesModel.setStackIndex(1);
  }
)
```

This Scaffold has a floatingActionButton, which is how the user will add a new note. This floats in the lower right, over the content of the screen. When tapped, the onPressed function fires, and we kick off entry. To do this, we begin by creating a new Note instance and storing it in the model as the entityBeingEdited. This is the object that will ultimately be saved to the database, once all the data the user enters is put into it (which you'll see in the next section about the entry screen).

One of the things the user can do on the entry screen is select a color for the note. Recall earlier when we talked about how the screen will re-paint itself when the model changes. Well, that's going to be necessary whenever the user selects a color. But, just having the color stored in that new Note object won't be enough since scoped_model won't see it change (because it's not a top-level property of the model – scoped_model can't see down into the properties of objects), so as you saw earlier, the NoteModel has a color property. Initially, we want there to be no color selected, hence the call to setColor(), passing it null, which sets the color property of the model and calls notifyListeners() so the screen updates (which doesn't really matter just yet since the entry screen isn't shown at this point, but it's still what happens).

Finally, we move the user to the entry screen by calling setStackIndex() and passing it a value of one, because the entry screen is the second thing on the IndexedStack (IndexedStack is zero-based obviously, and the list screen is at index zero).

After that, the body of the Scaffold is defined, and this is where we start drawing the list of notes:

```
body : ListView.builder(
  itemCount : notesModel.entityList.length,
  itemBuilder : (BuildContext inBuildContext, int inIndex) {
    Note note = notesModel.entityList[inIndex];
    Color color = Colors.white;
    switch (note.color) {
      case "red" : color = Colors.red; break;
      case "green" : color = Colors.green; break;
      case "blue" : color = Colors.blue; break;
      case "yellow" : color = Colors.yellow; ;
      case "grey" : color = Colors.grey; break;
      case "purple" : color = Colors.purple; break;
    }
```

We're using a ListView widget here because we want a scrolling list of items. This requires us to use the builder() constructor, which takes the number of items in the list via itemCount, and that's just the length of the entityList in the model, and then a function to actually build the widget for each item in the list. For each, we get the Note object from the list, and the first thing we need to do is deal with the color. By default, we'll assume no color has been specified, which means the note will be white. For all the others, we set the correct color from the Colors collection (note that the value of these constants are objects, not simple strings or numbers, which is why I didn't store those values directly, which necessitates this branching).

With the color figured out, the widget can be returned:

```
return Container(
  padding : EdgeInsets.fromLTRB(20, 20, 20, 0),
  child : Slidable(
    delegate : SlidableDrawerDelegate(),
    actionExtentRatio : .25,
    secondaryActions : [
      IconSlideAction(
        caption : "Delete",
        color : Colors.red,
        icon : Icons.delete,
        onTap : () => _deleteNote(inContext, note)
      )
    ]
```

It all starts with a Container, and we give it a little bit of padding around on the left, top, and right. This keeps the notes away from the edges of the screen, which is just aesthetically a little more pleasing, and ensures we have some space between notes.

Next, we come to that Slidable that we saw imported earlier. This widget is just a type of container that introduces some slide functionality. In many mobile apps, when there is a list of items, you can slide them left and/or right to reveal buttons for various functions. That's what this widget does for us. In simplest terms, you have to provide it a delegate that controls how the slide is animated (which here is just an instance of the SlidableDrawerDelegate(), also provided by this plugin). You also have to tell it how far the item can be slid, and here .25 means 25% of the way across the screen. Then, you have to specify the actions and/or secondaryActions properties. The actions property specifies what functions will be exposed with then item is slid to the right while secondaryActions are what functions will be exposed when the item is slid to the left. Here, we only have a delete action to implement, and most typically you see delete actions on the right (though there's no rule that says it *has* to be that way), so secondaryActions is all I used for sliding to the left.

Each of the objects in the secondaryActions list, of which you can have as many as you want and that fit, are IconSlideAction objects, also supplied by this plugin. These objects allow you to define what caption, icon, and color you want the actions to be, as well as what to do onTap of the items. We'll look at that _deleteNote() method soon, but there's still a bit more widget configuration to look at first:

```
child : Card(
  elevation : 8, color : color,
  child : ListTile(
    title : Text("${note.title}"),
    subtitle : Text("${note.content}"),
    onTap : () async {
      notesModel.entityBeingEdited =
        await NotesDBWorker.db.get(note.id);
      notesModel.setColor(notesModel.entityBeingEdited.color);
      notesModel.setStackIndex(1);
    }
  )
)
```

Inside the Container and Slidable, each note is represented by a Card, which you will recall provides a box with a drop shadow on it as per Google's Material design guidelines. These look a little bit like sticky notes to my eyes, so I felt this was a good choice here. I bump up the elevation a little bit to give them more pronounced drop shadows, and the color, of course, uses the color we determined earlier. Then, the child of the card is just a ListTile. This widget gives us a common way to lay out content with a title, which is the note title, and subtitle, which here I use to display the note's content. The note will expand vertically as much as necessary to show all the content. The ListTile is a very common widget that is typically used as the child of a ListView, but as you can see, it doesn't have to be a direct child of one (it doesn't even have to be an *indirect* child of one technically). You'll see more of this widget in the next chapter as well and see some other capabilities it has.

Now, when a note is tapped, we want the user to be able to edit it. This looks almost the same as creating a new note with one critical exception: the note is retrieved from the database. This is actually unnecessary since we already effectively have it in the entityList property in the model. However, for demonstration purposes, I thought it was better to show it coming from the database (there's also something to be said for having the database be the Single Source Of Truth™ for the app, which wouldn't be the case if we took it from entityList).

Finally, we have that _deleteNote() method that we skipped earlier:

```
Future _deleteNote(BuildContext inContext, Note inNote) {

  return showDialog(
    context : inContext,
    barrierDismissible : false,
    builder : (BuildContext inAlertContext) {
      return AlertDialog(
        title : Text("Delete Note"),
        content : Text(
          "Are you sure you want to delete ${inNote.title}?"
        ),
        actions : [
          FlatButton(child : Text("Cancel"),
            onPressed: () {
              Navigator.of(inAlertContext).pop();
            }
          ),
          FlatButton(child : Text("Delete"),
            onPressed : () async {
              await NotesDBWorker.db.delete(inNote.id);
              Navigator.of(inAlertContext).pop();
              Scaffold.of(inContext).showSnackBar(
                SnackBar(
                  backgroundColor : Colors.red,
                  duration : Duration(seconds : 2),
                  content : Text("Note deleted")
                )
              );
```

```
            notesModel.loadData("notes", NotesDBWorker.db);
        }
      )
    ]
  );
 }
);

}
```

As with most delete operations, confirming the user's intent is a nice thing to do, so we'll launch a dialog to do that with showDialog(). In order to do that, we need the BuildContext in effect where the dialog is shown from, which is passed in, along with the Note instance so that we can use some of its data (the title) in the dialog. Then, inside the builder() function that showDialog() requires, we construct an AlertDialog, the content of which asks for confirmation and shows the note's title. Then, for the actions, we build two: a cancel FlatButton, which simply pop()'s the dialog away, and the delete FlatButton. When the latter is tapped, we call the delete() method of the NotesDBWorker (it's db property technically, which actually *is* the NotesDBWorker singleton instance), passing it the id of the note. Then, we pop() the dialog away, and use the showSnackBar() method of the Scaffold to show a message indicating the note was deleted. This will show for two seconds as per the Duration. Finally, the loadData() method of notesModel needs to be called so that the list will be refreshed. Recall that loadData() will re-load all the notes from the database and then call notifyListeners(), which triggers re-painting of the screen. This has to happen after removing a note; otherwise, it would be deleted from the database but not reflect that on the screen.

The Entry Screen: NotesEntry.dart

Now we come to the final part of the notes puzzle, the entry screen. It's a simple screen, as you can see in Figure 5-4.

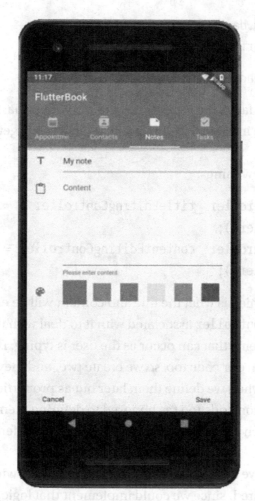

Figure 5-4. *The Notes edit screen*

The title (which I've entered here) and the content (which I haven't entered) are required (and you can see the error message for content where I've tried to save without entering anything). The color boxes are optional, but here I've selected red (which you can't see on a black-and-white printed page, so just trust me, m'kay?!), indicated by it being a bit bigger. There's a Cancel and a Save button, the former returns the user to the list screen, and the latter, of course, saves the new note (and, as I'm hoping you've realized by now, triggers re-painting of the list screen to show the new note).

As always, imports kick things off:

```
import "package:flutter/material.dart";
import "package:scoped_model/scoped_model.dart";
```

```
import "NotesDBWorker.dart";
import "NotesModel.dart" show NotesModel, notesModel;

class NotesEntry extends StatelessWidget {
```

Nothing new here as far as the imports go, and the widget class start is also what you've seen before. Keep in mind that this is still a stateless widget, despite having to deal with some state.

Now, we have two new things:

```
final TextEditingController _titleEditingController =
  TextEditingController();
final TextEditingController _contentEditingController =
  TextEditingController();
```

A TextFormField, which is what the title and content will be entered with, needs to have a TextEditingController associated with it to deal with things like its default value and the various events that can occur as the user is typing. But, we're going to need access to these from our code too, so we create two, and they will be hooked up to the TextFormFields when we define them later but as properties of our class, are available to our application code too (as opposed to defining them inline with the TextFormFields, in which case we wouldn't have any way to reference them, not without hackery anyway!)

But first, since we have the notion of required fields to deal with, we're going to have a form (which isn't required, since we could implement that logic ourselves, but as you saw in the previous two chapters, a form makes things easier), and a form requires a key:

```
final GlobalKey<FormState> _formKey = GlobalKey<FormState>();
```

We don't so much care what the key is, only that we have one, so a simple GlobalKey is created.

Next, we have some work to do when the class is created, so we have a constructor:

```
NotesEntry() {

  _titleEditingController.addListener(() {
    notesModel.entityBeingEdited.title =
      _titleEditingController.text;
  });
```

```
_contentEditingController.addListener(() {
  notesModel.entityBeingEdited.content =
    _contentEditingController.text;
});
}
```

See! We really *did* need access to those two controllers! The trick here is that any time the value of the TextFormField the controller is attached to changes, the corresponding value in entityBeingEdited needs to be updated. Calling addListener() and giving it a function to be called that does that accomplishes that goal. Without doing this, whatever the user enters on the screen wouldn't be reflected in the model, so we'd have nothing to save later.

Now, the build() method rears its head once more:

```
Widget build(BuildContext inContext) {

  _titleEditingController.text =
    notesModel.entityBeingEdited.title;
  _contentEditingController.text =
    notesModel.entityBeingEdited.content;
```

Since this screen can effectively be used in two modes, adding and maintaining a note, we'll want to make sure the previous values for title and content are on the screen when editing one. That's what these statements do. When the screen is in add mode, it will just be setting null values, since that's the default for a String, which is what the title and content properties of the Note class are. The TextFormField handles that nicely and just makes them blank as we want; otherwise, whatever the current value is when editing a Note will be shown.

Now we start to build up the top-level widget that build() returns:

```
return ScopedModel(
  model : notesModel,
  child : ScopedModelDescendant<NotesModel>(
    builder : (BuildContext inContext, Widget inChild,
      NotesModel inModel
    ) {
      return Scaffold(
```

So far, nothing new: it's just like the start of the widget on the list screen. But after that though, we have something new:

```
bottomNavigationBar : Padding(
  padding :
    EdgeInsets.symmetric(vertical : 0, horizontal : 10),
  child : Row(
    children : [
      FlatButton(
        child : Text("Cancel"),
        onPressed : () {
          FocusScope.of(inContext).requestFocus(FocusNode());
          inModel.setStackIndex(0);
        }
      ),
      Spacer(),
      FlatButton(
        child : Text("Save"),
        onPressed : () { _save(inContext, notesModel); }
      )
    ]
  )
)
```

The bottomNavigationBar of the Scaffold widget lets us put some static content at the bottom, content that won't scroll away even if what's above it requires scrolling. That's perfect for buttons, which is exactly what we have here. The first one is Cancel, which navigates the user back the list screen via a call to setStackIndex(). Just before that though, we need to hide the soft keyboard if it's open. Otherwise, it'll still be there obscuring the ListView on the notes list screen. The FocusScope class establishes a scope in which widgets can receive focus. Flutter keeps track via a focus tree of which widget is the user's current focus. When you get the FocusScope of a given context via the static of() method, you can then call the requestFocus() method to send focus to a specific place, but passing a new FocusNode() instance effectively results in focus not going anywhere, which causes the OS to collapse the keyboard and mission accomplished!

The second button is Save, and that's just a call to the _save() method, something we'll get to when we're done looking at the widget code. Speaking of which:

```
body : Form(
  key : _formKey,
  child : ListView(
    children : [
      ListTile(
        leading : Icon(Icons.title),
        title : TextFormField(
          decoration : InputDecoration(hintText : "Title"),
          controller : _titleEditingController,
          validator : (String inValue) {
            if (inValue.length == 0) {
              return "Please enter a title";
            }
            return null;
          }
        )
      )
    )
```

In the previous two chapters, you saw how you can optionally have a Form widget so that you can have, among other things, validation events for your entry fields. That's precisely what we want here, and of course, that _formKey that was created earlier is used here. The children are ListTile widgets, and here you can see one of the other things that widget provides: leading. This can be some content on the left side of the main content, and an Icon as shown here is typical. This widget also supports a trailing property to do the same on the right side, but that's not needed here.

The title of the ListTile is the first TextFormField. It might seem weird that a property named title isn't just a text string, but that's the beauty of everything being a widget in Flutter: it doesn't (usually) matter! You can put anything you want there, so long as it's a widget (whether it'll look good or work as you expect is another matter of course, but it will ostensibly work virtually all the time, that's the point). This TextFormField has a decoration whose value is an InputDecoration object that. This object has many properties including labelText (text that describes the field), enabled (for visually

217

enabling or disabling the field), suffixIcon (an icon that that appears after the editable part of the text field and after the suffix or suffixText, within the decoration's container), just to name a few. It also has a hintText property. Setting this as shown has the effect of showing the word "Title" as slightly dimmed text whenever the field is empty of user input. It serves the same function as a label in other words. As you can see, the controller property references the TextEditingController created earlier for this field, and there is a validator defined that checks to ensure something has been entered and which returns an error string if not that will be displayed in red below the field once the form is validated, which happens in that _save() method that we'll get into soon.

Before that though, we have another TextFormField for the content:

```
ListTile(
  leading : Icon(Icons.content_paste),
  title : TextFormField(
    keyboardType : TextInputType.multiline,
    maxLines : 8,
    decoration : InputDecoration(hintText : "Content"),
    controller : _contentEditingController,
    validator : (String inValue) {
      if (inValue.length == 0) {
        return "Please enter content";
      }
      return null;
    }
  )
)
```

It's almost the same as that of the title field, save for one thing: the *maxLines*. This determines how tall the field will be. Here, there will be enough space for eight lines of text. If you know HTML, this in effect makes this TextFormField work like a <textarea>.

Now we come to the part responsible for those color blocks that the user can use to select the note's color:

```
ListTile(
  leading : Icon(Icons.color_lens),
  title : Row(
    children : [
```

We start with another `ListTile`, with a `leading` that shows a color palette icon (Flutter calls it a color "lens," but whatever, looks like a palette to me!). The `title` this time is a `Row` so that all the blocks can be laid out next to each other.

Because of the repetitive nature of what follows, I'm going to show the code for just one block. The other blocks are identical to this code, save for the color references of course.

```
GestureDetector(
  child : Container(
    decoration : ShapeDecoration(
      shape : Border.all(width : 18, color : Colors.red) +
      Border.all(width : 6,
        color : notesModel.color == "red" ?
        Colors.red : Theme.of(inContext).canvasColor
      )
    )
  ),
  onTap : () {
    notesModel.entityBeingEdited.
    color = "red";
    notesModel.setColor("red");
  }
),
Spacer(),
...repeated for each color...
```

Each block beings with a `GestureDetector`, which is a widget that gives us an element that responds to various touch events. We only care about tap events here though, hence the `onTap()` function provided. That's jumping ahead though! Inside the `GestureDetector` is a `Container`, and this widget has a `decoration` that defines a box with a `Border` around all sides. The box is given a border eighteen pixels wide, which effectively results in a filled box since there is no content, so the borders in a sense "collapse" into a solid box. Then, another `Border` is added to that, again using the `all()` constructor, to put a six-pixel wide border around that box. If the `color` property in the model has a value of red, then the border's color is made red. Otherwise, it's made the same color as the background, which we can get by interrogating the Theme associated with this BuildContext. The canvasColor is the background that everything is drawn on, so that's the element of Theme that we want. The idea here is that the box will be made thicker by virtue of that outer border only when it's selected.

When the block is tapped, then the color is set in entityBeingEdited, and also it's set as the color attribute of the model via the call to setColor(). That call also results in notifyListeners() being called, which causes this screen to be re-painted, which finally results in the border now being shown in the box's color, and that's how the box appearing bigger effect is achieved.

The final bit of code to look at in this chapter is that _save() method that you saw called earlier:

```
void _save(BuildContext inContext, NotesModel inModel) async {

  if (!_formKey.currentState.validate()) { return; }

  if (inModel.entityBeingEdited.id == null) {
    await NotesDBWorker.db.create(
      notesModel.entityBeingEdited
    );
  } else {
    await NotesDBWorker.db.update(
      notesModel.entityBeingEdited
    );
  }

  notesModel.loadData("notes", NotesDBWorker.db);

  inModel.setStackIndex(0);

  Scaffold.of(inContext).showSnackBar(
    SnackBar(
      backgroundColor : Colors.green,
      duration : Duration(seconds : 2),
      content : Text("Note saved")
    )
  );
}
```

This, obviously, is what persists the note to the database. First, the form is validated, and if it's not valid, then the event is terminated via the early `return`. If it's valid, then the first thing to determine is whether we're creating a new note or updating one. Since there's no flag specifically for this purpose, we must interrogate the data to tell, and that's easy: a new note won't yet have an `id`, but one being updated will. So, we branch on `inModel.entityBeingUpdated.id` being `null` or not. If it is, then a call to the `create()` method of the `NotesDBWorker` is the right thing to do. Otherwise, we're updating, so it's the `update()` method that needs to be called. In either case, the `entityBeingEdited` is what gets passed to it. As you saw earlier, that will be converted to a map and saved to the database.

With the note saved, we just have some final tasks to accomplish to complete the process. First, a call to `loadData()` needs to be made so that the list screen will be updated to reflect the new note or the changes to an existing one. Then, we navigate the user back to the entry screen with the call to `setStackIndex()`. Finally, we snow a `SnackBar` message for two seconds to indicate that the note was saved.

And that, as they say, is a wrap on notes!

Caution   Something that has burned me time and again when working with Flutter that I want to bring to your attention is the persistence, or lack thereof, of hot-reloaded changes. While hot reloading is undoubtedly a tremendous productive gain, it can sometimes cause you problems if you don't remember that when you hot reload, the changes *do not persist* in your app. Meaning that if you have your app running in the emulator, you make a change and hot-reload it, you will see that change in the emulator as expected, but if you then close the app and re-start it in the emulator, your change *will not be there*. The change will only be present for that run of the app, or until you do a complete rebuild to effectively re-deploy the app, including the change. There have been times I've forgotten this, and I'm left banging my head against the desk because something that literally was *just* working suddenly seems not to for no apparent reason. I urge you to drill this fact into your head so you can avoid a trip to the doctor to address a frustration-induced concussion, like I probably have had a few times because I didn't remember this!

Summary

Hooray, we did it! We've got FlutterBook working, if not entirely completed yet! In your first experience building a real Flutter app, you saw quite a lot including overall application architecture, project configuration including adding plugins, navigating between parts of the app, state management, data storage with SQLite, and a whole lot of widgets! It's not a complete app yet of course, but it's an excellent start.

In the next chapter, we'll complete FlutterBook by adding the code for the other three entities: appointments, contacts, and tasks. In the end, you'll have a complete, usable app and a whole lot of excellent Flutter knowledge in your head!

CHAPTER 6

FlutterBook, Part II

In the last chapter, we began looking at the code of FlutterBook, the notes entity specifically. In this chapter, we'll close it out by looking at the tasks, appointments, and contacts.

That may seem like a lot of ground to cover, but here's the secret of why it's not: if you compare the code for the four entities, you'll see that they are probably 90% the same. The same structure is at play for all of them: a main code file (like `notes.dart`) and then a list screen and an entry screen, each in their own source files. The code in each will mostly be the same (or extremely similar) to that of the notes entity. The four list screens are all somewhat different though, so we'll be looking at those in some detail, but the entry screens are, for the most part, very similar, save for a few bits and pieces.

So, what I'm going to do is only show you the areas where things diverge from the code you saw in the last chapter. As such, we'll be looking at pieces of source files for the most part, not full source files. The bottom line is if I don't discuss it here then you can assume that it's not really any different than the notes code from the previous chapter (aside from small things like variable names and field names and such, the obvious things that don't have much impact to your learning).

Get 'Er Done: Tasks

The first entity we'll look at in this chapter is tasks. Tasks are straightforward things: they only require a line of text to describe them and optionally a due date. As you saw in the screenshot from the previous chapter, the list view allows the user to check off the tasks they have completed. As such, the code is quite simple, arguably even simpler than the notes code.

© Frank Zammetti 2019
F. Zammetti, *Practical Flutter*, https://doi.org/10.1007/978-1-4842-4972-7_6

TasksModel.dart

First, as you know, each entity has its own model, and a class that represents an instance of the entity. Tasks are no different: there is a `Task` class, and the only difference between the `Note` class from the last chapter and `Task` are the fields in the class:

```
int id;
String description;
String dueDate;
String completed = "false";
```

As usual, an instance of this class will be stored in the database, and so we need a unique `id` field. Beyond that, we have the `description` of the task, a `dueDate` (which will be optional) and a `completed` flag to tell if the task is done or not. You may think that completed should be a `bool`, and I would generally agree! But, since it's getting stored in a SQLite table, and SQLite doesn't offer us a boolean type natively, it'll have to be stored as a string. While converting from and to string when necessary so we're dealing with a `bool` in the Dart code would be doable, I don't see much point to it in this case, so a string it is!

After that comes the model:

```
class TasksModel extends BaseModel { }
```

Wait, did I make a mistake pasting the code in this chapter? Nope! The `TasksModel` really is empty! You see, there are no fields on the entry screen like there were with notes (dealing with the selected color) that we need to track on the screen. Therefore there doesn't have to be anything in the model. Recall that `BaseModel` provides the common code that all four of the models need to have, but tasks don't need anything beyond that; hence its just an empty object (empty aside from what `BaseModel` provides that is!).

TasksDBWorker.dart

Like notes, the tasks entity needs to have its database worker, but there's only one substantive thing different from the notes worker (again, aside from basic things like variable and method names and such), and that's the SQL executed to create the table for this entity:

```
CREATE TABLE IF NOT EXISTS tasks (
  id INTEGER PRIMARY KEY, description TEXT,
  dueDate TEXT, completed TEXT
)
```

Hopefully, that's exactly what you expected!

Tasks.dart

The starting point for the task entity's screen is, like `TasksDBWorker.dart`, nearly
identical to `Notes.dart` that you saw in the last chapter, the same screen structure with
the `IndexedStack` and all that is present here, so let's move on to some code that actually
has some differences to see, shall we?

TasksList.dart

As mentioned earlier, each of the four list views is a bit different from one another,
though even there you'll find that a large percentage of the code is identical. But, for
tasks, the primary difference is that tasks can be checked off when completed, so let's
see the widget returned by the `build()` function here, which is again a `ScopedModel`
wrapping a `Scaffold` and with the following `body`:

```
body : ListView.builder(
  padding : EdgeInsets.fromLTRB(0, 10, 0, 0),
  itemCount : tasksModel.entityList.length,
  itemBuilder : (BuildContext inBuildContext, int inIndex) {
    Task task = tasksModel.entityList[inIndex];
    String sDueDate;
    if (task.dueDate != null) {
      List dateParts = task.dueDate.split(",");
      DateTime dueDate = DateTime(int.parse(dateParts[0]),
        int.parse(dateParts[1]), int.parse(dateParts[2]));
      sDueDate = DateFormat.yMMMMd(
        "en_US"
      ).format(dueDate.toLocal());
    }
```

The due date, if there is one, gets split() into three individual parts (remember from the previous chapter that it's stored as "year,month,day") and those parts passed to the DateTime constructor to get a DateTime object for the specified due date. Then, we use one of the formatting functions that the DateFormat class offers. This class is a utility class from the intl package that provides numerous functions for formatting dates and times and dealing with other internationalization concerns. The intricacies of working with these functions is a little beyond our scope here. But, the bottom line is that calling the yMMMMD() function and then feeding the return value to the format() function and passing it the result of a toLocal() call on the dueDate DateTime object gives us back a nicely formatted version of the date suitable for display. And that's the whole point of this exercise!

Next, we can start building the UI which, like notes, uses a Slidable as the basis:

```
return Slidable(delegate : SlidableDrawerDelegate(),
  actionExtentRatio : .25, child : ListTile(
    leading : Checkbox(
      value : task.completed == "true" ? true : false,
      onChanged : (inValue) async {
        task.completed = inValue.toString();
        await TasksDBWorker.db.update(task);
        tasksModel.loadData("tasks", TasksDBWorker.db);
      }
    ),
```

This time though, the leading is where we find the Checkbox the user can check when the task is completed. The value is taken from the task reference, which as you can see is the next task in the list of tasks. Since completed is a string and not a boolean, it can't be the value of the value property directly, so a simple ternary expression gets the boolean that is needed. After that, we have to attach an onChanged event handler for when the Checkbox is checked (or unchecked). The work here is easy: take the boolean value passed into the onChanged function and set it as the value of task.completed by calling toString() on it. Then, ask TasksDBWorker to update the task, and finally tell the TasksModel to rebuild the list via a call to the loadData() method that you know is supplied by BaseModel. That's it, easy!

Continuing on, we have the rest of the configuration for the Slidable:

```
title : Text(
  "${task.description}",
  style : task.completed == "true" ?
    TextStyle(color :
      Theme.of(inContext).disabledColor,
      decoration : TextDecoration.lineThrough
    ) :
    TextStyle(color :
      Theme.of(inContext).textTheme.title.color
    )
),
subtitle : task.dueDate == null ? null :
  Text(sDueDate,
    style : task.completed == "true" ?
      TextStyle(color :
        Theme.of(inContext).disabledColor,
        decoration : TextDecoration.lineThrough) :
      TextStyle(color :
        Theme.of(inContext).textTheme.title.color)
  ),
onTap : () async {
  if (task.completed == "true") { return; }
  tasksModel.entityBeingEdited =
    await TasksDBWorker.db.get(task.id);
  if (tasksModel.entityBeingEdited.dueDate == null) {
    tasksModel.setChosenDate(null);
  } else {
    tasksModel.setChosenDate(sDueDate);
  }
  tasksModel.setStackIndex(1);
}
),
```

```
  secondaryActions : [
    IconSlideAction(
      caption : "Delete",
      color : Colors.red,
      icon : Icons.delete,
      onTap : () => _deleteTask(inContext, task)
    )
  ]
);
  }
)
```

That should all look pretty familiar to you given your exposure to the code for notes, but one thing to understand is that we don't allow the user to edit a task that is already completed, hence the check of `task.completed` in the `onTap()` event handler.

As with notes, there is a `deleteTask()` method here too that you can see called via the `secondaryActions` of the `Slidable`, but given that it's the same as for notes, we can skip looking at it and move on to the entry screen.

TasksEntry.dart

The entry screen, which you can see in Figure 6-1, is very sparse, as previously stated, just having two fields, only one of which (description) is required:

Figure 6-1. *The entry screen for tasks*

The only code we need to look at here is around the due date field:

```
ListTile(leading : Icon(Icons.today),
  title : Text("Due Date"), subtitle : Text(
    tasksModel.chosenDate == null ? "" : tasksModel.chosenDate
  ),
  trailing : IconButton(
    icon : Icon(Icons.edit), color : Colors.blue,
    onPressed : () async {
      String chosenDate = await utils.selectDate(
        inContext, tasksModel,
        tasksModel.entityBeingEdited.dueDate);
```

229

```
    if (chosenDate != null) {
      tasksModel.entityBeingEdited.dueDate = chosenDate;
    }
  }
 )
)
```

Here, we finally see the usage of that `utils.selectDate()` function that we looked at briefly in the last chapter. This function returns a string in the form "year,month,day" after the user selects a date, which you know is the form it's saved into the database. Of course, if `null` is returned, then no date was selected, so we only set the `dueDate` field of the task if `null` wasn't returned.

And that's it for tasks!

Make a Date: Appointments

Next up is the appointments entity, and here we have a few new things to look at, including a nice plugin for our main display on the list screen. But, before that, let's take a look at the model.

AppointmentsModel.dart

As with the tasks entity and note entity, we have a class to describe an appointment, not surprisingly named `Appointment`, and it has the following fields:

```
int id;
String title;
String description;
String apptDate;
String apptTime;
```

The `id` you know about and `title` and `description` are obvious. Like task, an appointment has a date, called `apptDate` this time, but unlike tasks, appointments also have a time, stored as `apptTime`. Both are strings again because that's how they ultimately get stored in the database, so naturally, we're going to have some conversion code somewhere, as you'll see soon.

After the class definition comes the model, and there's only a single method we need to add to it, the one dealing with the time and being able to display it on the entry screen:

```
class AppointmentsModel extends BaseModel {
  String apptTime;
  void setApptTime(String inApptTime) {
    apptTime = inApptTime;
    notifyListeners();
  }
}
```

As with tasks (and contacts, as you'll see later), the BaseModel chosenDate field and setChosenDate() method will be used for the appointment's date on the entry screen (because that's needed on multiple entry screens, putting it in BaseModel avoids some duplicate code). Since only appointments have a time though, we only need the apptTime and setApptTime() method in this model, but the code for the setApptTime() method is just like that of setChosenDate(): store the passed in value in the model and notify listeners, so the screen is rebuilt with the new value.

AppointmentsDBWorker.dart

As with notes and tasks, appointments have a database worker, and it's nearly identical to those two except for the table definition, which is as follows:

```
CREATE TABLE IF NOT EXISTS appointments (
  id INTEGER PRIMARY KEY, title TEXT,
  description TEXT, apptDate TEXT, apptTime TEXT
)
```

There are no other surprises here; you've essentially seen this already by virtue of seeing the database worker for notes, so let's go forward.

Appointments.dart

Again, like with tasks, the core screen definition for appointments is the same as that of notes, so we can jump into the list screen straight away, which does have some new stuff to see.

AppointementsList.dart

First up, we have some new imports, among a batch of others you've seen before:

```
import
  "package:flutter_calendar_carousel/"
  "flutter_calendar_carousel.dart";
import "package:flutter_calendar_carousel/classes/event.dart";
import
  "package:flutter_calendar_carousel/classes/event_list.dart";
```

The Calendar Carousel is a plugin (see here: https://pub.dartlang.org/packages/flutter_calendar_carousel) that provides to our app a calendar widget that can be swiped horizontally to move between months. It has many other options available to it such as showing indicators on dates that have events on them, a variety of display modes, and tap handlers to perform actions when a date is tapped.

All of which sounds like *precisely* the kind of thing we need for displaying appointments in something other than a simple list! Flutter doesn't offer such a thing out of the box, hence the need for a plugin, and Calendar Carousel fits the bill exactly.

So, let's start building the list screen widget and see how it's used:

```
class AppointmentsList extends StatelessWidget {

  Widget build(BuildContext inContext) {

    EventList<Event> _markedDateMap = EventList();
    for (
      int i = 0; i < appointmentsModel.entityList.length; i++
    ) {
      Appointment appointment =
        appointmentsModel.entityList[i];
      List dateParts = appointment.apptDate.split(",");
      DateTime apptDate = DateTime(
        int.parse(dateParts[0]), int.parse(dateParts[1]),
        int.parse(dateParts[2]));
```

```
_markedDateMap.add(apptDate, Event(date : apptDate,
  icon : Container(decoration : BoxDecoration(
    color : Colors.blue))
));
}
```

One of the things Calendar Carousel provides is a way to show some sort of indicator on dates that have events associated with them. To do this, it has a markedDatesMap property that accepts a value that is a map containing keys that are DateTime objects and corresponding values that are Event objects (the latter being a class it provides) that describe each event. When the calendar is rendered, it uses this map to show the indicators. Here, we're building up that map by iterating over the appointmentsModel.entityList, which you know from your experience with notes, since the logic is the same here, is an array of appointments retrieved from the database. For each, we split the apptDate property and then feed that to the DateTime constructor to get a DateTime instance for the appointment's date. Then, we construct an Event object and add it to the _markedDateMap map. The Event object takes the date in of course, and it also takes an icon property. This can be any widget you want, and it will wind up being the indicator shown on the date. Here, I use a simple Container widget that has a BoxDecoration as a decoration. With no further properties defined for the BoxDecoration or the Container, the result is that the box uses the minimum space it can, the result being a square just a few pixels wide and tall, as you can see in Figure 6-2.

Figure 6-2. *The appointments list screen with date indicators*

The 8th and 13th have appointments, hence the dots. Notice on the 13th that if there are multiple events, you'll get multiple dots. Perfect!

Now, we can move on to the widget returned from this build() method:

```
return ScopedModel<AppointmentsModel>(
  model : appointmentsModel,
  child : ScopedModelDescendant<AppointmentsModel>(
    builder : (inContext, inChild, inModel) {
      return Scaffold(
        floatingActionButton : FloatingActionButton(
          child : Icon(Icons.add, color : Colors.white),
```

```
        onPressed : () async {
          appointmentsModel.entityBeingEdited =
            Appointment();
          DateTime now = DateTime.now();
          appointmentsModel.entityBeingEdited.apptDate =
            "${now.year},${now.month},${now.day}";
          appointmentsModel.setChosenDate(
          DateFormat.yMMMMd("en_US").format(
              now.toLocal()));
          appointmentsModel.setApptTime(null);
          appointmentsModel.setStackIndex(1);
        }
      ),
```

It starts out the same as notes and tasks did, complete with a FAB for creating a new appointment. At this point, that code should be quite familiar, so no need to go over in detail again. Instead, let's see what comes next:

```
body : Column(
  children : [
    Expanded(
      child : Container(
        margin : EdgeInsets.symmetric(horizontal : 10),
        child : CalendarCarousel<Event>(
          thisMonthDayBorderColor : Colors.grey,
          daysHaveCircularBorder : false,
          markedDatesMap : _markedDateMap,
          onDayPressed :
            (DateTime inDate, List<Event> inEvents) {
              _showAppointments(inDate, inContext);
            }
        )
      )
    )
  ]
)
```

The goal here is to get the Calendar Carousel to expand to fill the screen. For that, an Expanded widget makes sense since that's expressly its purpose: it expands its child to fill the available space inside a Row, Column, or Flex. The important point is that the parent widget must have a flex capability, which limits it to those three shown. Which of those is used here wouldn't matter much given that this is the only widget on the screen (well, in the body more precisely), so I just went with the tried and true Column. Rather than put the CalendarCarousel widget directly as the child of the Expanded though, I put it inside a Container so that I could set some margin around it. I just felt it looked better not stretching all the way to the very edge of the screen, not to mention avoiding running into the TabBar at the top or the FAB at the bottom.

The CalendarCarousel itself is simple to define in our case (though it provides many configuration options, we only need a handful). I give each date a grey border, as well as ensuring they are square by setting daysHaveCircularBorder to false. Then, the markedDatesMap we talked about earlier is pointed to the _markedDateMap that was populated before. Finally, an event handler is hooked up to handle taps on the dates. When this occurs, I want to show the events for the selected date, if any, in a BottomSheet, thanks to the _showAppointments() method:

```
void _showAppointments(
  DateTime inDate, BuildContext inContext) async {

  showModalBottomSheet(context : inContext,
    builder : (BuildContext inContext) {
      return ScopedModel<AppointmentsModel>(
        model : appointmentsModel,
        child : ScopedModelDescendant<AppointmentsModel>(
```

This method starts by accepting the DateTime that was tapped, and the BuildContext associated with the widget that called it. Note that while the function defined for onDayPressed accepts a list of events, for the display to show what I want, I needed to get that data from the entityList in the model. That's because the Event objects passed in wouldn't have all the data I needed, so that argument is simply ignored here in favor of the code that follows. That's why the widget returned by the builder function of the showModalBottomSheet() call begins with a ScopedModel and references our AppointmentsModel.

The builder function comes next:

```
builder : (BuildContext inContext, Widget inChild,
  AppointmentsModel inModel) {
  return Scaffold(
    body : Container(child : Padding(
      padding : EdgeInsets.all(10), child : GestureDetector(
```

So far, nothing you haven't seen before, right? I again felt like some padding was in order here, so a Container starts off the body so that I could apply it.

After that, since what is shown in the BottomSheet, which you can see in the screenshot from the previous chapter, is a vertically scrolling list of appointments, a Column layout makes sense here:

```
child : Column(
  children : [
    Text(DateFormat.yMMMMd("en_US").format(inDate.toLocal()),
      textAlign : TextAlign.center,
      style : TextStyle(color :
        Theme.of(inContext).accentColor, fontSize : 24)
    ),
    Divider(),
```

The first child is just a simple Text element, centered on the BottomSheet via the textAlign property, and the value of which is the selected date, formatted nicely. Notice here the way the color of the text is retrieved: the Theme.of() function is always available and gets you a reference to the theme currently active for the app. Once you have that reference, you can access its members, one of which is accentColor, which for the default theme will be a nice shade of blue. The fontSize is also specified to make this text stand out from the rest. I also added a Divider widget after that to separate the date from the list of appointments.

After that comes another Expanded, so that the list of appointments will fill the remaining space inside the Column layout. Each child is then built from the entityList, which we must write some code to filter out any appointment not for the selected date:

```
Expanded(
  child : ListView.builder(
    itemCount : appointmentsModel.entityList.length,
```

```
itemBuilder : (BuildContext inBuildContext, int inIndex) {
  Appointment appointment =
    appointmentsModel.entityList[inIndex];
  if (appointment.apptDate !=
    "${inDate.year},${inDate.month},${inDate.day}") {
    return Container(height : 0);
  }
  String apptTime = "";
  if (appointment.apptTime != null) {
    List timeParts = appointment.apptTime.split(",");
    TimeOfDay at = TimeOfDay(
      hour : int.parse(timeParts[0]),
      minute : int.parse(timeParts[1]));
    apptTime = " (${at.format(inContext)})";
  }
```

For any appointment that's not for the selected date, we return a `Container` with a zero `height`. This is necessary because returning `null` from the `itemBuilder` function will result in an exception; Flutter expects *something* to be returned in all cases, so here it's something that won't display anything, so only appointments for this date will be visible in the end, just like we want.

The time of the appointment, if there is one, has to be split just like the date is, because it's stored as a string in "hh,mm" form in the database. Once that's done, we can pass those two pieces of information to the `TimeOfDay` constructor, which is just like `DateTime` but, obviously, for times! The `format()` method of `TimeOfDay` gives us back a nicely formatted time in the applicable local form.

Now, each appointment needs to be editable and deletable, and we've been doing that with the `Slidable` widget so far with other entities, and it's the same story here:

```
return Slidable(delegate : SlidableDrawerDelegate(),
  actionExtentRatio : .25, child : Container(
  margin : EdgeInsets.only(bottom : 8),
    color : Colors.grey.shade300,
    child : ListTile(
      title : Text("${appointment.title}$apptTime"),
      subtitle : appointment.description == null ?
        null : Text("${appointment.description}"),
```

```
    onTap : () async {
      _editAppointment(inContext, appointment);
    }
  )
),
```

If the appointment has a description, then that's shown as the subtitle text. Otherwise, the value there is null, and nothing is displayed. The _editAppointment method we'll look at shortly, but before that, we'll finish out the widget definition with the secondaryActions property of the Slidable:

```
secondaryActions : [
  IconSlideAction(caption : "Delete", color : Colors.red,
    icon : Icons.delete,
    onTap : () =>
      _deleteAppointment(inBuildContext, appointment)
  )
]
```

That's no different than what you saw for notes and tasks already, and in fact, the code of the _deleteAppointment() method is just like the delete method for those two entities, so we'll skip looking at it. However, we do still have that _editAppointment() method to look at, and it is this code:

```
void _editAppointment(BuildContext inContext, Appointment
  inAppointment) async {

  appointmentsModel.entityBeingEdited =
    await AppointmentsDBWorker.db.get(inAppointment.id);
  if (appointmentsModel.entityBeingEdited.apptDate == null) {
    appointmentsModel.setChosenDate(null);
  } else {
    List dateParts =
      appointmentsModel.entityBeingEdited.apptDate.split(",");
    DateTime apptDate = DateTime(
      int.parse(dateParts[0]), int.parse(dateParts[1]),
      int.parse(dateParts[2]));
```

```
    appointmentsModel.setChosenDate(
      DateFormat.yMMMMd("en_US").format(apptDate.toLocal())));
  }
  if (appointmentsModel.entityBeingEdited.apptTime == null) {
    appointmentsModel.setApptTime(null);
  } else {
    List timeParts =
      appointmentsModel.entityBeingEdited.apptTime.split(",");
    TimeOfDay apptTime = TimeOfDay(
      hour : int.parse(timeParts[0]),
      minute : int.parse(timeParts[1]));
    appointmentsModel.setApptTime(apptTime.format(inContext));
  }
  appointmentsModel.setStackIndex(1);
  Navigator.pop(inContext);

}
```

It too is nearly identical to its notes and tasks edit method counterparts like the delete code is, but here we must deal with the time. Since the date and time are optional for appointments, we have to check if they are null or not and only process them if they aren't. If they aren't, we have to parse out the date components and build a DateTime to pass to setChosenDate() in the model, and similarly, we have to parse out the time components to construct a TimeOfDay to pass to setApptTime().

AppointmentsEntry.dart

The final piece of the appointment puzzle is, of course, the entry screen, which is shown here in Figure 6-3.

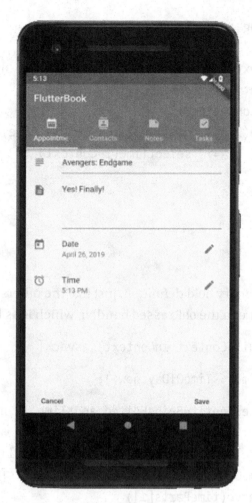

Figure 6-3. *The entry screen for appointments*

It's a simple enough screen, just a single required field in the title, a multi-line description field, and two fields for selecting a date and time. Technically, Date is required as well because an appointment without a date wouldn't make much sense (though time is not required because an appointment doesn't necessarily have to have a time associated with it logically). But, instead of dealing with validation, the date gets set to the current date by default, and there's no way to clear it. Therefore, an appointment is automatically going to always have a date, and it's up to the user to change it if the current date isn't appropriate.

As far as the code goes, there's nothing new there except for the piece about getting an appointment time, which is very similar to the date part, but let's take a look at the time code now anyway, beginning with the field definition:

```
      ListTile(leading : Icon(Icons.alarm),
        title : Text("Time"),
        subtitle : Text(appointmentsModel.apptTime == null ?
          "" : appointmentsModel.apptTime),
        trailing : IconButton(
          icon : Icon(Icons.edit), color : Colors.blue,
          onPressed : () => _selectTime(inContext)
        )
      )
    ]
  )
)
```

That's a perfectly ordinary field definition, just like the others you've seen so far, save for the call to _selectTime in the onPressed handler, which is as follows:

```
Future _selectTime(BuildContext inContext) async {

  TimeOfDay initialTime = TimeOfDay.now();

  if (appointmentsModel.entityBeingEdited.apptTime != null) {
    List timeParts =
      appointmentsModel.entityBeingEdited.apptTime.split(",");
    initialTime = TimeOfDay(hour : int.parse(timeParts[0]),
      minute : int.parse(timeParts[1])
      );
  }

  TimeOfDay picked = await showTimePicker(
    context : inContext, initialTime : initialTime);

  if (picked != null) {
    appointmentsModel.entityBeingEdited.apptTime =
      "${picked.hour},${picked.minute}";
    appointmentsModel.setApptTime(picked.format(inContext));
  }

}
```

Like I said, very similar to the code for getting a date that you saw earlier for tasks. If the user is editing an existing appointment, then we have to set the `initialTime` of the `TimePicker` that we'll show via the call to `showTimePicker()`. Therefore, we have to parse it out of the model, the `entityBeingEdited` specifically, since the list screen will have set that before navigating to the entry screen. Then, once the user selects a time, or cancels the `TimePicker`, the `apptTime` is updated in `entityBeingEdited` and then also in the model via the call to `setApptTime()` so that it gets reflected on the screen (remember, that method will call `notifyListeners()`, which will trigger Flutter updating the display based on the new model value).

Reaching Out: Contacts

The final entity to look at is contacts, and I left it for last because in some ways it's the most complex of the bunch, and for sure it offers you the opportunity to see some new things.

ContactsModel.dart

As with the other three entities, we'll start with the model for it, including the Contact class. And, like the other three entities, I'll just show you the fields in the class since it is otherwise the same as those others:

```
int id;
String name;
String phone;
String email;
String birthday;
```

A contact can, of course, have a great deal of information stored about it – if you open your phone's contact app right now, you'll see a whole host of attributes you can set – but I've chosen probably the key ones only, plus one more just for fun! The `name`, `phone,` and `email` fields are obviously key to a contact in this day and age, and I added `birthday` just to have another example of working with dates and the `DatePicker`.

Tip   I recommend extending the three apps in this book as learning exercises. All of them have things that can be done to make them better, by design for the most part, and adding more fields for contacts would be one relatively easy thing you could do to practice your skills.

As for the model, there's only one thing we need to have in it:

```
class ContactsModel extends BaseModel {
  void triggerRebuild() {
    notifyListeners();
  }
}
```

The `birthday` will be covered by the `chosenDate` field (and its associated setter method) from `BaseModel`, so this one `triggerRebuild()` method really is all that's specific to contacts. Since `notifyListeners()` must be called from within the model class, that's why we need this method, but in this case, that's the only task it has to accomplish. As you'll see, this method will be used when editing a contact, and an avatar image is selected so that the image gets displayed on the screen. Let's not get ahead of ourselves though; we'll get to that soon.

ContactsDBWorker.dart

The database worker code for contacts is once again identical to the three you've already seen, save for the creation SQL as usually, so here is that:

```
CREATE TABLE IF NOT EXISTS contacts (
  id INTEGER PRIMARY KEY,
  name TEXT, email TEXT, phone TEXT, birthday TEXT
)
```

By now, that shouldn't hold any surprises for you.

Contacts.dart

Similarly, the base layout of the contacts screen has nothing new to offer compared to the code for the other three entities, so let's get to where there is some new stuff.

ContactsList.dart

The list screen for contacts is just a simple ListView, much like you've seen in other areas, but we have an avatar image to deal with, potentially, for each contact, and that requires some new Flutter bits:

```
return ScopedModel<ContactsModel>(
  model : contactsModel,
  child : ScopedModelDescendant<ContactsModel>(
    builder : (BuildContext inContext, Widget inChild,
      ContactsModel inModel) {
      return Scaffold(
        floatingActionButton : FloatingActionButton(
          child : Icon(Icons.add, color : Colors.white),
          onPressed : () async {
            File avatarFile =
              File(join(utils.docsDir.path, "avatar"));
            if (avatarFile.existsSync()) {
              avatarFile.deleteSync();
            }
            contactsModel.entityBeingEdited = Contact();
            contactsModel.setChosenDate(null);
            contactsModel.setStackIndex(1);
          }
      )
  )
```

It all starts off ordinarily enough: the usual ScopedModel at the top, with the model referencing contactsModel, and then a child that is a ScopedModelDescendant. The builder function then is present, and it returns a Scaffold, which we need so we can have a FAB for creating a new contact.

Now, the onPressed event handler of the FAB is where we start to see some new and exciting stuff. What you're going to see is that when a contact is created, you can add an avatar image to it. The image will be stored in the app's documents directory, *not* in the database (that's on purpose because it provides an opportunity for you to see some file handling code). But, when editing a contact, whether new or existing, a temporary image file can be present if the user had previously been editing a contact. So, to start when creating a new contact, we have to make sure that the temporary file isn't there. The File class is a Dart class from the io package, and its constructor takes as an argument a path to a file. You saw the utils.docsDir retrieved in the previous chapter, and its path property is the path to the documents directory. So, passing that to the join() method, which is a function provided by the path library that knows how to concatenate file path parts to wind up with a proper platform-dependent path, along with the filename avatar, gets us a reference to that file, if it exists, wrapped in a File instance. The File class provides some methods, one of which is existsSync(). This returns true if the file exists, false if not, and it does so synchronously, which we need here. Otherwise, we'd have to await it (or otherwise wait for a Future to be resolved). There is also an exists() version that is asynchronous. If it exists then the deleteSync() method is called to get rid of it (and there is an asynchronous delete() method available as well). After that, a new Contact is created, and the user is navigated to the entry screen as usual.

Next up we have the ListView that contains the contacts:

```
body : ListView.builder(
  itemCount : contactsModel.entityList.length,
  itemBuilder : (BuildContext inBuildContext, int inIndex) {
    Contact contact = contactsModel.entityList[inIndex];
    File avatarFile =
      File(join(utils.docsDir.path, contact.id.toString()));
    bool avatarFileExists = avatarFile.existsSync();
```

Each contact is pulled out of the model in turn, and a reference to its avatar file is created, if it exists. The file uses the contact's id as a filename, so it's an easy link to the contact. This time, the result of the call to existsSync() is stored in avatarFileExists, for a reason you can see in the next chunk of code:

```
return Column(children : [
  Slidable(
    delegate : SlidableDrawerDelegate(),
```

```
actionExtentRatio : .25, child : ListTile(
leading : CircleAvatar(
  backgroundColor : Colors.indigoAccent,
  foregroundColor : Colors.white,
  backgroundImage : avatarFileExists ?
    FileImage(avatarFile) : null,
  child : avatarFileExists ? null :
    Text(contact.name.substring(0, 1).toUpperCase())
),
title : Text("${contact.name}"),
subtitle : contact.phone == null ?
  null : Text("${contact.phone}"),
```

Each child of the ListView is a Column layout and will have two items in it: a Slidable that contains a contact itself and a Divider, hence the Column being necessary. The Slidable is like all the others you've seen except for the leading. Here, it's a CircleAvatar, which is a widget that shows an image and condenses it down into a circular shape. It's typically used to display avatar images of people in a list, so it's a very fitting widget to use here. The only trick here is that the backgroundImage, which is how the image is specified, must be either a valid FileImage reference or null. That's where that avatarFileExists flag comes in. When it's true, the avatarFile, which remember is a File instance, is wrapped in a FileImage widget, which is a widget to display an image based on a reference to a file on the file system. When it's false, then backgroundImage will be null.

We also need that flag because when a contact has no avatar image, we want to show the first letter of their name, which is a typical pattern in contact apps. So, the child of the CircleAvatar will either be null when there is an image, or it will be a Text widget when it doesn't. In the latter case, the substring() method of the String class, of which contact.name is, of course, an instance, is used to get that first letter, and the toUpperCase() method is used to ensure its upper-case.

The rest of the configuration for the Slidable you already know, so let's look at the onTap handler for it, which is how we trigger editing of a contact:

```
onTap : () async {
  File avatarFile =
    File(join(utils.docsDir.path, "avatar"));
```

```
if (avatarFile.existsSync()) {avatarFile.deleteSync(); }
contactsModel.entityBeingEdited =
  await ContactsDBWorker.db.get(contact.id);
if (contactsModel.entityBeingEdited.birthday == null) {
  contactsModel.setChosenDate(null);
} else {
  List dateParts =
    contactsModel.entityBeingEdited.birthday.split(",");
  DateTime birthday = DateTime(
    int.parse(dateParts[0]), int.parse(dateParts[1]),
    int.parse(dateParts[2]));
  contactsModel.setChosenDate(
    DateFormat.yMMMMd("en_US").format(birthday.toLocal())
  );
}
contactsModel.setStackIndex(1);
}
```

This handler too is not too different from the others you've seen, but here again, we have to deal with the temporary avatar image that could be there, so that's deleted if it exists. The date has to be parsed apart too and set in the model for display on the edit screen, and then the usual screen navigation is done via the call to setStackIndex().

Just to complete the Slidable and ListView configuration, here's the secondaryActions:

```
secondaryActions : [
  IconSlideAction(caption : "Delete", color : Colors.red,
    icon : Icons.delete,
    onTap : () => _deleteContact(inContext, contact))
]
),
Divider()
```

You can also see the Divider there, and that completes the return in the itemBuilder() function.

Now, let's see about deleting a contact:

```
Future _deleteContact(BuildContext inContext,
  Contact inContact) async {

  return showDialog(context : inContext,
    barrierDismissible : false,
    builder : (BuildContext inAlertContext) {
      return AlertDialog(title : Text("Delete Contact"),
        content : Text(
          "Are you sure you want to delete ${inContact.name}?"
        ),
        actions : [
          FlatButton(child : Text("Cancel"),
            onPressed: () {
              Navigator.of(inAlertContext).pop();
            }
          ),
  FlatButton(child : Text("Delete"),
    onPressed : () async {
      File avatarFile = File(
        join(utils.docsDir.path, inContact.id.toString())));
      if (avatarFile.existsSync()) {
        avatarFile.deleteSync();
      }
      await ContactsDBWorker.db.delete(inContact.id);
      Navigator.of(inAlertContext).pop();
      Scaffold.of(inContext).showSnackBar(
        SnackBar(backgroundColor : Colors.red,
          duration : Duration(seconds : 2),
          content : Text("Contact deleted")));
      contactsModel.loadData("contacts", ContactsDBWorker.db);
    }
  )
```

Most of this is what by now can rightly be called the typical code of an entity delete function, but once more, we have the avatar files to deal with. Deleting a contact from the database isn't sufficient; we have to delete its avatar file too if it has one, so once more we get a reference to it and, if it exists, call `deleteSync()` to get rid of it. After that, it's just the usual database deletion and showing a `SnackBar` code to confirm, and we're all done!

ContactsEntry.dart

We have just one more piece of FlutterBook to look and, and it's the contacts entry screen, which you can glimpse in Figure 6-4.

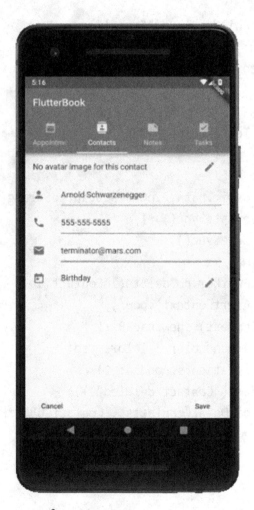

Figure 6-4. *The entry screen for contacts*

It's a simple enough screen: three `TextFormField` widgets, only one of which (name) is required, and then a birthday field with a trigger icon to show a DatePicker. As such, we'll get through this pretty quick, but I want to show the code anyway because the stuff about the avatar images is mixed in a few places, and that's where this code substantively diverges from the entry screen code for the other three entities a bit.

```
return ScopedModel(model : contactsModel,
  child : ScopedModelDescendant<ContactsModel>(
    builder : (BuildContext inContext, Widget inChild,
      ContactsModel inModel) {
      File avatarFile =
        File(join(utils.docsDir.path, "avatar"));
      if (avatarFile.existsSync() == false) {
        if (inModel.entityBeingEdited != null &&
          inModel.entityBeingEdited.id != null
        ) {
          avatarFile = File(join(utils.docsDir.path,
            inModel.entityBeingEdited.id.toString()
          ));
        }
      }
```

The first thing to deal with is the fact that this screen can be shown when creating a new contact or when editing an existing one. In the create case, there will be no avatar image, but when editing there might be: remember that `build()` will be called when the model changes, which is precisely what will happen when the user selects an avatar. So, being as we're inside the `build()` method here, we have to see if there is a temporary avatar image. If there isn't one, then we check the `entityBeingEdited`. If it has an `id`, which is only `true` when editing a contact, then we try to get a reference to its actual avatar file (as opposed to the file literally named `avatar`, which is the temporary one). We capture a reference to this for later. It will be needed when we start rendering fields, but first, we have some other "preliminary" stuff to do:

```
return Scaffold(bottomNavigationBar : Padding(
  padding :
    EdgeInsets.symmetric(vertical : 0, horizontal : 10),
```

```
child : Row(
  children : [
    FlatButton(child : Text("Cancel"),
      onPressed : () {
        File avatarFile =
          File(join(utils.docsDir.path, "avatar"));
        if (avatarFile.existsSync()) {
          avatarFile.deleteSync();
        }
        FocusScope.of(inContext).requestFocus(FocusNode());
        inModel.setStackIndex(0);
      }
    ),
    Spacer(),
    FlatButton(child : Text("Save"),
      onPressed : () { _save(inContext, inModel); })
  ]
)),
```

This is a typical entry form start, but in the Cancel button's onPressed handler we have some work to do around the possible temporary avatar file. Even though it's deleted before this screen is shown, it's still better to delete it now, if it exists (if the user had selected an avatar but then cancelled), so that's exactly what we do. Once that's done, the soft keyboard is hidden as previously discussed, and the user navigated back to the list screen. The Save button just calls _save() like always, and we'll see that later.

Before that though, let's start defining the actual form:

```
body : Form(key : _formKey, child : ListView(
  children : [
    ListTile(title : avatarFile.existsSync() ?
      Image.file(avatarFile) :
      Text("No avatar image for this contact"),
      trailing : IconButton(icon : Icon(Icons.edit),
        color : Colors.blue,
        onPressed : () => _selectAvatar(inContext)
      )
    )
```

Now, you can see where that avatarFile reference comes into play: the title of the ListTile will be either an Image or it will be a Text widget saying that no avatar image has been selected. When it's an Image, the avatarFile is passed to the Image.file() constructor and the avatar image is shown. Note that I did nothing fancy with scaling or constraints here. It will simply display the image in whatever size it is (you may want to change that as a suggested exercise – hint hint!). The trailing property of the ListTile provides an IconButton for the user to click to select an avatar image, and the code for this is something we'll look at soon because it's got some interesting new stuff to see!

First though, let's continue defining the form:

```
ListTile(leading : Icon(Icons.person),
  title : TextFormField(
    decoration : InputDecoration(hintText : "Name"),
    controller : _nameEditingController,
    validator : (String inValue) {
      if (inValue.length == 0) {
        return "Please enter a name";
      }
      return null;
    }
  )
),
ListTile(leading : Icon(Icons.phone),
  title : TextFormField(
    keyboardType : TextInputType.phone,
    decoration : InputDecoration(hintText : "Phone"),
    controller : _phoneEditingController)
),
ListTile(leading : Icon(Icons.email),
  title : TextFormField(
    keyboardType : TextInputType.emailAddress,
    decoration : InputDecoration(hintText : "Email"),
    controller : _emailEditingController)
),
```

```
ListTile(leading : Icon(Icons.today),
  title : Text("Birthday"),
  subtitle : Text(contactsModel.chosenDate == null ?
    "" : contactsModel.chosenDate),
  trailing : IconButton(icon : Icon(Icons.edit),
   color : Colors.blue,
   onPressed : () async {
     String chosenDate = await utils.selectDate(
       inContext, contactsModel,
       contactsModel.entityBeingEdited.birthday
     );
     if (chosenDate != null) {
       contactsModel.entityBeingEdited.birthday = chosenDate;
     }
   }
 )
)
```

That's all stuff you've seen before, aside perhaps from the keyboardType property, which allows us to specify a keyboard tailored to the type of data being input. As you can see, there are several properties available on it like phone and emailAddress, and their meanings I would think are self-explanatory!

Now, we come to the _selectAvatar() method that is called when the user clicks that IconButton next to the avatar Image widget:

```
Future _selectAvatar(BuildContext inContext) {

return showDialog(context : inContext,
  builder : (BuildContext inDialogContext) {
    return AlertDialog(content : SingleChildScrollView(
      child : ListBody(children : [
        GestureDetector(child : Text("Take a picture"),
          onTap : () async {
            var cameraImage = await ImagePicker.pickImage(
              source : ImageSource.camera
            );
```

```
    if (cameraImage != null) {
      cameraImage.copySync(
        join(utils.docsDir.path, "avatar")
      );
      contactsModel.triggerRebuild();
    }
    Navigator.of(inDialogContext).pop();
  }
)
```

The job here is to show a dialog where the user selects the source of the avatar image, which can either be from their gallery or the camera. So, we call showDialog() and then return an AlertDialog from its builder function. Inside the AlertDialog we start with a SingleChildScrollView, which is a widget that contains a single widget that can be scrolled. Why use that here? Honestly, there's no particular reason other than to show you an alternate way to do things. In this case, scrolling doesn't come into play, but what if you had a few more sources of images you wanted to provide? Rather than ensuring the dialog is big enough to fit them all, you can just allow it to scroll like this.

Anyway, inside the SingleChildScrollView goes a ListBody, which is a widget that arranges its children sequentially along a given axis and forces them to the dimensions of the parent in the other axis. Finally, because we need items that can be clicked, I decided to go with GestureDetector widgets here rather than buttons or something else, though not for any special reason. By doing so, we have an onTap event now that can be applied to this item, which is a Text widget that when clicked will launch the camera. The ImagePicker class is provided by the image_picker plugin which offers functions to access sources of images, the location you want to get the image from being specified by the source property passed to the ImagePicker. pickImage() function. Upon return from that call, if cameraImage isn't null (it would be null if no picture was taken), then we use the copySync() method, which is available because a File instance is what gets returned to us, to copy it to avatar, which you know now is our temporary avatar image file.

Then, we have to tell the model that it changed, even though in reality it hasn't! We have to do that because we need Flutter to call our build() method so that the image is shown (remember that code from earlier?). So, the contactsModel.triggerRebuild()

method is called, which you'll remember just calls notifyListeners(), and that causes the image to be shown as a result of the screen being redrawn. Then, we just pop() the dialog away by getting a reference to the BuildContext for the dialog, and we're good to go.

The other element in the dialog is for selecting an image from the gallery, and it's the same code, just with a different source specified in the call to pickImage():

```
GestureDetector(child : Text("Select From Gallery"),
  onTap : () async {
    var galleryImage = await ImagePicker.pickImage(
      source : ImageSource.gallery
    );
    if (galleryImage != null) {
      galleryImage.copySync(
        join(utils.docsDir.path, "avatar")
      );
      contactsModel.triggerRebuild();
    }
    Navigator.of(inDialogContext).pop();
  }
)
```

Finally, there is the _save() method, but just to wrap this up quickly, I'm just going to show you the small handful of lines that are different from the other _save() methods you've examined:

```
id = await ContactsDBWorker.db.create(
  contactsModel.entityBeingEdited
);
...some other code you're already familiar with...
File avatarFile = File(join(utils.docsDir.path, "avatar"));
if (avatarFile.existsSync()) {
  avatarFile.renameSync(
    join(utils.docsDir.path, id.toString())
  );
}
```

The only thing unique to contacts is, of course, the avatar image, and here we have to account for that. If the temporary `avatar` file is present, then we use the `renameSync()` function to give it a name matching the `id` of the contact. The `id` is captured from the call to the `create()` method of `ContactsDBWorker`, which is the only database worker class that does this, and is the ID that was assigned to the contact when it was stored to the database. Of course, when updating an existing contact, we already know that `id`, so we're good to go in either case.

And with that, we've completed our tour of the first app, FlutterBook!

Summary

In this chapter, we completed our look at the FlutterBook app. You saw how the appointments, contacts, and tasks entities were coded, including things like getting images from the gallery or camera and picking times and dates. With that, we have a complete PIM application that you could use for real if you wanted to, in keeping with the "practical" title of this book!

In the next chapter, we'll start building the second of our three apps and, in the process, you'll see some new capabilities of Flutter and even get a taste of some server-side programming and interfacing a Flutter app with it.

Sounds like good, educational fun, no? That's my goal!

CHAPTER 7

FlutterChat, Part I: The Server

With the last two chapters, we build an app that is an island unto itself: all its data lives on the device it's runnig on. That's fine for many kinds of apps, but for others, you're going to need a server to share some sort of data (or, just to make it available from places other than the device the app is running on). That's a big part of application development these days in fact.

With this chapter and the next, we'll build an app that bridges the divide into a larger world and uses a server. While this book is obviously not about building servers, that's precisely what we're going to do in this chapter for this project. So, you can consider this a little bit of bonus knowledge being dropped on 'ya!

First, we'll talk about what the project we're building is (it'd be weird *not* to start there, wouldn't it?!), and then we need to talk about two technologies that you probably have heard of: Node and WebSockets. If you're already familiar with these things, then you can skip those two sections and jump right into the application building section, but if not then read on to get a whirlwind introduction to these things – but first, let's talk about what we're building!

Can We Build It? Yes, We Can! But, uh, What IS "It"?!

The app we'll build will be christened FlutterChat, and just in case the name doesn't give it away, this will be a chat app! You'll be able to communicate with other users in real time with FlutterChat, in conjunction with the server.

259

© Frank Zammetti 2019
F. Zammetti, *Practical Flutter*, https://doi.org/10.1007/978-1-4842-4972-7_7

The app will provide users the ability to create rooms where they can congregate and talk to each other. There will be a lobby that lists all the rooms the server is aware of, and we'll also provide a way to list all the users the server is aware of.

Users will need to register with the server by providing a username and password, and they will be able to rejoin the server at any time with those.

Also, we'll provide the ability for users to specify that rooms are private. In those cases, only users who are invited will be able to join the room, so of course, we'll provide a mechanism to invite users.

Finally, the user that creates a room will have a few select "administrative" privileges: they'll be the only one that can close the room and also will be able to kick unruly users out of the room.

For this app, we're going to use the built-in navigation features of Flutter, something you didn't see in FlutterBook (remember, that was using something of a custom navigation mechanism). As far as the interface goes, we'll use the Drawer widget to control that navigation, giving the user the ability to jump between the lobby, whatever room they're currently in (if any), the user list, and also an About screen that we'll create, just for fun!

It's not a very complicated app really, and if you've ever used any kind of chat app that you're already familiar with most of the core concepts. But, it'll be an excellent demonstration of some things you haven't used in a real app yet and also will be a decent little app that you could use for real if you want to.

Now, let's talk about some server stuff before we get to Flutter code, beginning with Node.

Node

Ryan Dahl. That cat has some talent, I tell ya!

Ryan is the creator of a fantastic piece of software called Node (or Node.js, as it is sometimes written). Ryan first presented at the European JSConf in 2009, and it was quickly recognized as a potential game-changer, as evidenced by the standing ovation his presentation received.

Node is a platform for running primarily (though not exclusively!) server-side code that is high performance and capable of handling tons of request load with ease. It is based on the most widely used language on the planet today: JavaScript. It's straightforward to get started with and understand, yet it puts tremendous power in the hands of developers, in large part thanks to its asynchronous and event-driven model of programming. In Node, almost everything you do is non-blocking, meaning code won't hold up processing of other request threads. This, plus the fact that to execute code Node uses Google's popular and highly tuned V8 JavaScript engine, the same engine that powers its Chrome browser, makes it very high performance and able to handle a large request load.

It's no wonder that so many significant players and sites have adopted Node to one degree or another. Moreover, these aren't minor outfits either. We're talking about names you doubtless know, including DuckDuckGo, eBay, LinkedIn, Microsoft, Walmart, and Yahoo, to name just a few examples.

Node is a first-class runtime environment, meaning that you can do such things as interacting with the local file system, access relational databases, call remote systems, and much more. In the past, you'd have to use a "proper" runtime, such as Java or .Net to do all this; JavaScript wasn't a player in that space. With Node, this is no longer true. To be clear, Node isn't in and of itself a server, although it is most frequently used to create servers. But as a generic JavaScript runtime, it's the runtime that a great many non-server tools run in as well, including many of the developer tools you've probably encountered at some point, even if you didn't realize Node was involved!

Getting, installing, and running Node are trivial exercises, regardless of your operating system preference. There are no complicated installs with all sorts of dependencies, nor is there a vast set of configuration files to mess with before you can run a Node app. It's a 5-minute exercise, depending on the speed of your Internet connection and how fast you can type. There's only one address to remember: `http://nodejs.org`. That's your one-stop shop for all things Node, beginning, right from the front page, with downloading it, as you can see in Figure 7-1.

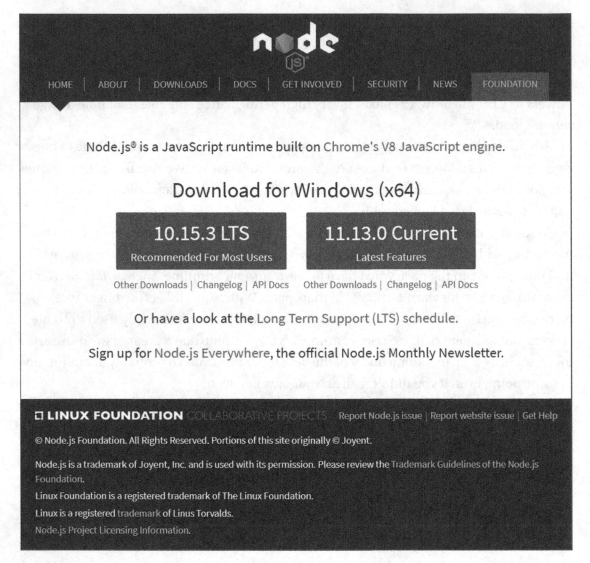

Figure 7-1. *Node has a simple web site, but it gets the job done*

Usually, I would tell you to install the latest version available, but in this case, it might be better to choose a long-term support (LTS) version, because they tend to be more stable. However, it shouldn't (he said, with fingers crossed) matter which you choose, for the purposes of this book. For the record, however, I developed all the code using version 10.15.3, so if you encounter any problems, I would suggest choosing that version, which you can get from the Other Downloads link and then the Previous Releases link (you'll be able to download any past version you like from there).

The download will install in whatever fashion is appropriate for your system, and I leave this as an exercise for the reader. For example, on Windows, Node provides a perfectly ordinary and straightforward installer that will walk you through the necessary (and extremely simple) steps. On MacOS X, a typical install wizard will do the same.

Once the install completes, you will be ready to play with Node. The installer should have added the Node directory to your path. So, as a first simple test, go to a command prompt, type `node`, and press Enter. You should be greeted with a > prompt. Node is now listening for your commands in interactive mode. To confirm, type the following:

```
console.log("test");
```

Press Enter, and you should be greeted with something like what you see in Figure 7-2 (platform differences excepted).

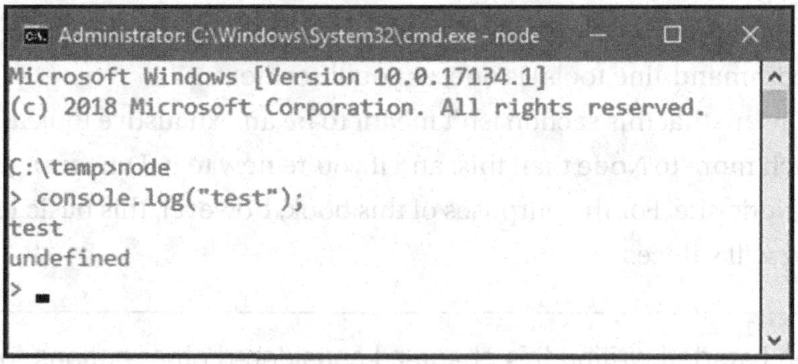

Figure 7-2. *Say hello to my little friend, Node*

Interacting with Node in CLI mode is fine but limited. What you really want to do is execute a saved JavaScript file using Node. As it happens, that's easy to do. Simply create a text file named test.js (it could be anything), and type the code below into it (and, of course, save it):

```
var a = 5;
var b = 3;
var c = a * b;
console.log(a + " * " + b + " = " + c);
```

To execute this file, assuming you are in the directory in which the file is located, you simply have to type this: `node test.js`. Press Enter after that, and you should be greeted with an execution, such as the one you see in Figure 7-3.

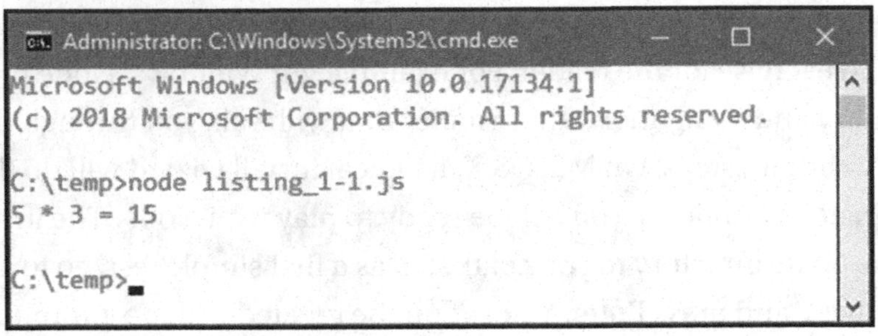

Figure 7-3. *An elementary Node example*

Clearly, this little bit of code is unexceptional, but it does demonstrate that Node can execute plain old JavaScript just fine. You can experiment a bit if you like, and you will see that Node should run any basic JavaScript that you care to throw at it. This capability, along with being a first-class runtime environment with access to many core operating system facilities, allows complex tools to be created, of which React Native (more precisely, its command-line tools) is one, as you'll see next.

Please be aware that this section isn't meant to be an exhaustive look at Node. There's so much more to Node than this, and if you're new to it, I encourage you to peruse the Node site. For the purposes of this book, however, this basic level of understanding will suffice.

Note   When I started writing this chapter, I considered other options for the server component of this project. I thought about creating a RESTful server using Express on top of Node, where Express is a library you can add that makes building RESTful servers very simple. But, given the real-time requirements of a chat application, that wouldn't have worked. I then thought about using Firebase, which is Google's real-time database system. The thing is though, there are lots of tutorials online about writing Flutter apps that hook up to Firebase, and there's even one or two that build a chat app with it. So, I decided to go a different route to, in a sense, add some content that may have been lacking into the developer education world. I think the approach outlined here also keeps things a bit simpler and certainly more self-contained, but either way I just wanted to provide some rationale for the choice here. Hopefully, it's a choice you agree with and like.

Keeping the Lines of Communication Open: socket.io

Now that you know something about Node, let's talk about the next component we're going to need: WebSockets and socket.io. But first, a bit of history to set the stage!

Note As I discuss this, it will be somewhat web-centric, web development-centric. But, rest assured, everything I'm talking about applies to mobile development as well, whether Flutter-based or not, because it's all an extension of the HTTP protocol, which applies to mobile development just as much as it does to web development. And with all the discussion in this chapter, don't worry if you don't know JavaScript – you won't have any problem understanding the code because I've written it very simply, and frankly it looks a bit like Dart anyway, a few syntactic differences aside. You're not going to be an expert JavaScript developer after this of course, but you shouldn't have any trouble following along even if you've never seen JavaScript before.

The Web (and by extension mobile apps that use the Web to communicate with other devices) was initially conceived as a place where it was the client's responsibility to request information from a server, but that eliminates a host of interesting possibilities, or at least makes them more difficult and non-optimal.

For example, if you have a machine that provides stock prices to a client to display in a dashboard, the client must continuously request updated prices from the server. This is the typical *polling* approach. The downside, primarily, is that it requires constant new requests from the client to server and also that the prices will only be as fresh as the polling interval, which you typically don't want to make too frequent, for fear of overloading the server. The prices aren't real-time, something that can be very bad if you're an investor.

After some time, something called AJAX came along. AJAX stands for Asynchronous JavaScript and XML. This is a technique that allows web pages to make requests to a server but to do so without refreshing the entire page, which is how web sites initially always worked. This was a game-changer! Now, the page could request data, those stock prices, for example, and just update a small part of the page, not the entire thing. Trust me, as someone who worked before and after that creation, it was huge!

Interestingly, the core concept behind AJAX means that it doesn't matter whether you use JavaScript or not, and it doesn't matter if you use XML or not. It's the *Asynchronous* part of the acronym that matters most.

265

With the advent of AJAX techniques, the next natural evolution was developers starting to investigate ways to have *bidirectional* communication, in which the server could push new stock prices out to the client without the client explicitly requesting anything as well. Some neat tricks were developed for this, one such method being long-polling. Sometimes called Comet, long-polling is a technique by which the client opens a connection with a server, as usual. But now, the server holds the request open, by never sending the HTTP response completion signal. Then, when the server has something to transmit to the client, the connection is already established, so it can do so immediately. This is referred to as a "hanging-GET" or "pending-POST," depending on the HTTP method used to create the connection.

This can be tricky to implement for many reasons, but probably the key one is that the connection processing thread is held on the server. Given that it's an HTTP connection, the overhead is not at all inconsequential. Before long, your server can be brought to its knees, without having all that many clients connected.

In more recent years, the WebSocket protocol was created to allow this sort of persistent connection without all the problems of long-polling, or other approaches, and this is precisely what we need for our chat app!

WebSocket is an Internet Engineering Task Force (IETF) standard that enables bidirectional communication between a client and a server. It does this by a special handshake when a regular HTTP connection is established. To do this, the client sends a request that looks something like this:

```
GET ws://websocket.apress.com/ HTTP/1.1
Origin: http://apress.com
Connection: Upgrade
Host: websocket.apress.com
Upgrade: websocket
```

Notice that Upgrade header value? That's the magic bit. When the server sees this, and assuming it supports WebSocket, it will respond with a reply such as this:

```
HTTP/1.1 101 WebSocket
Date: Mon, 21 Dec 2017
Connection: Upgrade
Upgrade: WebSocket
```

The server "agrees to the upgrade," in WebSocket parlance. Once this handshake completes, the HTTP request is torn down, but the underlying TCP/IP connection it rode in on remains. That's the persistent connection with which the client and server can communicate in real time, without having to reestablish a connection every time.

WebSocket also comes with a JavaScript API that you can use to establish connections, and both send and receive messages (and messages is what we call data that is transmitted over a WebSocket connection, in either direction). That's good for the Node side of the equation, writing the FlutterChat server using WebSockets, but it doesn't do us any good on the Flutter side, which of course is Dart-based.

Fortunately, there exists a library that sits on top of Node and which also is available as a Dart library for use in Flutter and that abstracts WebSockets a bit and gives us a nice, simple API to use in both places. This library is called socket.io, and it's what we're going to use for this project.

Simply stated, using socket.io, beyond the import of the library, requires little more than a few function calls: one to connect two devices (frequently a client and a server, but there's nothing that says two devices that aren't *servers* per se can't talk to each other), one when the code wants to send messages from one device to another (including sending a message to *all* connected devices, as you'll see later), and one to listen for messages from other devices.

Let's say that a client app (which, for the sake of this discussion, is assumed to be a JavaScript-based web app which is also using the socket.io library) stores its preferences on a server. Then, if the user wants to clear those preferences, it might send (or emit, as it's termed in socket.io land) a `clearPreferences` message to the server, along with an object that contains the ID of the user. To do this, it will need a socket.io server instance, which we'll assume has already been created and is referenced by the variable `io`. The client will use the `emit()` method to send the message, like so:

```
io.emit("clearPreferences", { "userID" : "user123" });
```

For this to do anything, the server must be listening for this message. You have to register a callback function with the socket.io instance for each message to listen for, and that's where the `on()` method comes into play:

```
io.on("clearPreferences", function(inData) {
  database.execute(
    `delete from user_preferences where userID=${inData.userID}`
  );
});
```

After that, any time the `clearPreferences` message is received, the callback function is executed and, in this case, a database query is executed to delete the preferences for the specified user (don't get hung up on the database stuff, it's not relevant for our needs here, it's simply an example).

Now, let's say you're migrating that web app to Flutter. On the Dart side, the concepts are the same, but the syntax is slightly different. There, rather than `emit()` to send a message, you use the aptly named `sendMessage()` method instead:

```
io.sendMessage("clearPreferences", { "userID" : "user123" });
```

As you can see, aside from the different method name, it looks identical. Similarly, registering a callback for a message is almost the same, but with Dart, you use the `subscribe()` method instead of `on()`:

```
io.subscribe("preferencesCleared", () {
  // Do something... or not - your choice!
});
```

To be clear, you can subscribe for messages on both the client and server, because of course, the server can emit messages to the client. I only mention this because we're not going to be writing a server in Dart and Flutter here, but the concept applies regardless because the line between client and server when working with WebSockets and socket.io is nebulous. There's nothing that really makes one device a client and one a server other than in a logical sense. That's the power of this mechanism!

As you can see, whether with the JavaScript version or the Dart version, whether the client-side or server-side of the equation, the socket.io API is incredibly simple yet simultaneously extremely powerful. It also offers more advanced capabilities, such as namespaces and rooms, which allow you to segregate messages into logical groupings, to name a few. However, for what we're doing in FlutterChat, this is about all you'll need to know. There's only one small bit beyond this related to establishing the connection, but that will be easier to explain within the context of FlutterChat's server code, which is what we're going to look at right now!

FlutterChat Server Code

To begin the server code, we have to create a Node app. Doing so is very simple: create an empty directory, and then execute the following in it:

```
npm init
```

"What the heck is NPM now?! You didn't mention that before!" I hear you exclaiming. Relax, it's easy to explain!

NPM is the Node Package Manager, and it's a tool that comes with Node that... wait for it... *manages packages*! Packages are just extra libraries and modules that can be added to a Node app, downloaded from a central repository that NPM knows about.

However, NPM does a few other things too, one of which is initializing a project. The result of executing the preceding command will be an interactive process that asks you some simple questions about your app, most of which frankly don't matter for our purposes here, so you could either accept the defaults or enter almost anything. The end result is what matters, and that's that will be a few files created in the directory, most importantly the one named `package.json`. This file describes your app to NPM and, ultimately, Node. It serves an analogous function to the `pubspec.yaml` file in a Flutter app, allowing you to specify things like dependencies. And, as luck would have it, that's precisely the thing we need to do!

Here, we have a choice: we could edit the `package.json` file, looking for the dependencies section, or add it if not present, and add the one dependency we need, socket.io, like so:

```
"dependencies": {
    "socket.io": "2.2.0"
}
```

After that, we can execute another command:

```
npm install
```

Doing that will cause NPM to read the `package.json` file, see the dependencies that are required, and install them for us from a central repository. Alternatively, we can skip editing the file directly and instead just execute this command:

```
npm install socket.io –save
```

This will cause NPM to download socket.io, "install" it into our project (which means creating a `node_modules` directory and putting socket.io's code there), and also automatically add the dependency to `package.json`. Either approach results in the same thing, but which way you prefer to do things is up to you. One difference to be aware of though is that the second approach results in your project getting the latest version of the requested module. This will usually be what you want, but if you need to specify a version explicitly, then you'll probably want to start with editing `package.json` (there are ways to specify a version from the command line, but that's a little more advanced).

Either way, once that's done, we're ready to start coding up the server.

Note   If you've download the source code for this book, which you most definitely should have done, you'll need to go to a command prompt in the `flutter_chat_server` directory and execute `npm install` before you can do anything else. Once that's done, you should be able to start the server by executing `npm start`. Because of the `main` property in `package.json`, npm knows that `server.js` is the main entry point to the app, and it will start Node, passing that file as an argument to it. Alternatively, you could do it manually by executing `node server.js`. Either way should get you to the same place, a running FlutterChat server.

Two Bits of State and an Object Walk into a Bar...

We're going to keep the server code as simple as possible, and part of that means there will be no persistence of any sort of data. Any data, or state, will only exist in memory while the server is running. That of course means that if the server restarts, then everything will be lost, but we can view that as a feature rather than a bug: it means the server is arguably more secure (to be clear, this app is in no way, shape, or form FBI/CIA/NSA-quality in terms of security – *far* from it).

With that said, we'll start by creating a `server.js` file that will house all our server code. In it, the first bit of code you find is this:

```
const users = { };
```

That's a map of users. This map will be keyed by username, and the value of each object, which we'll term a *user descriptor object*, will be in this form:

```
{ userName : "", password : "" }
```

Pretty simple, right?

After that, we have another map, this one for rooms:

```
const rooms = { };
```

The structure of the objects here, our *room descriptor objects*, are keyed by room name and will be in this form:

```
{ roomName : "", description : "", maxPeople : 99,
  private : true|false, creator : "",
  users : [
    <username> : { userName : "" }, ...
  ]
}
```

Each room can have a `description` to tell users what the topic of conversation is, and we'll also be able to specify the maximum number of users allowed in a room when the room is created via the `maxPeople` property. The `private` property tells us whether the room is private (`true`) or not (`false`) of course, and `creator` is the name of the user that created the room. The `users` map is keyed by username and is the collection of users currently in the room.

Those two variables are all the state the server needs to keep.

After that, we have a single object to create, and that's our socket.io object. It's done in a single line of code:

```
const io = require("socket.io")(
  require("http").createServer(
    function() {}
  ).listen(80)
);
```

I've formatted it here in a way that I hope is a bit clearer than the single, long line you'll find in the download bundle. The basic gist is that we create an HTTP server, which is something Node is very good at, by importing the `http` module, one of the many that Node ships with, which gives us an object of course, as a require() call does. Rather than keep the reference to the object, since I don't need it after this, I instead immediately call the createServer() method on it, passing it an empty function. Typically, without socket.io in the mix, you would go on to implement code in this function that would listen for requesting and respond to them – making web servers in Node is a piece of cake like this! Here though, since socket.io will be taking on that responsibility, an empty function is sufficient to fulfill the contract of the createServer() call. The value returned by the createServer() call is then started up by telling it to listen() for incoming requests on port 80, just like a good little HTTP server usually does!

However, since we're using socket.io for this project, we have one more step, which is to take the return value from the listen() call, which is a fully active HTTP server at that point, and pass it to the socket.io default constructor. This allows socket.io to take control of the server and implement its deepest, darkest black magic on it to make it a proper WebSocket server.

Of course, this server won't respond to anything at this point because we haven't told it what to respond to and how, but that's exactly what comes next!

The Big Hookup: Messages

It all starts with telling the socket.io server how to respond to the connection message, which is one of the few that socket.io itself defines:

```
io.on("connection", io => {
  console.log("\n\nConnection established with a client");
  // More stuff (coming soon to a chapter near you!)
});
```

Inside the function passed as the second argument to the io.on() call, we have a console.log() call so that we'll see a message in the console when a client connects. Then, there's... stuff... and that's it!

The "stuff" I'm referring to here is what the remainder of this chapter deals with: defining our app-specific messages and the code to execute in response to each. These message handler functions must be hooked up inside the handler for the connection message, so that's exactly what that comment there represents.

So now, let's see the first bit of that "stuff": the validate message handler.

Getting Through the Front Door: Validating a User

For all of the message handlers discussed from here on out, I'll show you a diagram that details the data coming into the handler (inData), as well as the data going out of the handler whether via callback or broadcast message (or both). A small handful of the handlers have some variation in their output depending on what happens in them, and that will be shown too as an alternate path. You should refer to these diagrams as you look at the code to get a holistic view of the data flow in and out of them. To begin with, Figure 7-4 shows such a diagram for the first handler we're discussing.

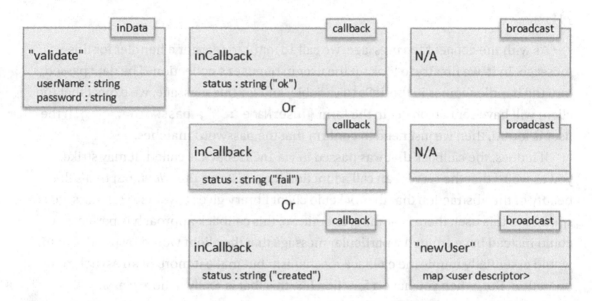

Figure 7-4. *Messaging details for the validate message handler*

The first thing that occurs when a user starts up the FlutterChat app on their mobile device is they are prompted for a username and a password (if it's their first time – subsequent times will do this automatically for them). They enter their credentials, and then the code emits a `validate` message. The server needs to respond to this to determine if the user is valid or not, and the code for it is as follows:

```
io.on("validate", (inData, inCallback) => {

  const user = users[inData.userName];
  if (user) {
    if (user.password === inData.password) {
```

273

```
        inCallback({ status : "ok" });
      } else {
        inCallback({ status : "fail" });
      }
    } else {
      users[inData.userName] = inData;
      io.broadcast.emit("newUser", users);
      inCallback({ status : "created" });
    }

  });
```

As with the `connection` message, we call `io.on()` to register a handler for this
message. In it, we first try to look up the user in our `users` collection. The data passed
into the handler comes in the `inData` variable, and for this message, we expect that the
client will have sent an object in the form `{ userName : "", password : "" }`. If the
user is found, then we just need to confirm that the password matches.

If it does, the callback that was passed in via `inCallback` is called. It may strike
you as weird that the server can call a function that exists on the *client*, but that's the
beauty of the abstraction that the socket.io client library gives us! Since this message is
specific to this user, there is nothing to emit. So, this callback approach is perfect. We
could instead have emitted a particular message that the client would respond to, which
would essentially mimic the callback mechanism but make it more of an asynchronous
operation. But, when you have a function like this that is really a more classic
request-response type of thing, the callback approach makes more sense.

If the password matches, we send back an object `{ status : "ok" }`. Otherwise,
we send back `{ status : "fail" }`. This "object with a `status` property" you'll see
is common to all the message handlers here, though it's entirely application-specific.
I could have just returned simple strings here instead, but I like the idea of all my calls
having the same basic sort of structure both on the input and output side, so I settled
on this paradigm (and, given that not all of the response are simple status messages,
consistently passing an object is, err, *consistent*!). But remember, socket.io doesn't
care; you can send and receive anything you like (as long as it can be marshaled and
unmarshaled on both sides of the communication).

As you'll see in the next chapter, these objects get marshaled into Dart maps, which
is precisely what we want and makes it easy to pass arbitrary data back and forth.

Now, if the user isn't found, that means this is a new user (or that the server has restarted, or that the user cleared the data for the app on their device). In all cases, we add the user to the `users` collection. Then, we do two things: make a call to `io.broadcast.emit()`, and then call the callback. Calling the callback you already understand, but what's the deal with `io.broadcast.emit()`?

The deal here is we want to let all connected clients know that there is a new user on the server. Remember that the app is going to have the ability to show a list of users on the server. Broadcasting this message provides an updated list of users on the server (as you can see, it's the second argument to `io.broadcast.emit()`, after the message to emit) which the app will then use to update the list on the screen, if it's showing. As you'll see in the next chapter, this results in the ScopedModel being updated with the list of users, so if the user list screen is showing it will automatically refresh, and if it's not, then no harm is done.

So yes, you absolutely can broadcast messages and call the callback from the same handler (and you can emit as many messages as you need, not just one, and technically you could call the callback multiple times, though I'm not sure why you'd ever want to do that).

That wasn't so tough, was it? Nah, pretty easy! That's a common theme in the remaining message handlers, thanks to socket.io, and in fact, I would suggest that this handler was probably the most complex of the bunch! Let's look at the next one and see!

Playing Carpenter: Creating a Room

The first function the server needs to support after validating users is the creation of rooms, diagrammed in Figure 7-5.

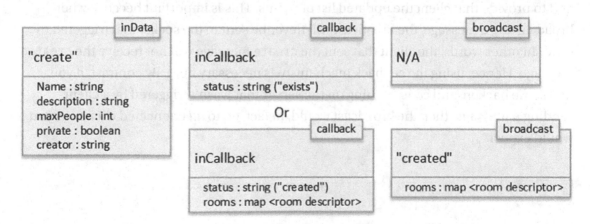

Figure 7-5. *Messaging details for the create message handler*

The code behind this is as follows:

```
io.on("create", (inData, inCallback) => {

  if (rooms[inData.roomName]) {
    inCallback({ status : "exists" });
  } else {
    inData.users = { };
    rooms[inData.roomName] = inData;
    io.broadcast.emit("created", rooms);
    inCallback({ status : "created", rooms : rooms });
  }

});
```

A quick check in the rooms collection tells us whether the room exists already or not, and if so an object with status of exists is sent back so the app can notify the user of this. Otherwise, an empty users collection is added to the incoming object, which is now our room descriptor object, and then that object is attached to the rooms collection by roomName.

Then, to alert all clients to the existence of this new room, the created message is emitted. The complete list of rooms is sent to all clients (not the most efficient mechanism, I admit, but it makes things simpler and, unless you've got an enormous number of rooms, really isn't *that* big a deal – again, I'm not claiming this is cloud-scale, production-ready code that can be used to support thousands of users!).

Finally, the callback is called to tell the user creating the room that the job was done and to provide that client the updated list of rooms. This is important because when broadcasting a message, the broadcast will never be sent to the socket that triggered the send. In other words, the client that sent the create message will not receive the created message. Hence, using the callback mechanism is necessary here. By contrast, if you had some background code running on the server that wasn't triggered by a client sending a message, then the broadcast would, in fact, go to *all* connected clients, as you would expect.

Show Me the Mon...err, Rooms: Listing Rooms

Now that we have a way to create rooms, it would be nice to have a way to list them, wouldn't it? I think you'll agree the answer is yes! For that, we'll have a `listRooms` message, and Figure 7-6 shows you that.

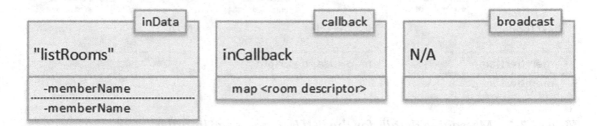

Figure 7-6. *Messaging details for the listRooms message handler*

I hope you're ready for some heavy typing because this code is a doozy. Are you ready? Are you *really* prepared for how overwhelmingly voluminous it's going to be? Okay then, here it comes:

```
io.on("listRooms", (inData, inCallback) => {

  inCallback(rooms);

});
```

Yep, that's it! All we have to do is return the `rooms` collection to the caller's callback function. This `listRooms` message is only needed in one case: when the user goes to the lobby screen for the first time. Remember that the `create` message handler broadcasts a complete list of rooms to all clients any time a room is created (and, as you'll see later, any time a room is closed). So, the clients will have an updated list of rooms any time those things happen, but they won't have it to begin with after a login. So, `listRooms` is sent in that case, but as you'll see in the next chapter, it's actually sent any time the user goes to the lobby. It's a bit redundant to do that given what the `create` (and `close`) message handlers do, but there's no harm in it either, and it makes the code simpler.

But, regardless, this is all the handler for this message needs to do, that's the bottom line. Oh yeah, and one final note: `inData` isn't needed here, but the handler function will always be passed something in its place, whether you need it or not or whether it is an empty object or even null or not, so we have to have it in the arguments' list of the anonymous function just to satisfy the API contract.

Don't Leave the People Out: Listing Users

Just like getting a list of rooms, we need to be able to get a list of users, and Figure 7-7 shows you what that's all about, and hopefully, it looks pretty familiar to you.

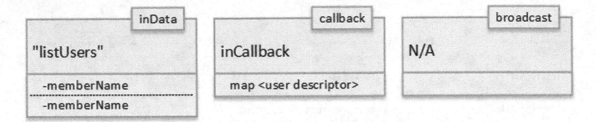

Figure 7-7. *Messaging details for the listUsers message handler*

The I/O model is the same as listing rooms, and so too is the code:

```
io.on("listUsers", (inData, inCallback) => {

  inCallback(users);

});
```

And, just like listing rooms, the clients will maintain a list of users on the server and will be notified any time a new user registers (though for users there is no way to "exit" the server, so no analogy to closing a room). But, they still need to get a list the first time, or, as you'll see, any time the user goes to the user list screen, just like going to the lobby for rooms.

A Knock at the Door: Joining a Room

Now that we can create and list rooms, the next step is being able to enter, or join, a room, and that's where the join message handler comes into play, with Figure 7-8 being your visual guide to that.

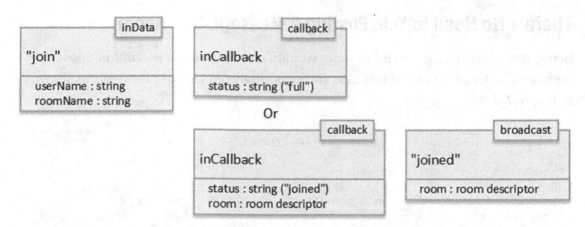

Figure 7-8. *Messaging details for the join message handler*

This one requires a little bit of logic, but not much, as you can see:

```
io.on("join", (inData, inCallback) => {
  const room = rooms[inData.roomName];
  if (Object.keys(room.users).length >= rooms.maxPeople) {
    inCallback({ status : "full" });
  } else {
    room.users[inData.userName] = users[inData.userName];
    io.broadcast.emit("joined", room);
    inCallback({status : "joined", room : room });
  }
});
```

First, we get a reference to the room descriptor object based on the requested name. Next, a check is done to see if the room is already full, and if so, an object with a status of full is returned. In that case, the client will tell the user they can't enter.

If the room isn't full though, then the user descriptor object for the inData.userName sent in is looked up in the users collection and is added to the users collection in the room descriptor object. That way, the room knows what users are in it.

Finally, a joined message is broadcast to all clients and, as with creating a room, the callback is called to provide the sender with the same information, which is the room descriptor object. The client will then navigate the user to the room screen and populate the list of users in the room, all of which you'll see in the next chapter. For any clients not in the room, this message will effectively be ignored since it isn't relevant to them.

279

There's No Need to Yell: Posting a Message to a Room

Being able to create, list, and join a room wouldn't be much use if we couldn't post messages, so let's take care of that next via the boringly named post message, as shown in Figure 7-9.

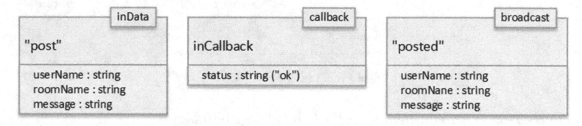

Figure 7-9. Messaging details for the post message handler

The handler for this is, perhaps surprisingly, sparse:

```
io.on("post", (inData, inCallback) => {

  io.broadcast.emit("posted", inData);
  inCallback({ status : "ok" });

});
```

This is a simple task: there's actually no persistence of messages involved, so all we have to do is relay the message to all connected clients via a broadcast of the posted message, along with the incoming data, which includes what room the message is for, what user posted it, and obviously the message itself. As with join message, any clients that aren't in the room at the time will ignore this message because it's irrelevant to them. Finally, although it's not technically necessary, the callback is called with a simple status of ok, just to ensure consistency of all these handlers.

Psst! Hey! You! Get in Here: Inviting a User to a Room

Once you're in a room, you can invite other users to join you. For this, a client sends an invite message, as Figure 7-10 details.

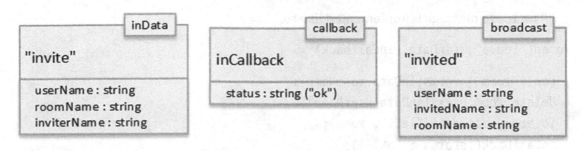

Figure 7-10. *Messaging details for the invite message handler*

The code behind this looks an awful lot like the handler for posting a message, as it turns out:

```
io.on("invite", (inData, inCallback) => {

  io.broadcast.emit("invited", inData);
  inCallback({ status : "ok" });

});
```

Although this obviously is for a specific user, the server has no way to identify a specific user's socket. Therefore, the invited message is broadcast to all clients, and only the one for the specified userName, which is included in inData (along with the room they're invited to and who invited them), will react. As with the post handler, the callback is called regardless of it not really being needed, just for the sake of consistency.

Okay, That's It, I've Had Enough: Leaving a Room

A user can leave a room any time they wish – this isn't a social prison after all! Figure 7-11 proves this is the case.

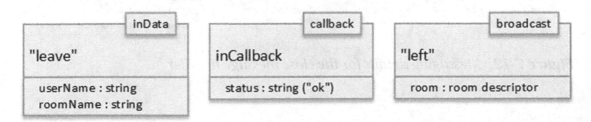

Figure 7-11. *Messaging details for the leave message handler*

The `leave` message is implemented like so:

```
io.on("leave", (inData, inCallback) => {

  const room = rooms[inData.roomName];
  delete room.users[inData.userName];
  io.broadcast.emit("left", room);
  inCallback({status : "ok" });

});
```

What it means for a user to leave a room is that they must be removed from the `users` collection in the room descriptor object for the named room, so first we get a reference to the room descriptor object, and then the user is deleted from the `users` collection thanks to this object being keyed by `userName`. After that, the code just has to emit the `left` message to give all clients an updated list of users in the room (really the entire room descriptor object, of which the list of users is part), and then a call to the callback is made so the client can complete its work of exiting the user from the room.

You Ain't Got to Go Home, but You Can't Stay Here: Closing a Room

Finally, we come to the first of the two creator functions that can only be used by the person who created a room, which are also the final two messages we need to look at. The first is for closing a room, with Figure 7-12 showing you the way.

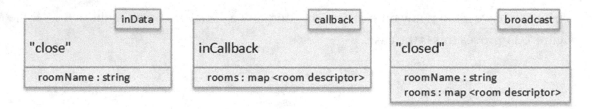

Figure 7-12. Messaging details for the close message handler

The code involved is short and sweet:

```
io.on("close", (inData, inCallback) => {

  delete rooms[inData.roomName];
  io.broadcast.emit("closed",
    { roomName : inData.roomName, rooms : rooms }
  );
  inCallback(rooms);

});
```

Closing a room results in the close message being sent and takes little more than deleting the room descriptor from the rooms collection and then broadcasting to clients the closed message with an updated list of rooms and the name of the room that was closed, plus calling the callback so that the caller has the same information. For the initiating client, they already know what room is being closed, so there's no need to send them the name of the room. But, for those receiving the broadcast, they will look at the roomName, and if it matches the name of the room they're in, then they will be booted out and told that the room was closed.

Somebody's Acting the Fool: Kicking a User Out of a Room

Finally, we have the kick message, which is sent by a room creator to forcibly remove a user from that room, as shown in Figure 7-13.

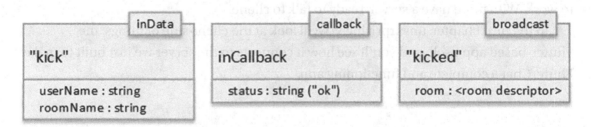

Figure 7-13. *Messaging details for the kick message handler*

There's only slightly more work involved in this creator function, as you can see for yourself:

```
io.on("kick", (inData, inCallback) => {

  const room = rooms[inData.roomName];
  const users = room.users;
  delete users[inData.userName];
  io.broadcast.emit("kicked", room);
  inCallback({ status : "ok" });

});
```

This requires getting the room descriptor object out of the `rooms` collection, then the `users` collection within it, and then deleting the user from it. After that, a `kicked` message is broadcast and sent to the updated room descriptor so that all users who are in that room can update the list of users in the room. The callback is called even though it's not required.

And with that final message handler, we have ourselves a complete server that implements all the functionality we need to make FlutterChat work!

Summary

In this chapter, we built the server side of the FlutterChat equation. Here, you got a look at Node and socket.io and saw the messages that needed to be implemented for the app to work. With it, we have a server, ready to talk to clients.

In the next chapter, unsurprisingly, we'll look at the client-side of things, the Flutter-based app itself, and you'll see how it connects to the server we just built to make FlutterChat a complete and functioning app.

CHAPTER 8

FlutterChat, Part II: The Client

In the previous chapter, we built the server side of FlutterChat, providing a WebSocket/socket.io-based API for the client-side of the app to use.

Now, it's time to build that client-side. Get ready, here comes FlutterChat: Flutter edition!

Model.dart

Although it might seem odd, rather than starting in the usual `main.dart` file, we're instead going to start with the source file `Model.dart`, which contains the code for the single scoped model that this app will use (so, as you saw with FlutterBook, `scoped_model` is a dependency in `pubspec.yaml` here as well). This file contains the class `FlutterChatModel` that extends from `Model` and includes the following properties:

- `BuildContext rootBuildContext` – The BuildContext of the root widget of the app. You'll see why this is needed shortly, but note that while it's not state per se, it is required in multiple places, so it makes some sense to be here. But, since there's never a case where we'd need to set it and call `notifyListeners()`, there's no explicit setter for it; the default is sufficient.

- `Directory docsDir` – The app's documents directory. See the comment about `rootBuildContext` and why it's in the model but with no explicit setter because it applies to this property as well.

- `String greeting = ""` – The greeting text that will be shown on the home screen (the first one the user sees, and where they wind up after various operations within the app like leaving a room).

© Frank Zammetti 2019

F. Zammetti, *Practical Flutter*, https://doi.org/10.1007/978-1-4842-4972-7_8

- `String userName = ""` – The username, obviously!

- `static final String DEFAULT_ROOM_NAME = "Not currently in a room"` – The text that will be shown on the `AppDrawer` when the user isn't in a room.

- `String currentRoomName = DEFAULT_ROOM_NAME` – The name of the room the user is currently in, otherwise the default string to indicate they aren't in a room at all.

- `List currentRoomUserList = []` – The list of users in the room the user is currently in.

- `bool currentRoomEnabled = false` – Whether the Current Room item on the `AppDrawer` is enabled (would only be if the user is in a room).

- `List currentRoomMessages = []` – The list of messages in the room the user is currently in since they entered.

- `List roomList = []` – The current list of rooms on the server.

- `List userList = []` – The current list of users on the server.

- `bool creatorFunctionsEnabled = false` – Whether the creator functions (Close Room and Kick User) are enabled or not.

- `Map roomInvites = {}` – The list of invites this user has received.

Note   For brevity, I've skipped printing all the imports in this and all source files going forward. If there are any new and exciting imports, I'll mention them, but otherwise, you can assume they're only modules you're already familiar with.

This is a typical model class like you saw in FlutterBook, so there are a series or property setters, like this one for greeting:

```
void setGreeting(final String inGreeting) {
  greeting = inGreeting;
  notifyListeners();
}
```

At the end, notifyListeners() is called so that any code interested in this change can react to it.

Just to save a little space, we'll skip looking at setUserName(), setCurrentRoom(), setCreatorFunctionsEnabled(), and setCurrentRoomEnabled() as they are the same as setGreeting(), just referencing a different property obviously.

Instead, let's jump to addMessage(), which is a bit different and is what will be called when the server informs the client of a new message having been posted to a room:

```
void addMessage(final String inUserName,
  final String inMessage) {
  currentRoomMessages.add({ "userName" : inUserName,
    "message" : inMessage });
  notifyListeners();
}
```

Here, instead of a simple property set, we need to use the add() method of the currentRoomMessages property since it's a List.

In a similar way, the setRoomList() method works a little differently:

```
void setRoomList(final Map inRoomList) {
  List rooms = [ ];
  for (String roomName in inRoomList.keys) {
    Map room = inRoomList[roomName];
    rooms.add(room);
  }
  roomList = rooms;
  notifyListeners();
}
```

We again are updating a List, so we use the add() method again, but this time the inRoomList the function is sent is a Map. So, we need to iterate the keys in that Map, and then, for each, pull out the room descriptor and add it to the rooms List.

After that is a setUserList() method and a setCurrentRoomUserList() method, and those are the same as setRoomList(), except for dealing with users instead of rooms, of course, so we can skip those as well.

Next up is the addRoomInvite() method:

```
void addRoomInvite(final String inRoomName) {
  roomInvites[inRoomName] = true;
}
```

An invite to a room results in a SnackBar being shown to the user for a few seconds. After it goes away, we still need to know if the user can enter a given private room, so the roomInvites collection is keyed by room name and where the value of each is a boolean. If true, then we'll know later that the user has an invite to the room and can enter. We'll also then need a way to remove an invite when a room is closed; otherwise, if someone creates a room with the same name, then a user may incorrectly appear to have an invite for the room, so we have the removeRoomInvite() method for that:

```
void removeRoomInvite(final String inRoomName) {
  roomInvites.remove(inRoomName);
}
```

When a user leaves a room, there will be some cleanup tasks as you'll see later, and one of those is clearing out the list of messages for the room, so we have the aptly named clearCurrentRoomMessages() method for that:

```
void clearCurrentRoomMessages() {
  currentRoomMessages = [ ];
}
```

Finally, an instance of this model is created:

```
FlutterChatModel model = FlutterChatModel();
```

That'll be the one and only instance of it used throughout the app, and with that, this source file is complete, and we have a scoped model ready for use!

Connector.dart

The next thing we're going to look at is the Connector.dart file. The goal with this file is to have a single module that communicates with the server and that the rest of the app uses. This keeps us from having duplicate code all over the place and keeps us from having to import some modules in multiple places (e.g., socket.io). For this file, we need two imports that are new to you:

```
import "package:flutter_socket_io/flutter_socket_io.dart";
import "package:flutter_socket_io/socket_io_manager.dart";
```

These are, obviously, the two imports needed to use socket.io. There are only two classes we're interested in: SocketIO from the flutter_socket_io.dart library and SocketIOManager from the socket_io_manager.dart library. But I'm getting ahead of myself a bit!

The actual code begins simply enough:

```
String serverURL = "http://192.168.9.42";
```

When you run the app, you'll need to change this to the IP address where your server is running. As a test of your abilities to this point, I offer you a suggestion: try to add a field for IP address to the login dialog that we'll be looking at the code for soon. That way, this hardcoding of server address can become dynamic and the app more useful as a result.

After that, we find a single instance of the SocketIO class:

```
SocketIO _io;
```

Well, technically that's a declaration of it, not an instance of it yet! That instance will be constructed very soon though. But before we get to that, we have two utility functions to talk about. Any time the server is called, the app will show a "please wait" mask over the screen. This keeps the user from doing anything that might break things and lets them know that communication is occurring. In many cases, the operation will be so fast that the user will see at most a flash on the screen, but that's fine. If an operation takes longer though, then this mask is nice to see. We're going to use a simple dialog for this, as you can start to see:

```
void showPleaseWait() {

  showDialog(context : model.rootBuildContext,
    barrierDismissible : false,
    builder : (BuildContext inDialogContext) {
      return Dialog(
        child : Container(width : 150, height : 150,
```

```
      alignment : AlignmentDirectional.center,
      decoration :
        BoxDecoration(color : Colors.blue[200])
```

The showDialog() function that you've seen before is called, and here we can see where that rootBuildContext model property comes into play. The issue is that this mask must mask the *entire* screen, the *entire* widget tree, not just some subset of it. So, we'll always want to set the context to that of the root widget. However, normally, that's not accessible from everywhere in the code. So, as you'll see when we look at the main.dart file next, we'll capture a reference to that widget during startup and set it on the model so it's available here and anywhere else it might be needed.

Setting the barrierDismissable property to false is key because, otherwise, the user would be able to dismiss our please wait dialog, which would defeat the purpose of it. After that, we're just building an ordinary dialog. The content of it boils down to some text to tell them what's going on and a spinning CircularProgressIndicator:

```
child : Column(
  crossAxisAlignment : CrossAxisAlignment.center,
  mainAxisAlignment : MainAxisAlignment.center,
  children : [
    Center(child : SizedBox(height : 50, width : 50,
      child : CircularProgressIndicator(
        value : null, strokeWidth : 10)
    )),
    Container(margin : EdgeInsets.only(top : 20),
      child : Center(child :
        Text("Please wait, contacting server...",
        style : new TextStyle(color : Colors.white)
      ))
    )
  ]
)
```

Placing the CircularProgressIndicator inside a SizedBox with a specific width and height gives us some control over the size of the indicator. It may seem odd to set the value property to null and never update it, but doing this causes the indicator to show an animation for an "indeterminant" ongoing operation. In simpler terms: it shows a spinning animation! If you had a finite operation, then you could update this value property little by little to give a real indication of the overall progress, but that's not the situation here. Note that I also set the strokeWidth to make the indicator fatter than usual, which I just felt looked better.

We also need a way to hide this dialog once the server responds, so we have the hidePleaseWait() function:

```
void hidePleaseWait() {
  Navigator.of(model.rootBuildContext).pop();
}
```

This is the usual way to hide a dialog, so nothing new, other than it must again make use of the rootBuildContext to get a reference to the dialog as it was shown.

Next up is the connectToServer() function, which you'll find is called from the login dialog once the user enters their credentials:

```
void connectToServer(final BuildContext inMainBuildContext,
  final Function inCallback) {
  _io = SocketIOManager().createSocketIO(
    serverURL, "/", query : "",
    socketStatusCallback : (inData) {
      if (inData == "connect") {
        _io.subscribe("newUser", newUser);
        _io.subscribe("created", created);
        _io.subscribe("closed", closed);
        _io.subscribe("joined", joined);
        _io.subscribe("left", left);
        _io.subscribe("kicked", kicked);
        _io.subscribe("invited", invited);
        _io.subscribe("posted", posted);
        inCallback();
      }
    }
  );
  _io.init();
  _io.connect();
}
```

Here is where that SocketIO object I mentioned earlier is created via the
SocketIOManager.createSocketIO() call and passing it the serverURL. This method
also takes a path and a query, neither of which are needed for this app, so default values
"/" and an empty string are passed for those (the first can be used if you set your server
up to listen at something like myserver.com/my/socket/io, and the query property can
be used to send arbitrary query parameters along with each request, perhaps for an
authentication mechanism on top of socket.io).

The socketStatusCallback property takes a function to call when the underlying
WebSocket's status changes. Several statuses can come back, but only one is essential to us
here: the connect status. This indicates a WebSocket connection has been established with
the server. When that happens, only then can we define the handlers for various messages
that the server can emit to clients. These are termed "subscriptions" to those messages, so
the subscribe() method is called, passing it the message and the handler function for it.

Finally, the init() and connect() methods must be called to actually initiate
the connection with the server and, if all goes well, get the callback defined earlier to
execute. Once that's done, our client is now able to emit a message to the server and
handle messages emitted by the server.

Server-Bound Message Functions

First, we'll look at functions that emit messages to the server, and the first such function,
called from the login dialog to validate what the user enters, is the validate() function:

```
void validate(final String inUserName, final String
  inPassword, final Function inCallback) {
    showPleaseWait();
    _io.sendMessage("validate",
      "{ \"userName\" : \"$inUserName\", "
      "\"password\" : \"$inPassword\" }",
      (inData) {
        Map<String, dynamic> response = jsonDecode(inData);
        hidePleaseWait();
        inCallback(response["status"]);
      }
    );
  }
```

The function takes in the user's name, their password, and a reference to a function to call when the server responds. To start, the showPleaseWait() function that we looked at earlier is called to mask the screen. Then, the sendMessage() method on the _io object is called, sending the server the validate message and a string of JSON that includes the user name and password. The callback function uses the Flutter/Dart-provided jsonDecode() function to generate a Dart Map that contains the data that was returned. Then, hidePleaseWait() is called to unmask the screen, and then the callback is called, passing it the status property from the Map.

In some cases, the entire Map will be sent to the callback, as is the case for the next function, listRooms():

```
void listRooms(final Function inCallback) {
  showPleaseWait();
  _io.sendMessage("listRooms", "{}", (inData) {
    Map<String, dynamic> response = jsonDecode(inData);
    hidePleaseWait();
    inCallback(response);
  });
}
```

These two functions, their basic structure, are replicated several times in other functions. The basic idea of showing please wait, sending a message, then in the callback decoding the response into a Map, hiding please wait, and sending the callback either certain properties from the Map or the entire Map repeatedly appears in them. The only difference is of course what message is sent, what arguments it takes, and what the server sends back. As such, I'm going to just summarize those functions here:

- create() – Called to create a room from the lobby screen. This is passed the name of the room, it's descriptor, the max number of people, whether it's private or not, the name of the creating user (the creator), and a callback (which is passed the status and rooms properties from the response, the latter of which is a complete and updated list of rooms on the server including the new one).

- join() – Called when the user clicks on a room from the room list on the lobby screen to join (or enter) it. This is passed the user's name, the room's name, and the callback (which is passed the status property from the response and the room descriptor).

- leave() – Called when the user leaves the room they're currently in. This is passed the user's name, the room's name, and the callback (which is passed nothing).

- listUsers() – Called to get an updated list of users on the server when the user selects the user list from the AppDrawer. This is passed just the callback, which is passed the entire response: a map of users.

- invite() – Called when the user invites another user to the room. This is passed the name of the user being invited, the name of the room they're being invited to, the name of the user inviting them, and the callback (which is passed nothing).

- post() – Called to post a message to the current room. This is passed the user's name, the room's name, the message being posted, and the callback (which is passed the status property from the response).

- close() – Called by the creator to close a room. This is passed the room's name and the callback (which is passed nothing).

- kick() – Called by the creator to kick a user from a room. This is passed the user's name, the room's name, and the callback (which is passed nothing).

Client-Bound Message Handlers

The next group of functions to look at deal with messages coming in from the server. These function names mimic the name of the message emitted by the server, the first of which is newUser():

```
void newUser(inData) {
  Map<String, dynamic> payload = jsonDecode(inData);
  model.setUserList(payload);
}
```

This is called when a new user is created. The server sends a complete list of users, and this function just sets that in the model.

The created() function, which handles the case where a new room is created, looks the same as newUser() except that it calls model.setRoomList() instead, so let's skip that one and get to one that's a bit different, closed():

```
void closed(inData) {
  Map<String, dynamic> payload = jsonDecode(inData);
  model.setRoomList(payload);
  if (payload["roomName"] == model.currentRoomName) {
    model.removeRoomInvite(payload["roomName"]);
    model.setCurrentRoomUserList({});
    model.setCurrentRoomName(
      FlutterChatModel.DEFAULT_ROOM_NAME);
    model.setCurrentRoomEnabled(false);
    model.setGreeting(
      "The room you were in was closed by its creator.");
    Navigator.of(model.rootBuildContext
    ).pushNamedAndRemoveUntil("/", ModalRoute.withName("/"));
  }
}
```

Here, we have a bit more work to do! First, the updated list of rooms is set in the model. Next, if the room that was closed is the one the user is currently in, then we have some cleanup to do. If there's an invite for this room, it must be removed (to avoid this user incorrectly having an invite for a room created with the same name later), and the list of users for the current room is cleared. The default text for what room the user is in is set, which will be reflected in the AppDrawer's header (which you'll see later when we look at that code). The Current Room link on the AppDrawer is disabled, and the greeting, which will show up on the home screen, reflects that the room was closed, so the user knows what happened. Finally, we need to navigate to that home screen, and that's accomplished with the help of the pushNamedAndRemoveUntil() method of the Navigator of the rootBuildContext. This ensures we're navigating with the correct Navigator (because you can nest Navigators, so there could be multiple). This function, one of several that can be used for navigation, ensures that we always go all the way back to the home screen and not just one screen. That way, our Navigator is always in a known, consistent state after this move.

When a user other than this user joins a room, the server emits a joined message, so we have a corresponding joined() handler function:

```
void joined(inData) {
  Map<String, dynamic> payload = jsonDecode(inData);
  if (model.currentRoomName == payload["roomName"]) {
    model.setCurrentRoomUserList(payload["users"]);
  }
}
```

We only care about this message when the user is currently in this room, and if they are, then the list of users sent by the server is set in the model. There is also a left() message handler for when a user leaves a room, and that does the same thing essentially, so we'll skip it.

When the room creator kicks a user from the room, the kicked() message handler, uh, *kicks* in! This function is basically the same as closed() because, from the user's perspective, the room in a sense did close – at least to them! The only difference is the text shown on the home screen, which reflects that they were kicked. So, let's save some time and not look at that one. Instead, let's see what happens when a user is invited to a room:

```
void invited(inData) async {
  Map<String, dynamic> payload = jsonDecode(inData);
  String roomName = payload["roomName"];
  String inviterName = payload["inviterName"];
  model.addRoomInvite(roomName);
  Scaffold.of(model.rootBuildContext).showSnackBar(
    SnackBar(backgroundColor : Colors.amber,
      duration : Duration(seconds : 60),
      content : Text("You've been invited to the room "
        "'$roomName' by user '$inviterName'.\n\n"
        "You can enter the room from the lobby."
      ),
      action : SnackBarAction(label : "Ok", onPressed: () {})
    )
  );
}
```

Here, we must pull out some information from the response, namely, the name of the room and the name of the user who invited them. Then, an invite is added for that room so that when (if) they click that private room in the lobby, we'll know to let them in. Then, we must show them a SnackBar to let them know about the invite. We'll leave it up for a full minute, so they (hopefully) don't miss it because otherwise there's no indication that they have an invite (hey, there's another suggested exercise for you: add some sort of indicator the room list in the lobby for that!). We'll also give them an Ok button to dismiss the SnackBar if they wish though, just to be thoughtful.

Finally, we come to the last message handler function, the one for handling messages posted to a room:

```
void posted(inData) {
  Map<String, dynamic> payload = jsonDecode(inData);
  if (model.currentRoomName == payload["roomName"]) {
    model.addMessage(payload["userName"], payload["message"]);
  }
}
```

Once again, we have a message that will be emitted to all users, so we have to ignore any message that isn't for the room this user is currently in. If they are in the room though, then a call to model.addMessage() adds the message to the list of messages for the room and triggers a notification to listeners, which will, of course, result in the message appearing on the screen for this user.

And with that, we now have a complete API for communication with the server against which we can write our client application code. And, the first piece of that puzzle is found in the usual spot: the main.dart file.

main.dart

As with FlutterBook, there are a few tasks to accomplish in main() before building the UI, and since these can take some time, we'll do them first again:

```
void main() {

  startMeUp() async {

    Directory docsDir =
      await getApplicationDocumentsDirectory();
```

297

```
  model.docsDir = docsDir;

  var credentialsFile =
    File(join(model.docsDir.path, "credentials"));
  var exists = await credentialsFile.exists();

  var credentials;
  if (exists) {
    credentials = await credentialsFile.readAsString();
  }
```

Once again, there's a startMeUp() function that will be called at the very end of main(), so we can do some async/await work within it. The first such task is getting the app's documents directory, as you saw in the previous project. That's because we're going to have a file to store the user's username and password – their *credentials*, in other words. So, the next step is to try to read that file. If it exists, then we read it in as a string. We'll deal with that in a moment, but before we do, we'll build the UI:

```
runApp(FlutterChat());
```

We'll get to the FlutterChat class in a moment, but before that, we have to deal with the credentials. The goal here is that if there is a credentials file, then we can immediately validate the user with the server. If there's not such a file, then we have to show them the login dialog. So:

```
if (exists) {

  List credParts = credentials.split("============");
  LoginDialog().validateWithStoredCredentials(credParts[0],
    credParts[1]);

} else {

  await showDialog(context : model.rootBuildContext,
    barrierDismissible : false,
    builder : (BuildContext inDialogContext) {
      return LoginDialog();
    }
  );

}
```

The contents of the file are a simple string in the form xxx=============yyy where xxx is the username and yyy is the password. Why the unusual 12 equals as a delimiter, you ask? Simple: the username and password are both constrained to ten characters, so by having a delimiter two larger than that, it means that even if a user enters ten equal signs for a username (which would be weird, but okay, to each their own!), then we'd still be able to tokenize this string, which is where that split() method comes in. It produces an array of string parts formed by breaking up the string on that 12-character equals delimiter. Yes, I could have used a single character, comma perhaps, and just disallowed commas in the username, but I wanted to give users full reign, even to enter something kind of silly!

As you can see, if the credentials file doesn't exist, then the login dialog is launched. We'll look at that in the next section, so for now, let's keep going. As mentioned, startMeUp() is called after this, and that's where execution really ostensibly begins.

Note   There is an edge case where if a user registers, but then the server restarts, and if a *different* user registers with the original user's userName, and then the original user tries to validate again, it will fail because the password (presumably) won't match. In that case, the code in validateWithStoredCredentials() will delete the credentials file and alert the user to this situation. Upon app restart, they'll be prompted for new credentials.

Now, going back to that FlutterChat class:

```
class FlutterChat extends StatelessWidget {
  @override
  Widget build(final BuildContext context) {
    return MaterialApp(
      home : Scaffold(body : FlutterChatMain())
    );
  }
}
```

It begins with a pattern you should be quite familiar with by now: a `MaterialApp` with a `Scaffold` nestled within it, sleeping comfortably in its... ah, wait, I forgot what kind of book I was writing there for a minute! The body points to the `FlutterChatMain` class, which is where our UI proper begins:

```
class FlutterChatMain extends StatelessWidget {

  @override
  Widget build(final BuildContext inContext) {

    model.rootBuildContext = inContext;
```

As you saw in the `Model.dart` file, the `rootBuildContext` is cached for use by other code, and since that's only introduced in the `build()` method, that's the first thing done. Next, the widget to return is built:

```
return ScopedModel<FlutterChatModel>(model : model,
  child : ScopedModelDescendant<FlutterChatModel>(
  builder : (BuildContext inContext, Widget inChild,
    FlutterChatModel inModel) {
      return MaterialApp(initialRoute : "/",
        routes : {
          "/Lobby" : (screenContext) => Lobby(),
          "/Room" : (screenContext) => Room(),
          "/UserList" : (screenContext) => UserList(),
          "/CreateRoom" : (screenContext) => CreateRoom()
        },
        home : Home()
```

Since we're going to use Flutter's built-in navigation capabilities in this app, rather than the "build it ourselves" approach taken in FlutterBook, the first task is to define the routes (read: screens) of the app. There's four of them: `/Lobby` (room list), `/Room` (inside a room), `/UserList` (the list of users on the server), and `/CreateRoom` (for creating a room of course). These are called *named routes* because, well, they have names! Without these, you can still navigate between screens, but then you have to push manually and pop specific widgets off the navigator stack, which tends to result in a lot of duplicate code all over the place. By using named routes, that code becomes much cleaner, as you saw in the `Connector.dart` code and that you'll see much more of as we progress.

As you can probably guess, the route names can be as complex as you like and can represent a hierarchy too. So, if you have page A, which has two "child" pages 1a and 2a, then you might name them /pageA, /pageA/1a and /pageA/2a. Here, they're all effectively at the same logical level, so I kept it simple (you could argue that since the room and create room screens launch from the lobby that they should be named /Lobby/Room and /Lobby/CreateRoom, and that's a fair argument to make – but either way works, that's kind of the main point here).

The initialRoute tells the Navigator what screen to show by default, and it corresponds to what the home property points to. Note that it's an error to have the home property and then also to specify a route named "/" in the routes map. But, if you drop the home property, then you can have "/" in the map, but then you'd need code to navigate to whatever your initial screen is, so it's usually easier to do it this way and let Flutter and the Navigator do it for you.

LoginDialog.dart

When there is no credentials file stored, the user is shown a login dialog, so they can register with (or be validated by, however you want to term it) the server. This is a standard-looking login dialog, as Figure 8-1 proves.

Figure 8-1. *The login (validate) dialog*

Just enter a username and password and click the Log In button and that's all there is to it. The code behind this starts typically enough:

```
class LoginDialog extends StatelessWidget {

  static final GlobalKey<FormState> _loginFormKey =
    new GlobalKey<FormState>();
```

We'll be dealing with a form, and there will be some validation involved, so we'll need a GlobalKey for it. Ultimately, we'll be populating two variables:

```
String _userName;
String _password;
```

After that comes the build() method:

```
Widget build(final BuildContext inContext) {
  return ScopedModel<FlutterChatModel>(model : model,
    child : ScopedModelDescendant<FlutterChatModel>(
    builder : (BuildContext inContext, Widget inChild,
      FlutterChatModel inModel) {
    return AlertDialog(content : Container(height : 220,
      child : Form(key : _loginFormKey,
        child : Column(children : [
          Text("Enter a username and password to "
            "register with the server",
            textAlign : TextAlign.center, fontSize : 18
            style : TextStyle(color :
              Theme.of(model.rootBuildContext).accentColor)
          ),
          SizedBox(height : 20)
```

As state is involved here, we wrap everything up in ScopedModel and under that a ScopedModelDescendant, a structure you should be familiar with after having looked at FlutterBook. The builder() function then builds the content, which begins with an AlertDialog. The content of that dialog is a Form, referencing the _loginFormKey from before, and then a Column layout begins the visual components, the first of which is the text heading at the top, again taking its color from the currently active Theme of the MaterialApp. Notice how that rootBuildContext is used here because that's the context that we want to take the Theme from. After that is a SizedBox, just to put some empty space between the heading text and the form fields, which come next:

```
TextFormField(
  validator : (String inValue) {
    if (inValue.length == 0 ||
      inValue.length > 10) {
      return "Please enter a username no "
        "more than 10 characters long";
    }
    return null;
  },
```

```
    onSaved : (String inValue) { _userName = inValue; },
    decoration : InputDecoration(
      hintText : "Username", labelText : "Username")
  ),
  TextFormField(obscureText : true,
    validator : (String inValue) {
      if (inValue.length == 0) {
        return "Please enter a password";
      }
      return null;
    },
    onSaved : (String inValue) { _password = inValue; },
    decoration : InputDecoration(
      hintText : "Password", labelText : "Password")
  )
```

There shouldn't be any surprises here by this point. There's a constraint on how many characters can be entered for a username (important, given the tokenization you saw in `main.dart`) and likewise a validation on password to ensure they entered something (ditto username). Otherwise, they're just boring 'ole `TextFormField` widgets!

The Log In button is next, and it's contained within the `actions` collection for the dialog (not so much a "collection" given there's only one, but I digress):

```
actions : [
  FlatButton(child : Text("Log In"),
    onPressed : () {
      if (_loginFormKey.currentState.validate()) {
        _loginFormKey.currentState.save();
        connector.connectToServer(() {
          connector.validate(_userName, _password,
            (inStatus) async {
            if (inStatus == "ok") {
              model.setUserName(_userName);
              Navigator.of(model.rootBuildContext).pop();
              model.setGreeting("Welcome back, $_userName!");
```

When pressed, and assuming the form passes validation, then the current form state is saved, triggering execution of the onSaved handlers on the fields, thus transferring the values into those _userName and _password variables from earlier. Next, a call to connector.connectToServer() is made. As you'll recall, this sets up a connection with the server and configures all the message handlers. This method is passed a callback to be called once the connection is established. This callback function calls the connector.validate() function, which passes the _userName and _password to the server for validation. If the status comes back ok, then the user is already known to the server and the password was correct, so we're good to proceed, which means storing the username in the model, pop()'ing the dialog away, and setting the greeting on the home screen (which we'll be looking at next). If the status is fail though, then a SnackBar is shown to indicate the username is already taken, as you can see here:

```
} else if (inStatus == "fail") {
  Scaffold.of(model.rootBuildContext
  ).showSnackBar(SnackBar(backgroundColor : Colors.red,
    duration : Duration(seconds : 2),
    content : Text("Sorry, that username is already taken")
));
```

The other possible condition is that the username is new to the server, in which case the created message comes back:

```
} else if (inStatus == "created") {
  var credentialsFile = File(join(
    model.docsDir.path, "credentials"));
  await credentialsFile.writeAsString(
    "$_userName=============$_password");
  model.setUserName(_userName);
  Navigator.of(model.rootBuildContext).pop();
  model.setGreeting("Welcome to the server, $_userName!");
}
```

Here, we need to store the credentials in the credentials file, so we create a File object instance, using the join() function to construct the path to the app's documents directory that was retrieved at startup of the app, and then await the writeAsString() method to write out the value, which again is the username and password separated by that oddly long delimiter! After that, we do the same setup as was done in the ok case, but with a slightly different greeting so it's distinct from an existing user logging in.

Existing User Login

Now, although this source file deals with the dialog for logging in, it also contains some code that deals with the case where the app starts and finds an existing credentials file. In that case, the server still has to be consulted, but there's no UI to go through; it happens automatically, which is where the `validateWithStoredCredentials()` function comes into play:

```
void validateWithStoredCredentials(final String inUserName,
  final String inPassword) {

  connector.connectToServer(model.rootBuildContext, () {
    connector.validate(inUserName, inPassword, (inStatus) {
      if (inStatus == "ok" || inStatus == "created") {
        model.setUserName(inUserName);
        model.setGreeting("Welcome back, $inUserName!");
```

As before, `connector.connectToServer()` is first called, and then `connector.validate()` is also called, passing it the username and password sent in, which will have been read from the credentials file. In this case, the logic is a little simpler because, from the perspective of the user, they are an existing user, but it's possible that the server was restarted, in which case, from the server's perspective, this is a new user, as long as the username isn't now taken by someone else. But of course, the server is a machine, so who cares about its feelings, right?! (unless we're in an episode of *Star Trek: The Next Generation*, where Data's personhood is being debated... but that's a much larger conversation!) We *do*, however, care about the user's feelings! So, whether we get back an ok or a `created` message, we'll show the message to indicate the user is a returning user, to make them feel like the server didn't forget them even though it kinda did!

Of course, there's a situation where we can get back fail, and that's if the username was taken by another user, in which case the password almost certainly will be wrong, as described in the logging in the case before. But, in this instance, we know the cause of the password being wrong: another user took this username after the restart and before this user tried logging in. So, we can handle this a little more robustly:

```
} else if (inStatus == "fail") {
  showDialog(context : model.rootBuildContext,
    barrierDismissible : false,
    builder : (final BuildContext inDialogContext) =>
    AlertDialog(title : Text("Validation failed"),
      content : Text("It appears that the server has "
        "restarted and the username you last used "
        "was subsequently taken by someone else. "
        "\n\nPlease re-start FlutterChat and choose "
        "a different username."
      )
```

Since this is basically a "game over" kind of scenario, we show an AlertDialog, and ensure it can't be dismissed in any way other than whatever actions we define, so barrierDismissable is set to false to ensure clicking anywhere outside the dialog doesn't dismiss it, as it the default. The verbiage of the message explains the situation, and then we provide a single Ok button to click in the actions:

```
actions : [
  FlatButton(child : Text("Ok"),
  onPressed : () {
    var credentialsFile = File(join(
      model.docsDir.path, "credentials"));
    credentialsFile.deleteSync();
    exit(0);
  })
]
```

Since we now know that this username can't be used, we need to delete the credentials file to avoid a loop at the next app startup. Finally, the exit() function is called, which is a function Flutter provides to terminate the app (the value passed to it doesn't matter in this case, though it can be used to return a value to the OS if needed). At the next app startup, the user will be prompted for a username and password, altering the flow as we need in this situation.

Now let's see where those greeting messages are used: the home screen.

Home.dart

The home screen, in the Home.dart file, is the first screen the user sees (and also what they get returned to when various events including room closure and being kicked from a room occur) and is a straightforward one, as you can see in Figure 8-2.

Figure 8-2. *The home screen*

The code for it is similarly direct:

```
class Home extends StatelessWidget {
  Widget build(final BuildContext inContext) {
    return ScopedModel<FlutterChatModel>(model : model,
      child : ScopedModelDescendant<FlutterChatModel>(
        builder : (BuildContext inContext, Widget inChild,
          FlutterChatModel inModel) {
          return Scaffold(drawer : AppDrawer(),
            appBar : AppBar(title : Text("FlutterChat")),
            body : Center(child : Text(model.greeting))
          );
        }
      )
    );
  }
}
```

Yep, that's really it! It is, in the final analysis, just a Text widget inside a Center widget. The Text widget will be updated from the model.greeting property to reflect things to the user. It is otherwise unremarkable, so I'll stop remarking on it now!

AppDrawer.dart

The AppDrawer, housed in the AppDrawer.dart file, is how the user navigates around the app and can be glimpsed in Figure 8-3.

309

Figure 8-3. *The app drawer*

At the top, we have a header with a pretty background, above which is shown the user's name and what room they are currently in, if any. Here, you can see that default room name that you saw in the Model.dart code. See, I told you then that you'd eventually come to know why that value is what it is!

The AppDrawer class begins as most that you've seen do:

```
class AppDrawer extends StatelessWidget {
  Widget build(final BuildContext inContext) {
    return ScopedModel<FlutterChatModel>(model : model,
      child : ScopedModelDescendant<FlutterChatModel>(
      builder : (BuildContext inContext, Widget inChild,
        FlutterChatModel inModel) {
```

```
    return Drawer(child : Column(children : [
      Container(decoration : BoxDecoration(image :
        DecorationImage(fit : BoxFit.cover,
          image : AssetImage("assets/drawback01.jpg")
      ))
```

It's ultimately a Drawer widget that is being built, and inside of it is a Column layout. The first item in that layout is a Container that is decorated with a DecorationImage. As the name implies, this is a widget that decorates a box with an image. That image is an AssetImage built from the drawback01.jpg file in the assets directory. Using the BoxFit.cover value for the fit property tells the Flutter to size the image as small as possible but still ensure that it covers the box, which is a good choice for a background image like this.

After that comes the child of the Container, which is where the username and current room are displayed:

```
child : Padding(
  padding : EdgeInsets.fromLTRB(0, 30, 0, 15),
  child : ListTile(
    title : Padding(padding : EdgeInsets.fromLTRB(0,0,0,20),
      child : Center(child : Text(model.userName,
        style : TextStyle(color : Colors.white, fontSize : 24)
    ))
  ),
  subtitle : Center(child : Text(model.currentRoomName,
    style : TextStyle(color : Colors.white, fontSize : 16)
  ))
```

First, a little padding is used to ensure nice spacing around these values. Then, a ListTile is used because I want the username to be bigger and the current room to be smaller, which logically makes them a title and subtitle, respectively. I also throw some padding on the title so that I can control the spacing between these two and avoid them bunching up too much. Of course, the color needs to be something other than the default black; otherwise the text won't show up well on the background, and I also adjust the fontSize to get them looking just how I want. The text displayed comes from the corresponding model fields so that they will get updated as appropriate automagically.

After that begins the three items that the user can tap to navigate the app, the Lobby:

```
Padding(padding : EdgeInsets.fromLTRB(0, 20, 0, 0),
  child : ListTile(leading : Icon(Icons.list),
    title : Text("Lobby"),
    onTap: () {
      Navigator.of(inContext).pushNamedAndRemoveUntil(
        "/Lobby", ModalRoute.withName("/"));
      connector.listRooms((inRoomList) {
        model.setRoomList(inRoomList);
      });
    }
  )
)
```

It is, again, a ListTile, with some padding thrown in, so I can space these items out nicely. Each of these three items will get an icon in the leading that makes sense for its functionality. When the onTap handler fires, a couple of tasks are necessary. First, we get a reference to the Navigator for inContext and call the pushNamedAndRemoveUntil() method, specifying the name of the route to navigate to. Then, a connector method is called to retrieve an updated list of rooms. In theory, this isn't necessary, since the server will emit a message when a room is added or closed, and the list would be updated then, but there's no harm in doing it here, just to be sure we have an updated list. Finally, the list of rooms is set on the model, and the lobby's list of screens will reflect the new list. Remember that the please wait mask will have been shown after the navigation, which is why the navigation occurred first: I wanted the lobby to be visible while awaiting the list of rooms since that's more like how you'd would, as a user, expect such a thing to work.

The next two items, Current Room and User List, are identical to the code you just looked at, save for one difference: there is no call needed to the server when navigating to the current room, and no model data to set, so that item just does the navigation and that's it. Oh, and of course, the User List item calls connector.listUsers() and model.setUserList() instead of the room methods, but I think you could have guessed that! So, we'll skip looking at the code for those here and instead get to the code for the lobby screen.

Lobby.dart

The lobby screen, shown in Figure 8-4 and contained within the `Lobby.dart` file, is a simple ListView that we've used a couple of times before, showing the rooms on the server. It shows a lock icon to denote whether the room is private or not, and it shows the room's name and its description, if any.

Figure 8-4. *The lobby (room list) screen*

Clicking one of them enters the room or else tells the user that the room is private and they can't enter (assuming they don't have an invite). There is also a FAB for creating a new room, which any user can do.

```
class Lobby extends StatelessWidget {
  Widget build(final BuildContext inContext) {
    return ScopedModel<FlutterChatModel>(model : model,
    child : ScopedModelDescendant<FlutterChatModel>(
      builder : (BuildContext inContext, Widget inChild,
      FlutterChatModel inModel) {
        return Scaffold(drawer : AppDrawer(),
          appBar : AppBar(title : Text("Lobby")),
          floatingActionButton : FloatingActionButton(
            child : Icon(Icons.add, color : Colors.white),
            onPressed : () {
              Navigator.pushNamed(inContext, "/CreateRoom");
            }
          )
```

It begins with the usual pattern, with everything wrapped up in our scoped_model, since without the data this whole thing won't work! Where it starts to get interesting is in the onPressed handler for the FAB. Here, we push a route, /CreateRoom, that will show the user the screen for creating a room. That's covered in the next section though, so we'll carry on:

```
body : model.roomList.length == 0 ?
  Center(child :
    Text("There are no rooms yet. Why not add one?")) :
    ListView.builder(itemCount : model.roomList.length,
    itemBuilder : (BuildContext inBuildContext, int inIndex) {
      Map room = model.roomList[inIndex];
      String roomName = room["roomName"];
      return Column(children : [
```

There's a possibility that there are no rooms, so rather than just have a blank screen, I decided to show a message right in the center of the screen. If there are rooms though, that's when we build the ListView. Each room descriptor is pulled out of the model. roomList map, and then a Column layout is started. I do this because I want to show the room in a ListTile and then also have a Divider after it, so I need a widget with a children property.

The ListTile for the room comes next:

```
ListTile(leading : room["private"] ?
  Image.asset("assets/private.png") :
  Image.asset("assets/public.png"),
  title : Text(roomName), subtitle : Text(room["description"]))
```

First, the lock icon, which is in the leading of the tile. The private element in the room map tells us whether the room is private or not, and it just so happens to be a boolean, so a simple ternary conditional is used to insert the appropriate Image widget. After that, the title and subtitle are shown, as per usual with a ListTile.

Each room can be tapped, so there is an onTap handler next:

```
onTap : () {
  if (room["private"] &&
    !model.roomInvites.containsKey(roomName) &&
    room["creator"] != model.userName) {
      Scaffold.of(
        inBuildContext).showSnackBar(SnackBar(
          backgroundColor : Colors.red,
          duration : Duration(seconds : 2),
          content : Text("Sorry, you can't "
            "enter a private room without an invite")
      ));
```

First, we see if the room is private. If it is, we check to see if the user has an invite. Also, we check to see if this is the user that created the room. If the room is private and the user doesn't have an invite, and they aren't the creator, then a SnackBar is shown indicating they can't enter the room without an invite.

Now, if it's not private, or if they have an invite, or if they are the creator, then the else branch is hit:

```
} else {
  connector.join(model.userName, roomName,
    (inStatus, inRoomDescriptor) {
    if (inStatus == "joined") {
      model.setCurrentRoomName(inRoomDescriptor["roomName"]);
      model.setCurrentRoomUserList(inRoomDescriptor["users"]);
```

```
model.setCurrentRoomEnabled(true);
model.clearCurrentRoomMessages();
if (inRoomDescriptor["creator"] == model.userName) {
 model.setCreatorFunctionsEnabled(true);
} else {
 model.setCreatorFunctionsEnabled(false);
}
Navigator.pushNamed(inContext, "/Room");
```

Entering a room entails some setup work. First, the server is notified of the user entering the room thanks to the `connector.join()` method emitting the `join` message. If the response comes back `joined`, then the user is entering the room. In that case, the current room name is recorded, along with the list of users in the room that the server will have returned. The current room `AppDrawer` item has to be enabled as well, and we have to make sure there's no list of messages floating around in case this isn't the first time the user has been in this room (the room will appear devoid of messages any time the user enters it whether the first time or not). If this user is the creator, then we enable the creator functions as well. Finally, the `/Room` route is pushed to show the room screen, which will be examined in the final section of this chapter.

One last case we must deal with is if the server responds indicating the room is full because each room can be created with a maximum number of people allowed in it. So, we find another logic branch:

```
} else if (inStatus == "full") {
  Scaffold.of(inBuildContext).showSnackBar(SnackBar(
    backgroundColor : Colors.red,
      duration : Duration(seconds : 2),
      content : Text("Sorry, that room is full")
  ));
}
```

As with not having an invite to a private room, a `SnackBar` is shown to let them know the room is full. And with that, the lobby is complete! Now, let's go back to what happens if you tap that FAB button, which finds us in the `CreateRoom.dart` file.

CreateRoom.dart

Now it's time to create some rooms! Ah, the power of a god, the power of creation, encapsulated in a Flutter form! Figure 8-5 shows this magical entity.

Figure 8-5. *The create room screen*

It's a simple enough screen, which makes sense given that creating a room isn't a complex thing. Just one piece of information is required, and that's the name of the room. A description is optional, and the maximum number of people in the room as a default value, though it can be adjusted using a Slider. A room can also be made private by actuating the Switch widget for that. Then, hit Save and you've got yourself a room!

Since this time around we'll be creating a stateful widget, we'll have two classes, the actual widget class and then it's corresponding state object, so we begin with the widget class:

```
class CreateRoom extends StatefulWidget {
 CreateRoom({Key key}) : super(key : key);
 @override
 _CreateRoom createState() => _CreateRoom();
}
```

That's just boilerplate code, of course, nothing special there, nothing new. So, let's move on to the _CreateRoom object, which extends from State:

```
class _CreateRoom extends State {

  String _title;
  String _description;
  bool _private = false;
  double _maxPeople = 25;
  final GlobalKey<FormState> _formKey= GlobalKey<FormState>();
```

There are a few variables we're going to need, one per field in the Form, and a GlobalKey for the Form itself. Then, the build() method can begin:

```
Widget build(final BuildContext inContext) {
  return ScopedModel<FlutterChatModel>(model : model, child :
    ScopedModelDescendant<FlutterChatModel>(
    builder : (BuildContext inContext, Widget inChild,
      FlutterChatModel inModel) {
        return Scaffold(resizeToAvoidBottomPadding : false,
          appBar : AppBar(title : Text("Create Room")),
          drawer : AppDrawer(), bottomNavigationBar :
            Padding(padding : EdgeInsets.symmetric(
              vertical : 0, horizontal : 10
            ),
            child :
              SingleChildScrollView(child : Row(children : [
```

As usual, when dealing with a model, we have a ScopedModel with a ScopedModelDescendant under it, and then a builder() function to return the widget that needs access to the model. As with the Home and Lobby screens, a Scaffold is built, and this time we introduce the resizeToAvoidBottomPadding property and set it to false. This property controls how floating widgets within the Scaffold resize themselves when the on-screen keyboard is shown. Typically, you want this to be set to true, the default, which normally allows the body and the widgets to avoid being obscured by the keyboard. However, in some cases, you'll find that this dynamic layout causes widgets to vanish when the keyboard is shown, as was the case here. In that situation, setting this property to false causes the keyboard to overlap the widgets, which initially seems worse (or at least no better), but if they're in a scrolling container, as they will be here, then the user can scroll them into view, which is what they will expect to be able to do. That aside, the appBar is set with the title of the screen and the AppDrawer is brought in. Then, we have a bottomNavigationBar with some Padding around it so that the buttons will be pushed in from the sides of the screen a few pixels (just for appearances' sake). Then, the buttons themselves are defined:

```
FlatButton(child : Text("Cancel"),
  onPressed : () {
    FocusScope.of(inContext).requestFocus(FocusNode());
    Navigator.of(inContext).pop();
  }
),
Spacer()
```

The Cancel button comes first, and all it must do when pressed is hide the keyboard and then pop the screen away (remember, this is a route, meaning a separate screen, not a dialog). Then comes a Spacer, which pushes the second button, the Save button, all the way to the right. That second button looks like this:

```
FlatButton(child : Text("Save"),
  onPressed : () {
    if (!_formKey.currentState.validate()) { return; }
    _formKey.currentState.save();
    int maxPeople = _maxPeople.truncate();
    connector.create(_title, _description,
      maxPeople, _private,
```

```
    model.userName, (inStatus, inRoomList) {
    if (inStatus == "created") {
      model.setRoomList(inRoomList);
      FocusScope.of(inContext).requestFocus(FocusNode());
      Navigator.of(inContext).pop();
    } else {
      Scaffold.of(inContext).showSnackBar(SnackBar(
        backgroundColor : Colors.red,
        duration : Duration(seconds : 2),
        content : Text("Sorry, that room already exists")
      ));
    }
  });
```

First, the Form is validated, and then its state saved, the typical first steps you're familiar with. After that, the value of _maxPeople needs to be truncated. That's because we want an integer value, but the Slider gives us a floating point. Once that's done, we can call the connector.create() method, which emits the create message to the server. Two possible outcomes must be handled: either the room was created, or it wasn't, and the latter can only happen if the name is already in use. So, we branch on the inStatus that is provided to the callback. If it's created, then that means the server sent back an updated list of rooms, so we set it in the model. Then, the keyboard is hidden, and the screen is popped off the Navigator stack, which takes the user back to the Lobby screen. However, if the room wasn't created, then a SnackBar is shown to let the user know that the name was already taken, giving them a chance to choose a new one.

Building the Form

Now, we just have to build the form itself. It is, for the most part, the same kind of code you've seen before with other forms.

```
body : Form(key : _formKey, child : ListView(
  children : [
    ListTile(leading : Icon(Icons.subject),
      title : TextFormField(decoration :
        InputDecoration(hintText : "Name"),
```

```
validator : (String inValue) {
  if (inValue.length == 0 || inValue.length > 14) {
    return "Please enter a name no more "
      "than 14 characters long";
  }
  return null;
},
onSaved : (String inValue) {
  setState(() { _title = inValue; });
}
)
)
```

Each field in the form is contained within a ListTile, beginning with the Name field. The validator ensures both that something is entered and that its length is 14 characters or less (I chose that length so that it displays well in all cases without wrapping or being cut off or anything else that a longer name could allow).

The Description field is similarly defined, though this time I didn't put any constraints on it, which means that wrapping is possible on the Lobby screen, but I felt that was acceptable for a description where it wasn't for the name.

```
ListTile(leading : Icon(Icons.description),
  title : TextFormField(decoration :
    InputDecoration(hintText : "Description"),
    onSaved : (String inValue) {
      setState(() { _description = inValue; });
    }
  )
)
```

Then comes the Max People field, and this is where we run into something new: the Slider widget:

```
ListTile(title : Row(children : [ Text("Max\nPeople"),
  Slider(min : 0, max : 99, value : _maxPeople,
    onChanged : (double inValue) {
```

```
      setState(() { _maxPeople = inValue; });
    }
  )
]),
trailing : Text(_maxPeople.toStringAsFixed(0))
)
```

It's a simple enough widget, just requiring a min and max value to define its endpoints, and in this case the value property ties to a state property, _maxPeople. There's no validation for this field, but any time the value changes, we need to set it in the widget's state. Finally, one problem that arose is that as the user is sliding the Slider, there is by default no way for them to know what the value currently is – it's not displayed anywhere, and there aren't even tick marks or something on the Slider to help. To alleviate this, I threw a Text widget in the trailing of the ListTile and took the value of _maxPeople to display. Of course, Text requires, well, *text*, to display, but _maxPeople is a number. Fortunately, a double in Dart has available several methods to convert it to a string, one of which is toStringAsFixed() (there is also toStringAsExponential() and toStringAsPrecision()). It does exactly what we need: convert the double to a string while also allowing us to set the precision shown after the decimal point. Of course, here, I want *no* numbers after the decimal point, which is exactly what passing zero to this method does.

Only a single field remains, and that's the one for making the room private:

```
ListTile(title : Row(children : [ Text("Private"),
  Switch(value : _private,
    onChanged : (inValue) {
      setState(() { _private = inValue; });
    }
  )
]))
```

For the first time, you see the Switch widget used. It seemed like a good choice here since it's a binary choice: the room is either public, or it's private. A Checkbox would have done the trick too, but since you haven't seen Switch in action yet, I figured I'd show you something new!

UserList.dart

The user list screen, as shown in Figure 8-6, is the next bit of code to look at and is contained within the UserList.dart source file.

Figure 8-6. *The user list screen*

The screen itself is very simple: it's just a GridView with an item for each user registered with the server. Each user grid item is housed in Card widget and has a generic icon, just for appearances' sake (one could imagine letting users choose an avatar icon like for the contacts in FlutterBook, but that's not done – but hey, that sounds like one of those suggested exercises I'm always on about, doesn't it?!)

The code begins thusly:

```
class UserList extends StatelessWidget {
  Widget build(final BuildContext inContext) {
    return ScopedModel<FlutterChatModel>(model : model,
      child : ScopedModelDescendant<FlutterChatModel>(
      builder : (BuildContext inContext, Widget inChild,
        FlutterChatModel inModel) {
        return Scaffold(drawer : AppDrawer(),
          appBar : AppBar(title : Text("User List")),
          body : GridView.builder(
            itemCount : model.userList.length,
            gridDelegate :
              SliverGridDelegateWithFixedCrossAxisCount(
                crossAxisCount : 3
              )
```

It opens like almost every other class you've seen has. We need data from the model obviously, so everything is housed in the usual ScopedModel/ScopedMod elDescendant/builder() hierarchy. We're building a screen, so the root widget returned is a Scaffold, and the AppDrawer is referenced on it so that we don't lose that on this screen. Then, the body begins. As I said, it's a GridView, so we use the builder() constructor of that class and feed it the length of the model.userList collection as the itemCount property value. Next, a gridDelegate is provided of type SliverGridDelegateWithFixedCrossAxisCount (Flutter isn't known for brevity of class name!). Here, we specify that we want three items per row with the crossAxisCount property.

Then, it's time to build our items, which the itemBuilder function does:

```
itemBuilder : (BuildContext inContext, int inIndex) {
  Map user = model.userList[inIndex];
  return Padding(padding : EdgeInsets.fromLTRB(10,10,10,10),
    child : Card(child : Padding(padding :
      EdgeInsets.fromLTRB(10, 10, 10, 10),
      child : GridTile(
        child : Center(child : Padding(
          padding : EdgeInsets.fromLTRB(0, 0, 0, 20),
```

```
        child : Image.asset("assets/user.png")
      )),
      footer : Text(user["userName"],
      textAlign : TextAlign.center)
    )
  )
));
}
```

For each item, we get the user descriptor from the userList map in the model. Then, a Card wrapped in a Padding with space defined all around it (so the items in the GridView don't bunch up unpleasantly) is built. The child of the Card is our friendly neighborhood GridTile, the usual child of a GridView (it doesn't have to be a *direct* child though, as you can see). The child of that is an Image widget that displays the user.png asset, wrapped in Padding to control the spacing around it (in this case, just to put some space on the bottom of it to separate it from the user's name) and that wrapped in a Center to center it on the Card. Finally, the footer of the Card is where the user's name goes, with textAlign set to TextAlign.center to center it, like the image above it.

And that's all there is to the user list! It's easy when there are no actions the user can take, but that's very obviously not the case for the room screen, which is what's up next to review (and is the last bit of code for this app in fact).

Room.dart

Finally, we now come to the code for the room screen, where most of the action takes place, and the most substantial chunk of code we need to look at. This is also where you'll be introduced to several new Flutter concepts! First, though, take a peek at Figure 8-7, so you know what it looks like.

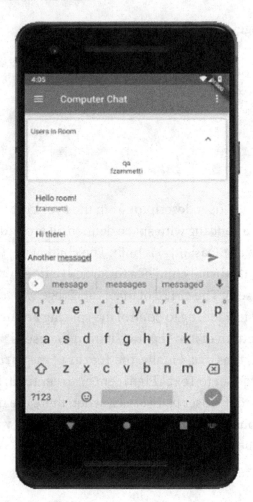

Figure 8-7. *The room screen*

At the top, you see an `ExpansionPanelList` widget. This is a widget that provides for having a list of child items which can be expanded and collapsed at the user's behest. In this case, we'll use it to show a list of users in the room. It should be expandable and collapsible because below that is the list of messages in the room, which of course is the primary purpose of this screen. At the bottom is an area for the user to enter a message and post it to the room, with an IconButton for doing this, which is a type of button that is just an icon. In the upper right is a three-dot menu, or overflow menu as it's sometimes called, where you find some functions: leaving the room, inviting a user to the room, kicking a user, and closing the room, the last two only being enabled if you're the user that created the room. The invite function will lead to a dialog to select a user from, but we'll get to all of that in just a bit.

Before that though, let's see how it all begins (imports aside of course):

```
class Room extends StatefulWidget {
 Room({Key key}) : super(key : key);
 @override
 _Room createState() => _Room();
}

class _Room extends State {
  bool _expanded = false;
  String _postMessage;
  final ScrollController _controller = ScrollController();
  final TextEditingController _postEditingController =
    TextEditingController();
```

This is a stateful widget; we're going to need some state local to this widget for expanding and collapsing the ExpansionPanelList. Of course, I could have put this in the scoped_model too. But, generally, for things that are truly local to a single widget, it probably makes more sense to make it a stateful widget and have that scope in the widget itself. But, as I've said before, Flutter is flexible, and there are no absolute rules about things like this.

There's a couple of class-level variables, namely, the one that determines whether the user list is expanded (when _expanded is true) or collapsed (when it's false). We also have a variable, _postMessage, that will contain the message the user posts. Also, we have a ScrollController referenced by the variable _controller. This is an object you typically don't need to deal with directly as most scrolling components have one automatically. However, in this app, there's a specific need for it that I'll get to a bit later when we look at the code behind the message list. After that, finally, is a TextEditingController, which you know is used when dealing with TextField widgets, which is exactly what's used for the user to enter a message in.

The Room Functions Menu

After that begins the build() method:

```
Widget build(final BuildContext inContext) {
  return ScopedModel<FlutterChatModel>(model : model,
    child : ScopedModelDescendant<FlutterChatModel>(
```

```
builder : (BuildContext inContext, Widget inChild,
  FlutterChatModel inModel) {
  return Scaffold(resizeToAvoidBottomPadding : false,
    appBar : AppBar(title : Text(model.currentRoomName),
      actions : [
        PopupMenuButton(
          onSelected : (inValue) {
            if (inValue == "invite") {
              _inviteOrKick(inContext, "invite");
```

Well, by this point, the beginning few lines of that should be almost boring to you, given how much you've seen it! In fact, it's all like that until you hit the PopupMenuButton line, which is new. A PopupMenuButton is a widget that provides a menu that, well, *pops up*, when you click the button (at least Google names their widgets descriptively!), as you can see in Figure 8-8.

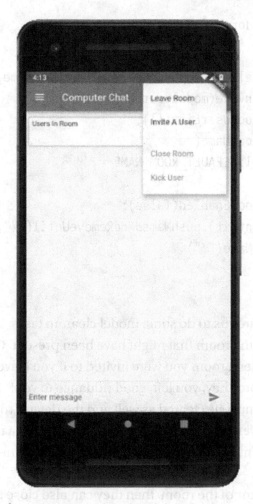

Figure 8-8. *The room functions menu*

Although we haven't constructed the menu items yet – that code is coming soon – we've already started in with the code that will execute when you select an item on the menu, contained within the onSelected handler function. This function receives the string value associated with a menu item that was tapped, so we start an if statement to take the correct course of action. In the case of the invite string, we're calling an _inviteOrKick() method, and we'll look at that later (that function handles both inviting a user and kicking a user out of the room).

After that is a branch for the `leave` string:

```
} else if (inValue == "leave") {
  connector.leave(model.userName, model.currentRoomName, () {
    model.removeRoomInvite(model.currentRoomName);
    model.setCurrentRoomUserList({});
    model.setCurrentRoomName(
      FlutterChatModel.DEFAULT_ROOM_NAME
    );
    model.setCurrentRoomEnabled(false);
    Navigator.of(inContext).pushNamedAndRemoveUntil("/",
      ModalRoute.withName("/")
    );
  });
```

Leaving a room requires us to do some model cleanup tasks, beginning with removing any invites for the room that might have been present. One could argue you should still be able to enter a room you were invited to if you leave, which is reasonable, but I guess I'm a little more "hey, you left, good riddance to you!" in my thinking. The list of users in the room must be cleared as well and the default room name string set again so that the `AppDrawer` again reflects the user not being in a room. Also related to the `AppDrawer`, the Current Room item must be disabled, and finally we navigate the user back to the home screen.

If the user is the creator of the room, then they can also close the room:

```
} else if (inValue == "close") {
  connector.close(model.currentRoomName, () {
    Navigator.of(inContext).pushNamedAndRemoveUntil("/",
      ModalRoute.withName("/")
    );
  });
```

There's no work to do here other than informing the server that the room is closed and then navigating to the home screen.

You can also give a user the boot:

```
} else if (inValue == "kick") {
  _inviteOrKick(inContext, "kick");
}
```

It's the same as the invite code, and again, we'll look at what's behind that function in a bit. Before that though, we gotta go back and actually construct the menu items with an itemBuilder function:

```
itemBuilder : (BuildContext inPMBContext) {
  return <PopupMenuEntry<String>>[
    PopupMenuItem(value:"leave",child:Text("Leave Room")),
    PopupMenuItem(value:"invite",child:Text("Invite A User")),
    PopupMenuDivider(),
    PopupMenuItem(value : "close", child : Text("Close Room"),
      enabled : model.creatorFunctionsEnabled),
    PopupMenuItem(value : "kick", child : Text("Kick User"),
      enabled : model.creatorFunctionsEnabled)
  ];
}
```

We must return an array of PopupMenuEntry widgets, and each PopupMenuEntry in that array has a value property (who's values you should recognize!) and a child Text widget for the actual text to be displayed. For the Close Room and Kick User options, the enabled property references the creatorFunctionsEnabled model property (just to show that you indeed can mix and match local state and global state, no problem) to determine whether those items are enabled or not.

The Main Screen Content

After the menu is built, we continue:

```
drawer : AppDrawer(),
body : Padding(padding : EdgeInsets.fromLTRB(6, 14, 6, 6),
  child : Column(
    children : [
      ExpansionPanelList(
```

```
      expansionCallback : (inIndex, inExpanded) =>
        setState(() { _expanded = !_expanded; }),
    children : [
      ExpansionPanel(isExpanded : _expanded,
        headerBuilder : (BuildContext context,
          bool isExpanded) => Text("  Users In Room"),
          body :
            Padding(padding:EdgeInsets.fromLTRB(0,0,0,10),
          child : Builder(builder : (inBuilderContext) {
            List<Widget> userList = [ ];
            for (var user in model.currentRoomUserList) {
              userList.add(Text(user["userName"]));
            }
            return Column(children : userList);
          })
        )
      )
    ]
  )
```

Ok, so, after the `drawer`, there's some new stuff here. First, a `Padding` is at the top so that I can control spacing around all the elements on the screen. I push everything down 14 pixels to clear the shadow under the status bar, and a few pixels on the left, right, and bottom, just because I think it looks better if things don't run right up against the screen edges.

After that comes a `Column` layout and its first child, the `ExpansionPanelList` where our list of users is displayed. The first thing we need to do is hook up an event handler to fire whenever the user expands or collapses the panel. Interestingly, by default, nothing will happen if you don't do this other than the little arrow on the right changing. Once that's done, it provides the flag we need in the first child of the `ExpansionPanelList`, which is the `ExpansionPanel` that houses our user list. The flag becomes the value of the `isExpanded` property, which is the `isExpanded` argument to the `headerBuilder` function. This function is where we build the header of the `ExpansionPanel`. That's just a simple `Text` widget, but not the two spaces at the start. This is another way to do padding, essentially. In this case, the `Text` by default will bump up right against the left edge of the panel, but as you know by now, I tend to not like this! But rather than wrap is in a

Padding, which certainly would have worked, I instead just add those two spaces, and we're good to go.

In addition to a header, an ExpansionPanel typically always has a body, and this one is no different. For this, I use a Padding to ensure some space below the user list, for similar reasons as in the header: without it, the last user in the list would be right up against that bottom edge, which just doesn't look right.

Now, the child of this Padding is something interesting. You've seen various builder functions plenty before, but I never showed that you could, in nearly all cases, have a generic Builder function any time you like. This is sometimes necessary because using it creates a closure, so if you need access to some data that you otherwise wouldn't (without resorting to putting everything in some common state object of course). In this case, there really wasn't that need, but I thought this would be an excellent place to demonstrate this anyway because obviously you can do it even if you don't need a closure. Again, Flutter gives you plenty of choices for how to solve problems.

Inside the Builder's builder() function is a simple iteration over the list of users in the room from state where each is a Text inside a Column, with the Column being what ultimately gets returned and displayed.

Following that comes the message list – well, with one thing before it:

```
Container(height : 10),
Expanded(child : ListView.builder(controller : _controller,
  itemCount : model.currentRoomMessages.length,
  itemBuilder : (inContext, inIndex) {
    Map message = model.currentRoomMessages[inIndex];
    return ListTile(subtitle : Text(message["userName"]),
      title : Text(message["message"])
    );
  }
))
```

The Container is yet another way to introduce padding into a layout. By defining it with no content but a defined height, I've added some separation between the user list and the message list without an explicit Padding widget. After that is a ListView for the messages, which hopefully is something that makes sense to you, both conceptually and in terms of the code, since you've seen ListView widgets a few times now. For each item in the list, a ListTile is created with the title being the message text and the subtitle being the name of the user that posted the message.

After that is a `Divider` widget, and then the area for the user to post a message:

```
Divider(),
Row(children : [
  Flexible(
    child : TextField(controller : _postEditingController,
    onChanged : (String inText) =>
      setState(() { _postMessage = inText; }),
    decoration : new InputDecoration.collapsed(
      hintText : "Enter message"),
  )),
  Container(margin : new EdgeInsets.fromLTRB(2, 0, 2, 0),
    child : IconButton(icon : Icon(Icons.send),
      color : Colors.blue,
      onPressed : () {
        connector.post(model.userName,
          model.currentRoomName, _postMessage, (inStatus) {
          if (inStatus == "ok") {
            model.addMessage(model.userName, _postMessage);
            _controller.jumpTo(
              _controller.position.maxScrollExtent);
          }
        });
      }
    )
  )
)
```

First things first: the entry area is a `TextField` and an `IconButton` right next to each other, so a `Row` layout makes sense. But I want to avoid having to set explicit widths for either since I don't know the dimensions of the screen. As it happens, Flutter provides a handy widget for such situations: `Flexible`. This allows you to control how components inside a `Flex`, `Row`, or `Column` widget flex and fill the available space. Here, the goal is simple: allow the `TextField` to fill as much space as is available once the `IconButton` is factored in. So, I place the `TextField` inside the `Flexible`, and then the `Flexible` inside the `Row` as the first child. The second child of the `Row` is a `Container` that contains the `IconButton`. It's an `IconButton` inside a `Padding` rather than just the `IconButton` by

itself again for spacing purposes so that I can have a few pixels to the left and right of the
IconButton. Then, the IconButton is constructed. Flutter gives us a nice icon for sending
a message, which I think works well for this situation.

When the button is pressed, the connector.post() method is called, passing it the
user's name, room name, and of course the message they entered. Assuming we get the
ok response back, then the message is added to the list of messages for the room, and
then, finally, that ScrollController I mentioned at the top is used. The goal here is
that since the message will appear at the bottom of the ListView, it may not be visible
if the number of messages overflows the screen (or if the user has scrolled back up to
read messages). So, with the _controller, we can use its jumpTo() method, passing it
_controller.position.maxScrollExtent, which is shorthand for "jump to the bottom
of the ListView," which is how you typically expect a chat room to work.

Inviting or Kicking a User

The final thing to look at is when the user wants to invite another user to the room or
kick a user out. When either of those menu items is tapped, a dialog like that shown in
Figure 8-9 appears, but of course, saying "kicked" instead of "invite" as appropriate.

Figure 8-9. *The invite user dialog*

So, the code begins like so:

```
_inviteOrKick(final BuildContext inContext,
  final String inInviteOrKick) {
  connector.listUsers((inUserList) {
    model.setUserList(inUserList);
```

The first thing we want to do is get an updated list of users on the server. As in a few other places, this *should* be superfluous, but better safe than sorry. Note that if we're kicking a user, this really is superfluous since the code already has the list of users in the room, but at this point, the code hasn't branched on the inInviteOrKick argument, so the server is consulted either way. It's a bit of inefficiency, but assuming our server is working well, it really shouldn't matter much.

Once the response comes back, we can then show the dialog:

```
showDialog(context : inContext,
  builder : (BuildContext inDialogContext) {
    return ScopedModel<FlutterChatModel>(model : model,
      child : ScopedModelDescendant<FlutterChatModel>(
        builder : (BuildContext inContext, Widget inChild,
          FlutterChatModel inModel) {
          return AlertDialog(
            title : Text("Select user to $inInviteOrKick"
          )
```

It all starts ordinarily enough, and in the AlertDialog constructor, you can see the first time something is different based on what function we're doing: the display of the title text.

Next, we begin to construct the content of the dialog:

```
content : Container(width : double.maxFinite,
  height : double.maxFinite / 2,
  child : ListView.builder(
    itemCount : inInviteOrKick == "invite" ?
      model.userList.length : model.currentRoomUserList,
      itemBuilder:(BuildContext inBuildContext, int inIndex) {
      Map user;
      if (inInviteOrKick == "invite") {
        user = model.userList[inIndex];
      } else {
        user = model.currentRoomUserList[inIndex];
      }
      if (user["userName"] == model.userName)
        { return Container(); }
```

Here, I want the dialog to fill the screen mostly, so I use a little trick by setting the width to the maxFinite constant of the double class and the height to half that value. This effectively forces Flutter to size the window to a maximum size that it determines will fill most of the screen.

Next, a `ListView` is built, since, of course, this is a list of users. Which list we get the data from, whether `model.userList` for an invite or `model.currentRoomUserList` for a kick, is determined both to get its `length` into the `itemCount` property as well as where we get the actual users from. When we hit the current user, it needs to be skipped, so an empty `Container` is returned. Flutter will collapse this into nothing, but we can't just return null from the `itemBuilder` function lest we get an exception, hence this empty `Container`.

If it's not the current user though, a `Container` with actual content is returned:

```
return Container(decoration : BoxDecoration(
  borderRadius : BorderRadius.all(Radius.circular(15.0)),
  border : Border(
    bottom : BorderSide(), top : BorderSide(),
    left : BorderSide(), right : BorderSide()
  )
)
```

First, I apply a `BoxDecoration` so that I can round the corners via the `borderRadius` property. You can round any or all corners this way – it's all of them here. Of course, without a border, this winds up looking a little funky to my eyes, so I apply a `Border` via the `border` property. The defaults work well enough for this, hence a simple `BorderSide` instance for all sides (again, you can apply borders arbitrarily to any or all sides as you see fit).

Now, I was feeling a bit psychedelic at this point, so I wanted some pretty colors! Fortunately, the `gradient` property of the `BoxDecoration` class allows for this:

```
gradient : LinearGradient(
  begin : Alignment.topLeft, end : Alignment.bottomRight,
  stops : [ .1, .2, .3, .4, .5, .6, .7, .8, .9],
  colors : [
    Color.fromRGBO(250, 250, 0, .75),
    Color.fromRGBO(250, 220, 0, .75),
    Color.fromRGBO(250, 190, 0, .75),
    Color.fromRGBO(250, 160, 0, .75),
    Color.fromRGBO(250, 130, 0, .75),
    Color.fromRGBO(250, 110, 0, .75),
    Color.fromRGBO(250, 80, 0, .75),
```

```
    Color.fromRGBO(250, 50, 0, .75),
    Color.fromRGBO(250, 0, 0, .75)
  ]
)),
margin : EdgeInsets.only(top : 10.0),
child : ListTile(title : Text(user["userName"])
```

There are a handful of *Gradient classes, LinearGradient being one that produces a gradient that goes straight up or down (RadialGradient and SweepGradient are the others). For this, you need to tell it where to begin and where to end, and in this case, I wanted it to start on the left and go to the right (technically it's the top-left and bottom-right, but it winds up being the same as left-to-right). You then need to define the stops along the gradient, which means what fraction of the total gradient will be each defined color. The values go from zero to one, and you can split them up however you want. Here, I want each color to take up equal space, so the stops are each a tenth of the way. The colors themselves are defined next. There are several ways you can define colors with Flutter, and you've seen the use of the Colors collection before, but here I wanted to be more explicit, so I use RGB values (red, green, blue). Technically, it's RGBO, where O is opacity, and in fact, the opacity is set to .75 for each, which makes them 75% translucent. It just blends in a little bit with the background that way, which dulls the colors a bit since the background color behind it is white. Finally, I apply some margin to the top so that there's space between the first user listed and the title text, and then, of course, a ListTile is built for each user.

Finally, we need to implement what happens when a user is tapped:

```
onTap : () {
  if (inInviteOrKick == "invite") {
    connector.invite(user["userName"],
      model.currentRoomName, model.userName, () {
      Navigator.of(inContext).pop();
    });
  } else {
    connector.kick(user["userName"],model.currentRoomName,() {
      Navigator.of(inContext).pop();
    });
  }
}
```

This is easy: if we're inviting a user, then we call `connector.invite()` and pass it the selected user's name, the current room name, and the name of the user inviting the other so that it can be displayed to the invited user. Or, if we're kicking a user, then it's a call to `connector.kick()` instead, passing it the name of the `userName` of the selected user and what room they're being kicked from. And, in both cases, the dialog is dismissed.

Summary

In this chapter, we wrapped up the FlutterChat app, building the Flutter-based client-side of the app. In it, you saw some new things (or some not new things that we haven't used in a real app before) like stateful widgets, the `PopupMenuButton` widget, the `ExpansionPanel` widget, real use of the `GridView` widget, the `Slider` and `Switch` components, and of course socket.io and WebSocket communications. As a bonus, you got to play around with Node a bit and write a server!

In the next chapter, we'll start building the last of our three apps, and this one will take you in a totally new direction and give you a somewhat different view of Flutter: we're building a *game*!

CHAPTER 9

FlutterHero: A Flutter Game

All work and no play makes Jack a dull boy (and a murderer at a snowy resort lodge, as we learned in *The Shining*).

With luck, you'll avoid that fate, but the point stands: if you don't stop to smell the roses every now and again, you tend not to have as good a life as you should. This is true for mobile development and Flutter too! (You didn't think I would be able to pull this back to relevance, did you?)

Throughout this book, you've seen Flutter through the lens of writing actual useful code and applications. But nothing says that's all you can do with Flutter. No, you can do something more frivolous, something more fun, something like, say, write a game!

Games are excellent projects for any developer to undertake because they touch on so many different disciplines in programming, from graphics and sound to AI, data structures, algorithmic efficiency, and so on. In my position as a lead architect, I'm sometimes asked by developers how they can sharpen their skills. My answer is always the same: write a game! I don't believe any other project provides the diversity and level of creativity that games do and, therefore, opportunity for learning.

Plus, by their very nature, games are fun to write!

In this chapter, you'll use Flutter to write a game. The benefit in terms of this book is that you'll get to see a few new Flutter facilities and see others in ways you maybe haven't before. In the end, you'll learn while, hopefully, having fun!

So, let's kick things off by figuring out what kind of game to make and coming up with what every great game needs: a story!

The Story So Far

The inhabitants of Gorgona 6 are a cosmic contradiction: a technologically advanced civilization that is simultaneously kinda backward intellectually! For example, they visited their own moon before figuring out that they should put wheels on luggage and,

© Frank Zammetti 2019
F. Zammetti, *Practical Flutter*, https://doi.org/10.1007/978-1-4842-4972-7_9

more importantly for the purposes here, they can build fast, sleek spaceships, but they are wimpy ships that can't survive much of anything! Just a bump into a space fish is enough to do them in (and being a peaceful people, the Gorgonians never develop weapons of any sort).

Yes, I said space fish! But I digress.

This situation is problematic for them because their star system has a vermin problem: it's lousy with spaceborne critters and dangers! They have the gargantuan space fish of the third moon of Valtrax, the naturally occurring sentient machine beings of protoplanet 10101110, space aliens (but who doesn't have space aliens in their solar system, amiright?), and your basic rogue asteroids tumbling about. These things gum up the works of the shipping lanes and pleasure cruise trails (though how anyone can derive pleasure from a cruise where your piece of garbage ship could be destroyed at any moment by the slightest impact is yet another contradiction embodied by the Gorgonians).

Fortunately, there is a solution to these problems: on the outskirts of the solar system is a massive crystal of unknown origin that emits a special type of energy that kills the space vermin, at least for a little while. The Gorgonians have figured out how to collect this energy, little by little. So, they send out ships that are essentially space tankers (but being Gorgonian ships, they at least look cool!) to collect the energy and return it to the homeworld.

Your job, as one of the brave – some might say *hero* even – pilots of the "crystal tanker fleet," is to make your way through the space vermin to extract energy from the crystal and then bring it home. When you collect enough energy, the vermin are destroyed, and you're a Gorgonian hero!

At least for a little while.

You get some points or something for doing this, of course – let's call 'em space credits – with which you can maintain your hallucinogenic Gorgonian lizard-licking habit.

And that, friends, is how you conceive a simple game that you can code up with Flutter. I mean, I'll say up front that if you're expecting Apex Legends, Halo, or Red Dead Redemption levels of gameplay, then you're going to be sorely disappointed. This ain't gonna be no AAA title, and it's not a game you'll want to be repeatedly playing (probably – hey, you could wind up loving it I suppose!). But it'll be a good learning experience, which of course is the goal here.

So, with the story in place, let's get to work because those vermin aren't going to destroy themselves (well, probably – they could be as stupid as the Gorgonians I suppose).

The Basic Layout

So, what does this game look like? Well, if you happened to have ever played an old 8-bit game with, say, a frog that hops across lanes of traffic of various types to get to a goal on the other side, well, this game may or may not be conceptually like that. To be more precise, Figure 9-1 shows what it looks like.

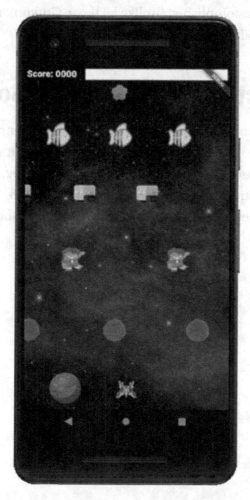

Figure 9-1. *Maybe I should have called it Space Frogger instead?*

Your ship starts at the bottom of the screen, near the homeworld. You control the ship by placing your finger anywhere on the screen, which becomes the "anchor" point, or zero position, of a virtual joystick. Now, just move your finger in any of the eight compass directions, and your ship moves in that direction. Your goal is to move through the lanes of vermin (asteroids, aliens, sentient machines, and space fish, starting from the bottom). When you reach the top, you touch the crystal, and the energy bar at the top fills. Then, you return through the vermin, touch your homeworld, and the energy is transferred, at which point all the vermin explode, you get some points, and the vermin come back so you can do it all over again. Of course, you explode if you touch anything but the crystal or your homeworld.

As I said, it's not exactly a complex, top-tier game, but it *is* a game, and it *is* made with Flutter, so, mission accomplished (unlike all those Gorgonian ship captains lost in the line of duty – we, the Flutter coders of Earth, salute you!)

Directory Structure and Component Source Files

Let's begin by talking about the directory structure and, more importantly, some of the files it contains. Figure 9-2 shows you the pertinent details. It's an entirely standard Flutter application structure as you've come to know and, I hope, love. In the `assets` directory, you'll find a bunch of images and some audio files. For the images, the names should give away what they each are, but the numbers require some explanation.

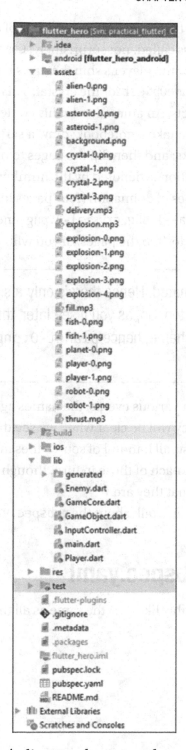

Figure 9-2. *The application's directory layout and constituent source/asset files*

As you'll see soon, each of the images represents part of an object in the game which will be used by a common class called, not surprisingly, GameObject. For example, there is a player GameObject for the player's ship that uses images player-0.png and player-1.png, and a crystal GameObject for the crystal. This common class includes logic for animating these objects. An animation in this context is just like the old trick when you were a kid where you take a notebook; draw a series of "frames," maybe a stick figure doing jumping jacks; and then flip the pages to produce the animation. Here, each frame of the animation is denoted by the number in the filename. So, for the crystal, there are four frames of animation (four pages in your notebook, so to speak): crystal-0.png, crystal-1.png, crystal-2.png, and crystal-3.png, and the GameObject class knows how to "flip the pages," if you will.

Note   The planet isn't animated. Hence there's only a single frame. But it gets wrapped in a GameObject too. So, as you'll see later, this requires the filename to use the same numbering scheme, hence planet-0.png so that the GameObject class can still work with it.

The MP3 files are audio for various events, the names again hopefully being self-explanatory, but if not, they will be clear when we see them used.

Beyond that, you've got a small handful of source files in lib aside from the required main.dart file, and we'll get to each of those in turn, though like the assets, the names should give you a good clue what they are.

Before any of that though, let's talk about the pubspec.yaml a bit.

Configuration: pubspec.yaml

The pubspec.yaml file is probably like 99% the same as all the others you've seen, save for one new element:

```
name: flutter_hero
description: FlutterHero
version: 1.0.0+1
environment:
  sdk: ">=2.1.0 <3.0.0"
```

```
dependencies:
  flutter:
    sdk: flutter
  cupertino_icons: ^0.1.2
  audioplayers: 0.11.0
dev_dependencies:
  flutter_test:
    sdk: flutter
flutter:
  uses-material-design: true
  assets:
    - assets/
```

This is a game, and most games have audio, so we should probably have some audio too! At the time of this writing, Flutter, perhaps surprisingly, doesn't have a good API for audio, at least not in the way you need for a game in terms of just being able to play arbitrary sound files included in the project any time you want (and sometimes simultaneously). So, we'll need a plugin for that. Fortunately, there are a few choices, but perhaps the most popular is the audioplayers plugin (https://pub.dartlang.org/packages/audioplayers). This is a fork of an earlier plugin named audioplayer (yes, the new one just has an added s on the end!) that extends the functionality of the old one. This plugin allows us to play audio files stored remotely on the Internet, locally from the user's device or, critically for us, as assets in our project. With this plugin, you can play files, control their playback (pause, stop, seek to a specific location in the audio), loop the audio if you like (good for background music), and listen for events during playback so you could, for example, show a progress bar if you wanted to.

For FlutterHero, we won't need most of that! We'll just need to be able to play our sounds when specific events occur. We'll look at the API for this plugin when we hit the first sound usage, but as you'll see, it's quite minimal.

Aside from that dependency, the assets directory is referenced in the catch-all way you've seen previously, so all of our assets are available, image and audio alike. I considered splitting them into assets/images and assets/audio, but that would require a tad more work in terms of getting audioplayers to be able to find them, and given the relatively small number of assets required, I decided to just dump them all in the single assets directory.

The GameObject Class

Now, we start to get to some code! Usually, I would begin with `main.dart`, but in this case, I want to talk about that `GameObject` class I mentioned earlier first. Some of what you'll see here might not immediately be clear, but it will quickly become so when you see this class and its subclasses used.

Speaking of subclasses, that's right, `GameObject` is a parent class to two others, as Figure 9-3 shows.

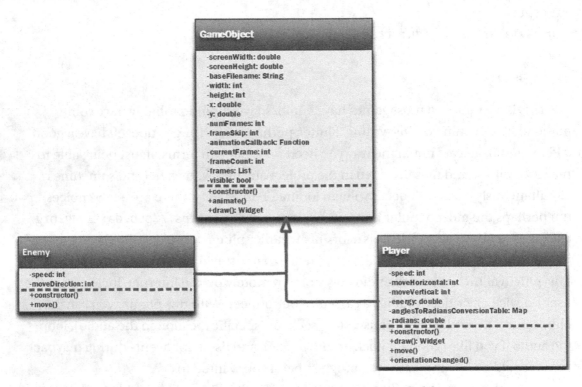

Figure 9-3. *The hierarchy of classes: GameObject and its children*

The basic idea here is simple Object-Oriented Programming: the `GameObject` class has data and functionality common to all objects in the game (which we call game object, as opposed to the `GameObject` class that is the code implementation of that general concept), and then the subclasses extend that data and functionality as required. So, for example, every game object (player, crystal, vermin, and planet) needs data like

- The width and height of the screen

- The base filename of their images ("planet-*.png" or "crystal-*.png," for example, where * will be the frame numbers)

- The width and height of the object

- The x and y location of the object

- The total number of frames in the animation cycle; how many game frames to skip between animation frame cycle changes (I know that's a little confusing, but don't worry, it won't be for long!); what the current frame of the animation cycle is; a counter for determining when it's time to flip to the next animation frame; a function that will be called when the animation cycle completes; and of course all the animation frame images

- Whether the object is visible or not

Also, every game object has some common functionality:

- A constructor for setting it up

- A method to animate it

- A method to draw it on the screen

But, the Enemy subclass, which will represent the fish, robots, aliens, and asteroids, has some additional needs:

- How fast they move across the screen

- What direction they're moving (left or right)

The Player class obviously represents the player's ship, and it too has some specific needs beyond those supplied by GameObject:

- How fast it moves

- Whether it's moving left or right (horizontal movement) and/or up or down (vertical movement)

- How much of the crystal's energy is onboard

- How many degrees (in radians) it's rotated (allows us to have a single image that can be in any orientation depending on the direction of travel) plus some data tables that save us from doing math repeatedly, to boost performance a little (it's always good to think about performance in games!)

- A method to be used any time the ship's orientation changes (based on the direction of movement) so that it can be rotated appropriately

So, now that you have a high-level idea of what these classes are about, let's get to the actual code of GameObject:

```
class GameObject {

  double screenWidth = 0.0;
  double screenHeight = 0.0;
```

It starts off as an ordinary class, not extending from anything else, and we have the first two data properties, namely, the width and height of the screen. As you'll see later, Flutter provides an API to get this information, and it is retrieved during application startup and is handed to any instance of GameObject during instantiation. This just avoids having to call a potentially expensive API over and over again, but this information is needed by the game objects in various ways, so doing it in one place and giving it to the instances works well.

```
String baseFilename = "";
```

The baseFilename is the portion of the filename of the images for this game object that doesn't change. Put more simply, it's the name of the object, be it fish, player, planet, or whatever else.

```
int width = 0;
int height = 0;
```

The width and height of the object are naturally needed too. I'm sure it would have been possible to find a Flutter API to get this information from the loaded images, but it's just simpler to provide it in the code when it's not something that's going to change ever.

```
double x = 0.0;
double y = 0.0;
```

The horizontal (x) and vertical (y) location of the game object on the screen is clearly something every game object will need, so that's here too.

```
int numFrames = 0;
int frameSkip = 0;
int currentFrame = 0;
int frameCount = 0;
List frames = [ ];
Function animationCallback;
```

These six properties are all related to animation. The `numFrames` property is how many total frames there are. The `frameSkip` property determines how many ticks of the main game loop must elapse before the next animation frame is shown (we'll talk about the main game loop later, but as a brief preview, it's something that will happen 60 times a second, executing our game logic, including animating each game object, at the same interval). The `currentFrame` property is simply which animation frame is currently showing. The `frameCount` property gets incremented with every tick of the main game loop, and when it hits the value of `frameSkip`, the value of `currentFrame` is incremented. The frames property is a list of the Flutter image assets for the game object, one per animation frame. Finally, the `animationCallback` property is an (optional) reference to a function that will be called any time the animation cycle end. You'll see why that's needed, along with all of these, very soon, but for now, let's press on.

```
bool visible = true;
```

The vermin and player need to be hideable at certain times, and the `visible` property determines when a game object is visible or not.

With the properties out of the way, we next come to the constructor:

```
GameObject(double inScreenWidth, double inScreenHeight,
  String inBaseFilename, int inWidth, int inHeight,
  int inNumFrames, int inFrameSkip,
  Function inAnimationCallback) {
  screenWidth = inScreenWidth;
  screenHeight = inScreenHeight;
  baseFilename = inBaseFilename;
  width = inWidth;
  height = inHeight;
  numFrames = inNumFrames;
  frameSkip = inFrameSkip;
  animationCallback = inAnimationCallback;
  for (int i = 0; i < inNumFrames; i++) {
    frames.add(Image.asset("assets/$baseFilename-$i.png"));
  }
}
```

Pretty straightforward, right? All the incoming arguments get stored in the appropriate properties, and then we need to load the animation frames. Here, you can see how each is an Image widget, loaded with its asset() constructor and using the baseFilename to construct the filename for each frame to load. This again is primarily done for performance: only loading the frames once is a good idea. Flutter may be smart enough to cache them if we were to load the same image twice, but it's much better not to assume that and instead architect our app to ensure it – it also makes the animation code easier to write in my opinion.

Speaking of animation code:

```
void animate() {
  frameCount = frameCount + 1;
  if (frameCount > frameSkip) {
    frameCount = 0;
    currentFrame = currentFrame + 1;
    if (currentFrame == numFrames) {
      currentFrame = 0;
      if (animationCallback != null) { animationCallback(); }
    }
  }
}
```

The logic is simple: every time this is called – which you'll see later is once per main game loop tick, which means 60 times a second – the frameCount is bumped up. When that value reaches the frameSkip value, then we increment to the next frame. When we reach the end of the frames, we reset it back to the first frame and, if one is supplied, call the animationCallback.

In addition to animating, a GameObject needs to know how to draw itself. As everything is a widget in Flutter, as you well know by now, the goal here is to get the proper widget for inclusion in a widget tree returned by some build() method somewhere (I'm being vague because we obviously haven't gotten to that yet, but we will!). The draw() method accomplishes this:

```
Widget draw() {
  return visible ?
  Positioned(left : x, top : y, child : frames[currentFrame])
    : Positioned(child : Container());
}
```

Not to jump the gun, but we'll be using a Stack widget as the parent to all our game objects. That's because within a Stack, you can have Positioned widgets which can be positioned absolutely inside the Stack. If the Stack covers the entire screen then, effectively, we've got ourselves a canvas perfectly suitable for game development because we can control the precise location of everything on the screen down to the pixel level. That's exactly what we're going to do, so draw() needs to return a Positioned widget that wraps the Image widget associated with the current animation frame of the object. In addition, an object can be hidden. How you do this is something you may find a little weird about Flutter. To hide a widget, regardless of what it is, you simply don't include it in the widget true! There's no hidden:true or something like that on widgets as seen in many other frameworks, no hide() method to call. However, as you'll see later, returning null from this method, as would probably be your first thought, wouldn't work because it would break the widget tree it'll eventually be a part of. So instead, an empty Container is returned when this game object isn't visible. That accomplishes the goal, even if in a somewhat weird way (I know it seemed a little weird to me at first at least!)

Extending from GameObject: The Enemy Class

With the basic GameObject coded, we can now look at the two subclasses, beginning with Enemy. The primary thing that makes an Enemy different from a plain GameObject is that an Enemy can move.

```
class Enemy extends GameObject {

  int speed = 0;
  int moveDirection = 0;
```

The movement of an enemy is simple though: it just moves either left or right and at a given speed (where *speed* here means how many pixels it moves per main game loop tick). So, that's what the speed and moveDirection properties denote. The value of moveDirection will be 0 for left or 1 for right.

Then, we have a constructor:

```
Enemy(double inScreenWidth, double inScreenHeight,
  String inBaseFilename, int inWidth, int inHeight,
  int inNumFrames, int inFrameSkip, int inMoveDirection,
  int inSpeed) :
```

```
    super(inScreenWidth, inScreenHeight, inBaseFilename,
    inWidth, inHeight, inNumFrames, inFrameSkip, null) {
  speed = inSpeed;
  moveDirection = inMoveDirection;
}
```

Now, since this class extends GameObject, it means that it supports all the same properties as GameObject, so those need to be set too. That's where the super() call comes into play. As you can see, the signature of the Enemy constructor includes everything the GameObject constructor does plus the items specific to Enemy, so first the super() call sets the properties common to GameObject, then the code inside the Enemy constructor sets the additional properties specified to Enemy.

And with all that data set, we can implement the move() method:

```
void move() {
  if (moveDirection == 1) {
    x = x + speed;
    if (x > screenWidth + width) { x = -width.toDouble(); }
  } else {
    x = x - speed;
    if (x < -width) { x = screenWidth + width.toDouble(); }
  }
}
```

You can now see why the width and height of the screen are needed: that's how we know when a given enemy has moved off the screen when it's moving in either direction. Then, it helps us set its new location. So, to go through this conceptually: a given enemy fish is moving right across the screen (the first if branch). When it's beyond the right edge of the screen (the second if branch), its x location is set to a negative value, which puts it on the left of the screen. Then it continues moving as before and does this again. For left movement (the else branch), the same is done, but in reverse. That's all there is to the enemy movements, very simple.

Extending from GameObject: The Player Class

The other class that extends from GameObject is for the player:

```
class Player extends GameObject {

  int speed = 0;
  int moveHorizontal = 0;
  int moveVertical = 0;
```

Like the vermin, the player obviously can move, so we need to know how fast it can move (speed) and in what direction it's moving (moveHorizontal and moveVertical). Unlike the enemy vermin, the player can move up, down, left, and right, plus the four combinations of each. Hence, we need two variables to track which way it's moving instead of just one like for the enemies. But the player can also be not moving, So, each of these has three possible values instead of only two for the enemies: 0 for either means no movement in that direction while for moveHorizontal -1 means left and 1 means right while for moveVertical -1 means up and 1 means down.

```
double energy = 0.0;
```

The player can also, at any moment in time, have some of the crystal's energy onboard. So, we need a variable to track that too.

```
Map anglesToRadiansConversionTable = {
  "angle45"  : 0.7853981633974483,
  "angle90"  : 1.5707963267948966,
  "angle135" : 2.3387411976724017,
  "angle180" : 3.141592653589793,
  "angle225" : 3.9269908169872414,
  "angle270" : 4.71238898038469,
  "angle315" : 5.497787143782138
};
double radians = 0.0;
```

One of the things that makes game development somewhat unique is that you are almost always looking for little tricks to optimize things, to save some memory or cycles here or there. In this case, there are two tricks to be played with the player's ship. First, the ship should always be pointed in the direction of movement (or remain in whatever position it was going when it last stopped). So, that would mean that we need eight different images: one each for when moving up, down, left, right, up/left, up/right, down/left, and down/right. But, since the ship is animated, and assuming all use two frames, that would mean we need *16* different images! That seems inefficient. So instead, as you saw earlier when we looked at the assets, there's only two, one for each frame. In order to provide the eight different orientations, those two images will be rotated in real time to the correct orientation. Flutter provides several means to rotate an image, but we'll get to how to actually rotate the image shortly. Before that, the second trick comes in, and that's to avoid some calculations. As you'll see, to rotate the ship, we'll need to tell Flutter how much to rotate it, and that's provided in radians. But, from our perspective, we really want to rotate it some number of degrees. So, we could, of course, do a degrees-to-radians calculation every time we need to rotate, but avoiding that calculation saves us some cycles, so that's what we'll do! The simplest approach is to just precalculate the radians for each angular degree measure we want to rotate by and store those values in a map for easy lookup, and that's precisely what the `anglesToRadiansConversionTable` property is for. The actual number of radians rotated is something we'll need to keep track of too, and that's where the `radians` property comes in. You'll see both in use very soon.

The constructor comes next:

```
Player(double inScreenWidth, double nScreenHeight,
  String inBaseFilename, int inWidth, int inHeight,
  int inNumFrames, int inFrameSkip, int inSpeed,
) : super(inScreenWidth, inScreenHeight, inBaseFilename,
  inWidth, inHeight, inNumFrames, inFrameSkip, null) {
  speed = inSpeed;
}
```

Since `Player` extends from `GameObject`, we need to call the `GameObject` constructor first, and then set the `speed`, which is the only value specific to the `Player` that needs to be set during construction. Note the null as the last argument to the `GameObject` constructor – that's the animation callback, which isn't needed for the player, hence passing `null`.

Now, GameObject provides a draw() method, but for the player, the act of drawing itself is a little different, so we need to override that method:

```
@override
Widget draw() {
  return visible ?
  Positioned(left : x, top : y, child : Transform.rotate(
    angle : radians, child : frames[currentFrame]))
  : Positioned(child : Container());
}
```

The difference here, of course, is the rotation discussed earlier. For that, we wrap the Image widget in a Transform widget, which is one Flutter provides to apply a transformation to a child before it's painted. While using Transform itself requires you to provide a transformation matrix, which can be complicated and math-intense depending on what you're trying to achieve, this class helpfully provides a handful of constructors for the most common transformations. These include Transform. scale() for scaling the child, or making it bigger or smaller in other words; Transform. translate() for translating the child, or shifting it in other words; and most importantly for us now, Transform.rotate() to rotate the child around its axis. As you can see, this constructor requires the angle of rotation in radians, so here you can see that radians property being used. How that value gets set is done in the orientationChanged() method, which you'll learn later is called from the code that handles user input:

```
void orientationChanged() {
  radians = 0.0;
  if (moveHorizontal == 1 && moveVertical == -1) {
    radians = anglesToRadiansConversionTable["angle45"];
  } else if (moveHorizontal == 1 && moveVertical == 0) {
    radians = anglesToRadiansConversionTable["angle90"];
  } else if (moveHorizontal == 1 && moveVertical == 1) {
    radians = anglesToRadiansConversionTable["angle135"];
  } else if (moveHorizontal == 0 && moveVertical == 1) {
    radians = anglesToRadiansConversionTable["angle180"];
  } else if (moveHorizontal == -1 && moveVertical == 1) {
    radians = anglesToRadiansConversionTable["angle225"];
  } else if (moveHorizontal == -1 && moveVertical == 0) {
```

```
    radians = anglesToRadiansConversionTable["angle270"];
  } else if (moveHorizontal == -1 && moveVertical == -1) {
    radians = anglesToRadiansConversionTable["angle315"];
  }
}
```

A check is performed for each of the four cardinal directions, plus the four combinations, to determine which way the player is moving. Once that's determined, a lookup into anglesToRadiansConversionTable is done and the resultant radians stored in the radians property. It's not fancy code, but it gets the job done nicely and, again, all while avoiding a potentially costly mathematical operation here.

Tip   It wouldn't be all *that* costly in practice, but again, in games, it's always better to be thinking about optimizations as you code. This is true generally in all kinds of programming, but more so in games where every cycle factors into the main game loop, as we'll discuss soon. Of course, you have to avoid taking this exercise *too* far and stretch into premature optimization territory, which is something you should always try to avoid — but a precalculated lookup table like this is quite common.

The final method is for moving the player:

```
void move() {
  if (x > 0 && moveHorizontal == -1) { x = x - speed; }
  if (x < (screenWidth - width) && moveHorizontal == 1) {
    x = x + speed;
  }
  if (y > 40 && moveVertical == -1) { y = y - speed; }
  if (y < (screenHeight - height - 10) && moveVertical == 1) {
    y = y + speed;
  }
}
```

This will be called once per main game loop tick. We do horizontal movement direction, and then vertical movement, separately. Recall that there are eight possible directions the player can be moving. The four cardinal directions are handled obviously, but the other four that represents the combinations are also handled by virtue of horizontal and vertical movement being handled separately. Since it's possible for one of the if statements dealing with x to fire while one of those dealing with y also fires, that yields a combination of vertical and horizontal movement. Of course, we must ensure that the player doesn't go off the screen too, which is what the bounds checks in each of the if statements do for us. These consider the side of the player as well as the space for the score and energy bar as well.

Where It All Starts: main.dart

As always, our app starts off in the main.dart source file:

```dart
import "package:flutter/material.dart";
import "package:flutter/services.dart";
import "InputController.dart" as InputController;
import "GameCore.dart";

void main() => runApp(FlutterHero());

class FlutterHero extends StatelessWidget {
  @override
  Widget build(BuildContext context) {
    SystemChrome.setEnabledSystemUIOverlays(
      [SystemUiOverlay.bottom]
    );
    return MaterialApp(
      title : "FlutterHero", home : GameScreen()
    );
  }
}

class GameScreen extends StatefulWidget {
  @override
  GameScreenState createState() => new GameScreenState();
}
```

The `services.dart` module is something new. This module provides us some device service access for things like interacting with the clipboard, generating haptic feedback (device shaking), playing system sounds, and selecting text, just to name a few. Something else it lets us do is control the "chrome" that is visible around our app, that is, the system status bar at the top and, on Android at least, the row of soft input buttons at the bottom. If you jump down to the top-level `FlutterHero` class here, in its `build()` method, you'll see a call to `SystemChrome.setEnabledSystemUIOverlays()`. This is provided by the services module, and this method allows us to pass it an array of chrome identifiers to enable. Here, I specifically enable the `SystemUiOverlay.bottom` element, which are the soft navigation buttons in Android. Since that's all that's in the array, the status bar at the top will be hidden, providing our game a (nearly) full-screen experience.

Of course, before that, you'll notice that we're building a stateful widget in `GameScreen`, which is the home screen defined in the `MaterialApp` of the `FlutterHero` class, a pattern you've seen before, and the necessary `main()` method is defined above that.

As you should expect, given that `GameScreen` is a stateful widget, there will be an associated `State` class, and there is: `GameScreenState`:

```
class GameScreenState extends State with
  TickerProviderStateMixin {
  @override
  Widget build(BuildContext inContext) {
    if (gameLoopController == null) {
      firstTimeInitialization(inContext, this);
    }
```

For this app, we're not going to use scoped_model and instead just use the basic state facilities that Flutter provides. But, in addition to the `State` stuff, this class has something new: the `TickerProviderStateMixin`. We'll get to what that's all about in the next section, but just as a preview I'll tell you that it has to do with the main game loop that will tick by 60 times a second throughout the lifetime of the game.

The `build()` method begins with a check of the `gameLoopController`, which you're going to see is part of the `GameCore.dart` file. Ignoring for the moment what that is, if it's `null`, then a call to `firstTimeInitialization()` is made, passing it the `BuildContext` and also a reference to the `GameScreenState` class itself using `this`. That function too will be examined in the next section, but I'm sure you can guess from the name that it performs some tasks that happen the first time the `build()` method executes (remember that build() will fire many times throughout this game). The issue here is that there are some tasks that must be done to set up the game that can only occur when we have that BuildContext. So, those tasks must be done in the build() method. But, they must only happen once, hence why that check of gameLoopController is done.

But like I said, we'll get to all of that in the next section!

Continuing in the build() method, we begin to build our widget tree:

```
List<Widget> stackChildren = [
  Positioned(left : 0, top : 0,
    child : Container(width : screenWidth,
      height : screenHeight,
      decoration : BoxDecoration(image : DecorationImage(
        image : AssetImage("assets/background.png"),
        fit : BoxFit.cover
    ))
  )
),
```

Interestingly, in all previous build() methods you've seen, you almost immediately have seen a return statement to return a widget, and all the child widgets were defined "inline" with that widget. Here though, we're constructing a list first. The situation here is that there is some logic that has to occur while building the widget tree, some loops and such, none of which could be done in a single monolithic inline widget tree like we normally do. Because the widget we ultimately want to return is a Stack (well, a Stack inside a GestureDetector inside a Scaffold, if you want to be pedantic) and because a Stack takes a list as its children, we can do all of the logic and looping outside the widget definition, build the list separately, and then just reference it in the final Stack definition. That's what's happening here. The first element in the list is a Positioned wrapping a Container that uses a BoxDecoration to show the background image. The fit specified as BoxFit.cover ensures that the background fills the screen regardless of its physical dimensions. The width and height of the Container are the values of the screenWidth and screenHeight variables. As you'll find out in the next section (or, well, now I guess, as it happens!) those values are queried during first-time initialization and retrieved from the operating system so that anywhere that information is needed, it will be available without having to do that query many times.

```
Positioned(left : 4, top : 2,
  child : Text('Score: ${score.toString().padLeft(4, "0")}',
    style : TextStyle(color : Colors.white,
      fontSize : 18, fontWeight : FontWeight.w900)
  )
),
```

After the background is another `Positioned` wrapping a `Text` this time. That's our score display. As you can see, this widget is placed at x/y location 4/2 as per the `left` and `top` properties. That's the whole point of using a `Stack`: we can absolutely position these elements as we see fit. The `Stack` will by default fill its parent, which happens to be the screen, so we have absolute positioning capability across the entire screen. Handy for a game, don't you think?!

After that comes another Positioned, this time with a `LinearProgressIndicator` inside for the energy bar:

```
Positioned(left : 120, top : 2, width : screenWidth - 124, height : 22,
  child : LinearProgressIndicator(
    value : player.energy, backgroundColor : Colors.white,
    valueColor : AlwaysStoppedAnimation(Colors.red)
  )
),
crystal.draw()
];
```

The `valueColor` property is important here because by default, a progress indicator in Flutter, whether linear or circular, wants to animate. It will spin if it's circular, or fill up if it's linear. But, that's not what we want. We want a bar that fills up little by little when the ship is in contact with the crystal and empties little by little when in contact with the planet to indicate energy filling or draining to and from the ship, all under the control of our code, not what Flutter wants to do with it (waah, this is my game, do it my way, Flutter!). So, rather than specifying just a single color to indicate what color to make the filled portion of the indicator, we instead use an instance of the `AlwaysStoppedAnimation` widget. This is a special widget that the progress indicator classes know how to deal with that provides an indicator that isn't constantly animating, precisely as we need! Of course, what color the filled portion should be is still important information, so it's passed to the `AlwaysStoppedAnimation` constructor. Note too that the width of the `Positioned` that the `LinearProgressIndicator` is in is set dynamically using the width of the screen minus the space the score takes up. This way, the energy bar fills whatever space is left after the score.

The crystal is also added here, which is the last element in the list that's added during its declaration (inline, if you will).

After that, we have to add our enemy vermin:

```
for (int i = 0; i < 3; i++) {
  stackChildren.add(fish[i].draw());
  stackChildren.add(robots[i].draw());
  stackChildren.add(aliens[i].draw());
  stackChildren.add(asteroids[i].draw());
}
```

There's three of each, so it's a simple loop – but this loop is the primary reason we needed to build this list in the first place! Trying to do it all inline would have meant having to write out 12 enemy references here since we couldn't use a loop construct.

Next, the planet and player are added:

```
stackChildren.add(planet.draw());
stackChildren.add(player.draw());
```

It's important to realize that with a `Stack`, there is a z-axis at play. That means that elements added later in the list will appear on top of those added before. So, we have to ensure that, to the extent it matters in this game, we add things in the proper order. So, the player must be added after the planet, for example, so that the ship isn't occluded by the planet when the player flies near it. The ship should remain visible, on top of the planet. Hence it needs to be higher in the z-order and so has to be added after the planet.

Now, although they won't be visible except at specific times, we need to add any explosions needed to the list next:

```
for (int i = 0; i < explosions.length; i++) {
  stackChildren.add(explosions[i].draw());
}
```

Recall that if any given game object isn't currently visible, its `draw()` method will return an empty `Container`. Explosions are when that's most obvious because while most of the game objects are nearly always visible, explosions are obviously transient in nature. So, this loop may be drawing a bunch of empty Container widgets most of the time, but that's fine, that's just the way visibility is controlled in Flutter.

Finally, the widget to return is constructed:

```
return Scaffold(body : GestureDetector(
  onPanStart : InputController.onPanStart,
  onPanUpdate : InputController.onPanUpdate,
  onPanEnd : InputController.onPanEnd,
  child : Stack(children : stackChildren)
));
```

The body of the Scaffold returned isn't the Stack directly, as you might have anticipated. We're going to need to work some method for the player to control his ship in, and given that most modern mobile devices are touchscreen-oriented, it makes sense that touch will be our control mechanism. So, we need a widget to recognize touch events, and that's exactly what the GestureDetector widget is for.

This widget recognizes all sorts of various gestures, taps and such, and one such gesture is a pan. This is simply the user putting their finger down and then moving it around. If you were developing a web site where users use a mouse most of the time, then you would recognize events like mouseDown, mouseMove, and MouseUp. But, we don't have those here, even though conceptually those are what we need. But, three pan events conceptually mimic those (taking the player's finger to be basically what the mouse pointer is): onPanStart for mouseDown, onPanUpdate for mouseMove, and onPanEnd for mouseUp. The code that handles those events represents the functionality that the InputController class encapsulates, but we'll get to that later. Before that though, you can see that the Stack is the child of the GestureDetector, which means that gestures anywhere on the screen will be handled because recall that the Stack takes up the whole screen (it fills its parent by default, as does its parent GestureDetector). Finally, as previously mentioned, the children of the Stack references the list that was built up before here.

Remember that everything we just talked about is inside the build() method of the top-level widget, and remember that we're dealing with a stateful widget. That means that any time state changes, build() will be called again and the screen re-rendered. That's the key to making this all work as a game. Next, we need to talk about that main game loop I've mentioned several times, as well as the core logic that makes up the game, all of which ties into this build() method because ultimately, all of this logic mutates state and triggers this build() method being executed over and over again to move all our game objects.

The Main Game Loop and Core Game Logic

The core logic of the game is contained within the GameCore.dart file, and it begins, as always, with import:

Kicking It Off

```
import "dart:math";
import "package:flutter/material.dart";
import "package:audioplayers/audio_cache.dart";
import "InputController.dart" as InputController;
import "GameObject.dart";
import "Enemy.dart";
import "Player.dart";
```

The math package is necessary because we're going to need to generate some random numbers, and that functionality is included there. The audio_cache.dart module is part of the audioplayers plugin and is the interface we'll use to load and play the sound assets, as you'll see. The others are the various source files for FlutterHero as needed.

Then, we have a whole bunch of variables:

- State state – This is a reference to the State class.

- Random random = new Random() – The Random class allows us to… you guessed it… generate random numbers! I instantiate it once here because while we'll need it multiple times, there's no sense having more than one instance.

- int score = 0 – The current score of the game.

- double screenWidth – The width of the screen.

- double screenHeight – The height of the screen.

- AnimationController gameLoopController – We'll talk about this in a moment!

- Animation gameLoopAnimation – This goes along with gameLoopController.

- `GameObject crystal` – The one and only crystal game object.

- `List fish` – A list of fish enemy vermin game objects.

- `List robots` – A list of robots enemy vermin game objects.

- `List aliens` – A list of aliens enemy vermin game objects.

- `List asteroids` – A list of asteroids enemy vermin game objects.

- `Player player` – The one and only player game object.

- `GameObject planet` – The one and only planet game object.

- `List explosions = [ ]` – A list of explosions (which are `GameObject`) instances (this is empty when there are no explosions currently on screen).

- `AudioCache audioCache` – A cache of audio assets that can be played (more on this later).

With the variables out of the way, we can now get to the code that uses them.

First Time Initialization

The first bit of code is the `firstTimeInitialization()` function that you saw called from the `build()` method of the main widget, remember? It's the call that was made if and only if the `gameLoopController` variable was `null`. Well, here it is finally:

```
void firstTimeInitialization(BuildContext inContext,
  dynamic inState) {

  state = inState;
```

The code in this module will need some access to the `GameScreenState` object since it contains the state for the main widget, so a reference to it is passed in and that reference stored in the `state` variable.

Next, it's time to deal with audio:

```
audioCache = new AudioCache();
audioCache.loadAll([ "delivery.mp3", "explosion.mp3",
  "fill.mp3", "thrust.mp3" ]);
```

The audioplayers plugin has a couple of different ways to deal with audio, one of which is the AudioCache class. This is used to preload audio and play it efficiently, something that's important in a game. This is also, a little oddly in my mind, necessary to be able to play sounds that are assets in our app. So, weird or not, we instantiate the class and then call its loadAll() method, passing it a list of audio filenames to load, after which we're ready to play those sounds any time we want, as you'll see later.

We then need to get the dimensions of the screen:

```
screenWidth = MediaQuery.of(inContext).size.width;
screenHeight = MediaQuery.of(inContext).size.height;
```

The MediaQuery class is provided by the material.dart library and which allows us to retrieve information about a given piece of media, the screen for example. Calling its of() method for the incoming BuildContext gets us a MediaQueryData object about the given context, which we can then drill down into to get the screen width and height.

Next, it's time to create some game object!

```
crystal = GameObject(screenWidth, screenHeight, "crystal",
  32, 30, 4, 6, null);
planet = GameObject(screenWidth, screenHeight, "planet",
  64, 64, 1, 0, null);
player = Player(screenWidth, screenHeight, "player",
  40, 34, 2, 6, 2);
fish = [
  Enemy(screenWidth,screenHeight, "fish", 48, 48, 2, 6, 1, 4),
  Enemy(screenWidth,screenHeight, "fish", 48, 48, 2, 6, 1, 4),
  Enemy(screenWidth,screenHeight, "fish", 48, 48, 2, 6, 1, 4)
];
```

The crystal and planet are plain old GameObject instances, while the player and the enemy vermin are Player and Enemy instances correspondingly. The robots, aliens, and asteroids are created the same way the fish are, so no point in showing those I figured. Note that they had to be created here because we need the screenWidth and screenHeight to have been queried already, hence why this couldn't have been done as part of the declaration of these variables, or even in a constructor, both of which would seem like natural choices otherwise.

Flutter Animation in Brief

Flutter provides rich animation support in various ways, but it ultimately comes down to a few key classes, even if you don't use them explicitly (in the case, for example, of widgets that do their own animation – they're using these classes under the hood). You firstly need a `Ticker` object, then you need an `Animation` object, and finally, you need an `AnimationController` object.

A `Ticker` object is one that sends a signal at a regular interval that is typically 60 times a second. Every time this object ticks, some callback functions are executed to perform animation-related things.

The `Animation` object is concerned with generating a number on each tick. This number is part of a sequence between two defined values over a defined period of time and can be generated in a simple linear fashion or via complex curves.

The `AnimationController` is an object that controls an animation. It can start, stop, and pause an animation. It can also reverse the animation (and remember here that "animation" means nothing but the generation of the next value in the sequence – none of this thus far has any knowledge of what's on the screen).

An `AnimationController` gets bound to a `Ticker`, which most typically is bound to a `State` object in your app. So, every time the `Ticker` ticks, the `AnimationController` is sent a signal. It then sends a signal to the `Animation` object which then generates a new value. Then, your code hooks into lifecycle events on the `Animation` and does whatever is necessary to draw the animated elements on the screen. It's ultimately your code (or the code in a Flutter widget you're using) that is responsible for actually putting object on the screen and moving them (or otherwise altering them because remember that animation is a generic concept here and doesn't have to mean movement – we might be animating the size of an object, for example).

So, imagine you have a `Ticker` ticking off 60 times a second. Also, imagine that an `Animation` is spitting out a linear set of numbers between 0 and 500 under the control of an `AnimationController`. Finally, imagine that you hook into the lifecycle of the `Animation` so that every time a number is generated, you update the X location of one of our enemies on the screen. This will, of course, trigger the `build()` method to fire again, thus updating the screen. Suddenly, you've got a moving object on the screen. In other words, you've got animation!

That's the core concept, so now let's look at the actual code that puts this theory into practice:

```
gameLoopController = AnimationController(vsync : inState, duration :
Duration(milliseconds : 1000));
gameLoopAnimation = Tween(begin : 0, end : 17).animate(
  CurvedAnimation(parent : gameLoopController,
    curve : Curves.linear)
);
gameLoopAnimation.addStatusListener((inStatus) {
  if (inStatus == AnimationStatus.completed) {
    gameLoopController.reset();
    gameLoopController.forward();
  }
});
gameLoopAnimation.addListener(gameLoop);
```

First, an `AnimationController` is instantiated. The `sync` property associates a `Ticker` with it, and in this case, it's our `GameScreenState` object. If you look back on that code, you'll see that it extends that class with the `TickerProviderStateMixin`. That turns it into a `Ticker`! We also tell the `AnimationController` how long we want the values animated for, and it's one second in this case (1,000 milliseconds).

Next, we have to create an `Animation` object and associate it with the `AnimationController`. There are a few subclasses we could choose from, and here I've used perhaps the simplest: `Tween`. This allows us to define a sequence from a `begin` to an end value, which is 0 to 17 here.

Why those values? Well, the goal here is to create what's called a main game loop. That's a fancy way of saying we want some function, our main game loop function, to execute once per frame (drawing frame that is). But, how long does each execution take? Well, what we do here is divide the total time by the number of ticks. That means 1,000 divided by 60. That comes out to 16.666667. Round that up to 17 and that's the range. To put this all succinctly: we want the main game loop function to execute once every 17 milliseconds, which means it will execute 60 times per second (roughly). That's what this `Animation` does: it spits out a number between 0 and 17 (linearly, because of the curve property being set to `Curves.linear`, a standard curve Flutter provides) over the course of 1 second, once every 17 milliseconds.

Now, with all that doing what we want, we have to hook into the lifecycle to do our work. That comes in two places. First, you should recognize that after one second, that animation would be complete. The sequence of values would be exhausted. Obviously, we need it to happen again, and again, and again. So, we set a listener function any time the status of the `Animation` changes. This function will be called in a couple of different situations, when the animation starts and finishes being two of them. We only care about when it finishes, so we look at the status passed in, and when it's completed, then we call the `reset()` and `forward()` methods on the `AnimationController`. This does exactly as the name implies: resets all the values to their starting points and starts the `Animation` sequence again in the forward direction (counting from 0 to 17 again over the course of one second).

We then need to be informed every time a number is generated so that we can call the main game loop function. The `addListener()` method on the `Animation` instance does precisely that.

With the main game loop hooked up and ready to go, we just need to reset all game state variables:

```
resetGame(true);
```

We're going to look at this next, so let's skip discussing it for now. After that is:

```
InputController.init(player);
```

The `InputController` object is responsible for handling user input, but that too is something we'll look at later, so for now, we'll skip it too and find that there's only one more line after that in this function:

```
gameLoopController.forward();
```

That effectively starts the game loop, which means our game is now running. Woo-hoo! Things are moving on the screen!

Resetting Game State

When things start up, and after the player explodes or the energy is delivered to the planet, the game needs to be reset. For that, we have the resetGame() function:

```
void resetGame(bool inResetEnemies) {

  player.energy = 0.0;
  player.x = (screenWidth / 2) - (player.width / 2);
  player.y = screenHeight - player.height - 24;
  player.moveHorizontal = 0;
  player.moveVertical = 0;
  player.orientationChanged();
```

First, we clear the energy from the ship and reposition the ship to the center of the screen and a few pixels away from the bottom of the screen. Then, we have to make sure the player isn't currently moving, and also reset its orientation so that it's facing up via the call to orientationChanged().

```
crystal.y = 34.0;
randomlyPositionObject(crystal);
```

After the player, the crystal gets reset. Note that after the first call to this function, there's no point in setting the y property since it doesn't change, but there's no harm either, so it's done to avoid any logic. The x property is set by the randomlyPositionObject() function, which we'll look at later, but the name tells you exactly what it does!

The planet is done next in basically the same way:

```
planet.y = screenHeight - planet.height - 10;
randomlyPositionObject(planet);
```

The y property needs to consider the height of the planet though so that it doesn't hang off the bottom of the screen (10 pixels is just an arbitrary value, but it's one I chose so that the starting position of the ship looks roughly centered on the vertical axis of the planet).

Next comes the enemies (maybe):

```
if (inResetEnemies) {
  List xValsFish = [ 70.0, 192.0, 312.0 ];
  List xValsRobots = [ 64.0, 192.0, 320.0 ];
  List xValsAliens = [ 44.0, 192.0, 340.0 ];
  List xValsAsteroids = [ 24.0, 192.0, 360.0 ];
  for (int i = 0; i < 3; i++ ) {
    fish[i].x = xValsFish[i];
    robots[i].x = xValsRobots[i];
    aliens[i].x = xValsAliens[i];
    asteroids[i].x = xValsAsteroids[i];
    fish[i].y = 110.0;
    robots[i].y = fish[i].y + 120;
    aliens[i].y = robots[i].y + 130;
    asteroids[i].y = aliens[i].y + 140;
    fish[i].visible = true;
    robots[i].visible = true;
    aliens[i].visible = true;
    asteroids[i].visible = true;
  }
}
```

When resetGame() is initially called from firstTimeInitialization(), true is passed to it. This causes the preceding block to execute. When the player explodes, false is passed to skip this setup since there's no point in resetting their positions (and when the energy is delivered to the planet, true is again passed).

The reset logic here is simple: we have four lists, one for each type of enemy, that contains the x location values for each enemy. Rather than calculate these dynamically, I felt it was simpler to "magic number" them. Importantly, this made it easy to introduce some variation without a lot of code: the spacing is mixed up a bit across the enemies to avoid any repeating gaps that the player can too easily get through, improving the challenge of the game. For the y location values, I build from the previous row of enemies such that the rows get a little closer together as you get closer to the top. This again is done to make it just a little harder the further up the screen you move. We also need to ensure that all the enemies are visible at this point because after they all explode when energy is delivered to the planet, they will be hidden as the explosions occur (you'll see this later), so they have to be shown again, so the game resets appropriately.

Only two small tasks remain:

```
explosions = [ ];
player.visible = true;
```

You'll see how explosions are dealt with later, but at this point, it's enough to know that the list of them, if any, needs to be cleared, and there's no easier way than setting explosions to an empty list. Finally, the player is made visible again so that if they just exploded, they're back to life and ready to try again.

The Main Game Loop

Now, finally, we come to the main game loop function, the function that is called 60 times a second, every 17 milliseconds, as a result of the animation setup code you explored earlier:

```
void gameLoop() {

  crystal.animate();
```

The first thing done is to request the crystal to animate itself. As you know from looking at the GameObject code, this just means cycling through the animation frames which, for the crystal, just makes it cycle through some colors.

Next, we have to animate and move the vermin:

```
for (int i = 0; i < 3; i++) {
  fish[i].move();
  fish[i].animate();
  robots[i].move();
  robots[i].animate();
  aliens[i].move();
  aliens[i].animate();
  asteroids[i].move();
  asteroids[i].animate();
}
```

Each vermin, three of each type, get a chance to animate and then move. Keeping the logic for these functions in the `GameObject` and `Enemy` classes should make sense to you now: it keeps us from having to write a lot of ultimately repetitive code to do it all here.

Then, it's time for the player to move and animate:

```
player.move();
player.animate();
```

Note that for the most part, the exact order of all these calls doesn't really matter much. If we called `player.animate()` before `player.move()` that would be fine, and if we did the player before the vermin, it too wouldn't make much of a difference.

Now, we get to some good old-fashioned demolitions:

```
for (int i = 0; i < explosions.length; i++) {
  explosions[i].animate();
}
```

There might be no explosions on the screen at this time, or there might be one (if the player hit an enemy), or there may be twelve (if they just delivered the energy to the planet and now all the vermin are exploding). So, it's a simple loop where each iteration gives any explosions in the `explosions` list a chance to animate.

So far, this has been very straightforward and just producing updates to the location and appearance of our various game objects. But, that's not all there is to it of course: we also must have some logic to make this an actual game, and that comes next:

```
if (collision(crystal)) {
  transferEnergy(true);
} else if (collision(planet)) {
  transferEnergy(false);
} else {
  if (player.energy > 0 && player.energy < 1) {
    player.energy = 0;
  }
}
```

The first part of that logic is to see I the player is in contact ("collided with") the crystal or the planet. The `collision()` function implements that check, but we'll look at that next. For now, know that it simply returns `true` if the player and the game object passed in have collided, false otherwise. If they are touching the crystal, then we need to transfer energy to the ship (or to the planet *from* the ship in the case of the planet), which there is a function for, not surprisingly called transferEnergy() (which we'll look at shortly). Passing true to it tells that the collision was with the crystal, while false means the planet, as you can see in the else if branch.

The else branch covers a "cheat" condition: if the player has energy, but the ship isn't 100% full of it, then dump it all out. Without this, the player would be able to grab just a tiny bit of energy, but then return it to the planet and be given full credit for the delivery. That would be terrible for the economics of the Gorgonian solar system (and sociologically would probably lead to wars between the ship captains, and since we've already established their ships are weak that would probably be a short war – but I digress), so we'll just put a stop to it right here and now! Since this situation can *only* arise if they are not in contact with *either* the crystal or planet, the else branch is the right place for that logic.

Next, we need to check for collisions with the vermin:

```
for (int i = 0; i < 3; i++) {
  if (collision(fish[i]) || collision(robots[i]) ||
    collision(aliens[i]) || collision(asteroids[i])) {
    audioCache.play("explosion.mp3");
    player.visible = false;
    GameObject explosion = GameObject(screenWidth,
      screenHeight, "explosion", 50, 50, 5, 4,
      () { resetGame(false); }
    );
    explosion.x = player.x;
    explosion.y = player.y;
    explosions.add(explosion);
    score = score - 50;
    if (score < 0) { score = 0; }
  }
}
```

Obviously, we need to check each enemy, hence the loop. To avoid nested loops, I check one of each enemy with each iteration of the loop. If any collision occurs, then first we play the explosion sound. The audioCache that we set up earlier provides a play()

method for this, and all you do is give it the name of the file to play (sans `assets/` prefix, it should be noted, since audioplayers assumes that's where the files are by default). Piece of cake! Next, the player needs to be hidden. That's because an explosion is going to be shown in its place, which is exactly what we do next: instantiate a `GameObject` for the explosion. It gets positioned right where the player is (err, was!) and then that `GameObject` gets added to the `explosions` list (which, you'll recall from earlier in this function, means it will be animated beginning with the next frame). The effect of all of that is an exploding ship! A few points are deducted from the player's score for the mishap (which we must ensure doesn't go negative) and we're done.

Only one task remains, a single line of code, but it is absolutely critical:

```
state.setState(() {});
```

Without this, to put it succinctly: nothing happens! Without updating state, Flutter doesn't know anything has changed and so `build()` won't fire again and the screen won't update. Kind of an important step, don't you think?!

Next, let's look at that `collision()` function and see what it's all about.

Checking for Collisions

Most video games require the ability to detect when two objects collide with each other. Here, we need to know when the ship hits any of the vermin. There are several ways to do this, each having their pluses and minuses. One simple approach is called bounding boxes. This method simply checks the four bounds of the objects, and if the corner of one object is within the bounds of the other, then a collision has occurred.

As illustrated in the example in Figure 9-4, each game object has a square/rectangular area around it called its bounding box. This box defines the boundaries of the area the object occupies. Note in the diagram how the upper-left corner of object 2's bounding box is within the bounding box of object 1. This represents a collision. You can detect a collision by running through a series of simple tests comparing the bounds of each object. If any of the conditions are untrue, then a collision cannot possibly have occurred. For instance, if the bottom of object 1 is above the top of object 2, then there's no way a collision could have happened. In fact, since you're dealing with a square or rectangular object, you have only four conditions to check, any one of which being false precludes the possibility of a collision.

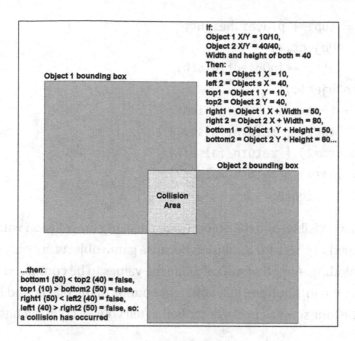

Figure 9-4. *The basic idea behind bounding boxes*

This algorithm does not yield perfect results though. For example, you will sometimes see the ship "hitting" an object when it clearly did not really touch. Other times, they may appear just barely to collide, but it won't register as a collision. The rotation of the ship also plays a role in this because this simple version of the algorithm can't handle the altered geometry of the ship from something that isn't (roughly) square and aligned perfectly vertically or horizontally. This could be fixed with a more complex version of the algorithm, or with pixel-level detection, meaning checking each pixel of one object against all the pixels in the other (or at least the pixels on their edges). However, the bounding boxes approach shown here gives an approximation that yields "good enough" results in many cases – the game isn't unplayable even with this margin of error – so all is right with the world.

With all that explained, let's see that collision() function that was referenced in the previous section:

```
bool collision(GameObject inObject) {
  if (!player.visible || !inObject.visible) { return false; }
  num left1 = player.x;
  num right1 = left1 + player.width;
  num top1 = player.y;
```

```
num bottom1 = top1 + player.height;
num left2 = inObject.x;
num right2 = left2 + inObject.width;
num top2 = inObject.y;
num bottom2 = top2 + inObject.height;
if (bottom1 < top2) { return false; }
if (top1 > bottom2) { return false; }
if (right1 < left2) { return false; }
return left1 <= right2;
```

If the player isn't visible, or if the object we're checking for collision with isn't visible, then there's no need to check for a collision because game objects are only ever not visible when they're exploding. After that, we calculate the values to be compared, which means the coordinates of the top, bottom, left, and right bounds of the player and the target object. Finally, it's just the four simple checks described to tell you if a collision has occurred.

Randomly Positioning an Object

After the player picks up all the energy from the crystal, or when they have transferred all the energy back to the planet, or when the game resets, the crystal and planet get randomly positioned via a call to randomlyPositionObject():

```
void randomlyPositionObject(GameObject inObject) {
  inObject.x = (random.nextInt(
    screenWidth.toInt() - inObject.width)).toDouble();
  if (collision(inObject)) {
    randomlyPositionObject(inObject);
  }
}
```

The Random object created during startup is used by calling its nextInt() method. The value we want must be in the range zero to the width of the screen minus the width of the object, so that it's always on the screen and not hanging off the left or right edge. Only the horizontal position of the object is random, so the resultant random value is set to its x property. The other consideration is that the object can't be in the same place as the player. So, we call collision() to check for that condition and if a collision occurs then randomlyPositionObject() is recursively called until a non-collision position is selected.

Transferring Energy

When the ship "collides" with the crystal or planet, energy must be transferred to or from the ship. The `transferEnergy()` function is called for that purpose:

```
void transferEnergy(bool inTouchingCrystal) {

  if (inTouchingCrystal && player.energy < 1) {
```

If the caller indicates that the crystal is being touched, then we have to ensure that the ship isn't already full. The values run from 0 to 1 because that's what the `LinearProgressIndicator` widget wants for its value range. However, I found that if a check isn't done to be sure the value never goes over one then the bar "bounces" at the end a little bit, which looks bad.

When the first contact occurs, we need to play the appropriate sound:

```
  if (player.energy == 0) { audioCache.play("fill.mp3"); }
```

At the first touch, the energy would be zero, of course, that's why this condition is checked.

After that, it's a simple matter of incrementing the energy and capping it at one:

```
player.energy = player.energy + .01;
if (player.energy >= 1) {
  player.energy = 1;
  randomlyPositionObject(crystal);
}
```

Also, when the ship is full, the crystal gets randomly repositioned so that the ship is no longer sucking energy (not that it would anyway with the conditions checked for here, but this way it *visually* isn't there to be siphoned from).

The `else if` branch comes next and that's for contact with the planet:

```
} else if (player.energy > 0) {
```

This only has an effect when the ship has energy onboard of course, so we check for that.

CHAPTER 9 FLUTTERHERO: A FLUTTER GAME

Then, similar to the first contact with the crystal, we want to play a different sound upon the first contact with the planet, so:

```
if (player.energy >= 1) {
  audioCache.play("delivery.mp3");
}
```

And, as with the crystal, the energy on the ship is adjusted:

```
player.energy = player.energy - .01;
```

Of course, with the energy being adjusted and state being set, the bar will fill or unfill as appropriate, just like we want.

Now, there's some other logic we need to implement when depositing energy to the planet, and that's when all the energy is delivered:

```
if (player.energy <= 0) {
  player.energy = 0;
  audioCache.play("explosion.mp3");
  score = score + 100;
  for (int i = 0; i < 3; i++) {
    Function callback;
    if (i == 0) {
      callback = () { resetGame(true); };
    }
    fish[i].visible = false;
    GameObject explosion = GameObject(screenWidth,
      screenHeight, "explosion", 50, 50, 5, 4, callback);
    explosion.x = fish[i].x;
    explosion.y = fish[i].y;
    explosions.add(explosion);
    robots[i].visible = false;
  }
}
```

Here, we ensure that the energy is at zero, not below, and the explosion sound is played, and the player's score bumped up. That's because it's time to blow up the vermin! The loop executes and for each vermin, it's hidden, and an explosion shown in its place. Note that the animation callback you saw earlier when looking at the GameObject class

380

now is used: the first (and only the first) vermin has this callback hooked up so that when the animation cycles completes, we can reset the game, including resetting the position of the enemies.

Note   The code you see here for the fish is repeated for the robots, aliens, and asteroids, so I saved a little space by not showing them here.

The result of all of this is shown in Figure 9-5: beautiful vermin carnage!

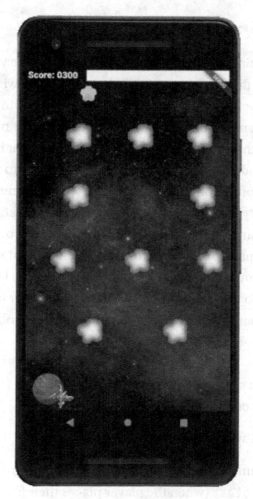

Figure 9-5.   *Boom! We all fall down!*

Of course, they come right back, so it's a short-lived victory for our hero ☹

Taking Control: InputController.dart

The final bit of code we need to look at is the InputController class, the one you saw get hooked up to the GestureDetector's event properties earlier. It implements all the player motion controls and begins thusly:

```
import "package:flutter/material.dart";
import "Player.dart";

double touchAnchorX;
double touchAnchorY;
int moveSensitivity = 20;
```

After what I would think are obvious imports, we have three variables. The way the control scheme works is that the player places their finger any where on the screen and that becomes the "anchor point." Picture a video game joystick in your mind. The center position represents this anchor point. Now, any time the player moves their finger, the new position relative to that anchor point represents movement in that direction. If their finger is, say, 20 pixels above the anchor point, then they want to move the ship up. If they lift their finger and put it somewhere else, then we have a new anchor point. They can, in a sense, create a "virtual joystick" anywhere on the screen that is convenient for them. So, we need two variables to record the X and Y location of the anchor point. We also need to know how many pixels away from the anchor point will register a move, a "sensitivity" setting if you will, and after some experimenting, I landed on 20 being a pretty good value: not too touchy but not too difficult to register a move either.

We also need a reference to the player, which should seem obvious:

```
Player player;
```

And, that reference it stored when the init() method here is called from the firstTimeInitialization() method:

```
void init(Player inPlayer) { player = inPlayer; }
```

Now, you'll recall from earlier that we need to handle three events from the GestureDetector: onPanStart (when the player places their finger down), onPanUpdate

(when they drag their finger) and onPanEnd (when they lift their finger). First up is
onPanStart() for handling the onPanStart event:

```
void onPanStart(DragStartDetails inDetails) {
  touchAnchorX = inDetails.globalPosition.dx;
  touchAnchorY = inDetails.globalPosition.dy;
  player.moveHorizontal = 0;
  player.moveVertical = 0;
}
```

The task here is simple: record the new anchor point and ensure the player isn't
moving. The object passed into this method is a DragStartDetails object that contains
a few pieces of information, most critically to us being globalPosition.dx and
globalPosition.dy for the horizontal (x) and vertical (y) position of the drag event.

Next is the onPanUpdate() function, which is where the majority of the work that this
class does is found:

```
void onPanUpdate(DragUpdateDetails inDetails) {
  if (inDetails.globalPosition.dx <
    touchAnchorX - moveSensitivity) {
    player.moveHorizontal = -1;
    player.orientationChanged();
  } else if (inDetails.globalPosition.dx >
    touchAnchorX + moveSensitivity) {
    player.moveHorizontal = 1;
    player.orientationChanged();
  } else {
    player.moveHorizontal = 0;
    player.orientationChanged();
  }
  if (inDetails.globalPosition.dy <
    touchAnchorY - moveSensitivity) {
    player.moveVertical = -1;
    player.orientationChanged();
  } else if (inDetails.globalPosition.dy >
    touchAnchorY + moveSensitivity) {
    player.moveVertical = 1;
```

```
      player.orientationChanged();
    } else {
      player.moveVertical = 0;
      player.orientationChanged();
    }
  }
}
```

It may look like a lot of code, but it's straightforward: if the horizontal location of the drag update event, as indicated by the DragUpdateDetails object's globalPosition. dx property, is more than 20 pixels to the left of the anchor point, then the player's moveHorizontal value is -1, and the call to player.orientationChanged() results in the proper rotation being applied. Similarly, if the event happened more than 20 pixels to the right, then the player is moving right (moveHorizontal gets a value of one). If neither of those conditions applies, then there is no horizontal movement (moveHorizontal is set to zero). Then, the same logic is applied for the vertical position but using the inDetails.globalPosition.dy property. The result is the movement control mechanics described, the virtual joystick, so to speak.

Finally, we just have to handle the onPanEnd event in the onPanEnd() handler function:

```
void onPanEnd(dynamic inDetails) {
  player.moveHorizontal = 0;
  player.moveVertical = 0;
}
```

All we need to do here is stop any movement that may be occurring, and we have a fully controllable player and a fully playable game thanks to Flutter!

Summary

That's it! You made it! Three complete Flutter apps, the final one a game! In this chapter, you learned about some new things such as the Positioned widget, Random number generation, handling pan input events, AnimationController, Tween and Animation for performing – after a fashion – animation, and audio. You also, if it was something you hadn't seen before, learned a little bit about how to architect a game.

It is my sincerest hope that you've enjoyed Practical Flutter and that you've learned a lot from it. The goal was never to make you an absolute expert in all things Flutter – it's way too big of a thing for a single book to pull that off! But, if I've done my job even close to properly, then you now have a solid foundation on which to build your Flutter knowledge, and with luck, I've provided you the necessary building blocks to start creating your own Flutter apps.

So, get to it, start twiddling some bits, go forth and create greatness thanks to Flutter and, in some small part I hope, this book!

Index

A

addListener() method, 370

addRoomInvite() method, 288

AlertDialog widget, 128, 129

Align widgets, 89

AlwaysStoppedAnimation widget, 362

Android Studio, 19–20

    hot reload icon, 30

    .idea directory, 34

    virtual machine dropdown, 24

AnimatedContainer widget, 141–142

AnimatedCrossFade widget, 142–143

Animation object, 368, 369

animationCallback property, 351

AnimationController, 368–370

Animations and transitions, 140

    AnimatedContainer widget, 141, 142

    AnimatedCrossFade widget, 142, 143

    AnimatedDefaultTextStyle, 144, 145

    AnimatedOpacity widget, 145

    AnimatedPositioned widget, 145

    Animated* widget, 145

    Stack widget, 145

    *Transition widget, 145

APIs, 167, 168

Application

    build() method, 28

    Center widget, 29

    Column widget, 29

    FAB, 25

main() method, 28

MaterialApp widget, 28

MyApp class, 28

MyHomePage class, 28

runApp() method, 28

Scaffold, 29

structure, 31, 32

    android directory, 33

    .gitignore, 34

    *.iml, 34

    ios directory, 33

    lib directory, 33

    .metadata, 34

    .packages, 34

    pubspec.lock and pubspec.yaml, 34

    readme file, 35

    res directory, 33

    test directory, 33

Appointments entity, 230

    Appointments.dart, 231

    database worker, 231

    list screen

        build() method, 234, 235

        Calendar Carousel, 232, 233, 236

        with date indicators, 234

        DateTime constructor, 233

        decoration, 233

        _deleteAppointment() method, 239

        Divider widget, 237

        _editAppointment method, 239

F. Zammetti, *Practical Flutter*, https://doi.org/10.1007/978-1-4842-4972-7

Printed in the United States
By Bookmasters